T0309869

Cruisy, Sleepy, Melancholy

Cruisy, Sleepy, Melancholy

Sexual Disorientation in the Films of Tsai Ming-liang

N I C H O L A S   D E   V I L L I E R S

UNIVERSITY OF MINNESOTA PRESS

MINNEAPOLIS • LONDON

The University of Minnesota Press gratefully acknowledges the financial assistance provided for the publication of this book by the University of North Florida.

Chapter 1 was originally published as "Spatial and Sexual Disorientation in the Films of Tsai Ming-liang," *IAFOR Journal of Literature & Librarianship* 2, no. 1 (2013), https://doi.org/10.22492/ijl.2.1.05. Chapter 2 was originally published as "Leaving the Cinema: Metacinematic Cruising in Tsai Ming-liang's *Goodbye, Dragon Inn*," *Jump Cut* 50 (Spring 2008), https://www.ejumpcut.org/archive/jc50.2008/DragonInn/.

Copyright 2022 by the Regents of the University of Minnesota

All rights reserved. No part of this publication may be reproduced, stored in a retrieval system, or transmitted, in any form or by any means, electronic, mechanical, photocopying, recording, or otherwise, without the prior written permission of the publisher.

Published by the University of Minnesota Press
111 Third Avenue South, Suite 290
Minneapolis, MN 55401-2520
http://www.upress.umn.edu

ISBN 978-1-5179-1317-5 (hc)
ISBN 978-1-5179-1318-2 (pb)

A Cataloging-in-Publication record for this book is available from the Library of Congress.

Printed in the United States of America on acid-free paper

The University of Minnesota is an equal-opportunity educator and employer.

UMP BmB 2022

Perhaps the immobility of the things that surround us
is forced upon them by our conviction that they are themselves,
and not anything else, and by the immobility of our conceptions
of them. For it always happened that when I awoke like this, and
my mind struggled in an unsuccessful attempt to discover
where I was, everything would be moving round me through the
darkness: things, places, years. My body, still too heavy with
sleep to move, would make an effort to construe the form which
its tiredness took as an orientation of its various members, so as
to induce from that where the wall lay and the furniture stood,
to piece together and to give a name to the house in which it
must be living.

— MARCEL PROUST, *Swann's Way*

Contents

Queer Metacinema

It's a Dream

> The work in the mirror and the work in the seed have
> always accompanied art without ever exhausting it. . . .
> By the same token, the film within the film does not signal
> an end of history, and is no more self-sufficient than is the
> flashback or the dream: it is just a method of working.
>
> —Gilles Deleuze, *Cinema 2: The Time-Image*

> As we see, what passes into the work is certainly the author's
> life, but a life *disoriented*.
>
> —Roland Barthes, *"Longtemps, je me suis couché
> de bonne heure"*

Tsai Ming-liang's short film *It's a Dream* (2007) contains *in nucleo* his understanding of cinema as a dreamlike state and his reflection on the cinema as a space so saturated with memory and *cruisy* queer desire that it can feel disorienting. A temporally disorienting autobiographical voice-over opens the film: "I dreamt of my father as a young man. He woke me in the middle of the night. We ate durians together. My mother was there too. She was already an old lady."[1] The soft-spoken voice-over places us within a distinct yet ghostly space: these family members are camped out in the aisle of a now derelict movie theater in Malaysia, the country where Tsai was born. A portable gas lamp illuminates Tsai's longtime "male muse,"[2] actor Lee Kang-sheng, playing Tsai's father as a young man, squatting on the ground, splitting and sharing out a durian fruit with the old lady (played by Tsai's actual mother) and the retrospective narrator as a young boy (here played by Lee Kang-sheng's nephew).[3]

Tsai's voice-over—like Marcel Proust's narrator—suggests that what passes into this work is the author's life, but a life *disoriented* by time, by Tsai's queer kinship with his cinematic muse, and by the affectively charged space of the cinema.[4] Over a shot of a framed portrait that sits in one of the cinema's chairs, the narration continues, still in a hushed tone: "This is my maternal grandmother. She loved the movies. Every time she took me to the cinema, she'd buy me pears on a skewer." The film thus harks back both to his own past experiences watching films in Malaysia with his maternal grandmother, and to the past of Chinese-language cinemas, especially the musicals and martial arts genre pictures Tsai pays homage to, queerly, in several of his films.[5]

An old-fashioned Mandarin pop song from the 1940s plays over the remainder of the shots from *It's a Dream,* all of which feature characters facing toward an unseen movie screen, leading us to speculate as to whether it might be diegetic sound (the soundtrack of the film they are watching but which we cannot see). The song features melancholy and philosophical lyrics:

> Last night, the moon was pale and mesmerizing
> Even the pine forest held its breath
> I thought of you in my dream
> My mind was caught between sadness and joy
> Tonight, the moon is bright like a mirror
> As we stroll together under the bridge
> Let me ask you in my dream
> Is this a dream or reality?[6]

While this song plays, we see actors who appeared (but did not meet onscreen) in Tsai's first feature film to be set in Malaysia, *I Don't Want to Sleep Alone* (2006):[7] we observe a woman (Pearlly Chua) eating pears on a skewer and then, without turning her head, she reaches the skewer back to the row behind her to share the sliced pears with a man (Norman bin Atun), who takes a bite between puffs on a cigarette. Picking up the cigarette motif, we see a shot of Lee Kang-sheng lighting a cigarette, with the boy seated next to him snacking from a paper packet. The final shot features only the family members, including the portrait of the maternal grandmother, seated together in one row, facing the screen, in an otherwise seemingly empty theater (Figure 1). The film acts as a kind of mirror for contemplating film spectatorship (and Tsai's own past), caught between sadness and joy.

It's a Dream condenses many of the central themes and motifs of Tsai's entire body of work: melancholy, nostalgia, familial intimacy, cruising, dreaming, and both temporal and spatial *disorientation*. It juxtaposes discontinuous generational time (including the afterlife and the temporal distortion of age in dreams) with apparently continuous screen time, and employs shifting spatial continuity in a nonetheless surreal location that acts as a kind of heterotopia.[8] This reflexive form of filmmaking—the film within the film in which "the moon is bright like

FIGURE 1. *It's a Dream* (Tsai Ming-liang, 2007). "Is this a dream or reality?" The cast seated in the dark, mostly empty movie theater represent Tsai's cinephile maternal grandmother (in a photograph), himself as a child, his "male muse" Lee Kang-sheng as his father, and his actual mother.

a mirror," or more generally films about filmmaking and film viewing—can be considered in terms of what Gilles Deleuze calls "the work in the mirror" and "the work in the seed."[9] What I am calling queer meta-cinema holds up a mirror to the cinema and its audience, but can also act like a seed encapsulating the queer potentiality of this space.

Tsai provocatively mixes the familial scene of relatives with the erotic cruising of strangers in the movie theater (recalling the provocative mixture of anonymous bathhouse cruising and filial relations in his early film *The River* [1997]).[10] He stages his complex vision of ethical relations via the shot of the woman sharing pears on a skewer with the man in the row behind her without looking at him. This is one of many scenes in Tsai's body of work in which he *queers heterosexual relations* via anonymity, cruising, female agency, and the eroticization of fruit.[11] The pears on the skewer nostalgically reference the food enjoyed with his maternal grandmother, but the durian is even more evocative as a notoriously culturally specific food (prohibited from certain enclosed places due to its pungent aroma, but also a marker of connoisseurship in Malaysia).

It's a Dream overlays motifs from *I Don't Want to Sleep Alone*, his film about spatial and sexual disorientation set in Malaysia's capital, Kuala Lumpur (the subject of chapter 1) and Tsai's metacinematic film *Goodbye, Dragon Inn* (2003), a melancholy ode to a "cruisy" old Taipei movie theater at its last screening (the subject of chapter 2). In an interview, Tsai explained how with *Goodbye, Dragon Inn*, "I feel like it was the theater that was calling me to make the film. That theater reminded me of my experience growing up in Malaysia. At that time there were seven or eight grand theaters like that, that have disappeared one by one over the past few years. Prior to making *Dragon Inn* I was having this recurring dream of this particular theater in Malaysia. It's almost like these images of childhood wouldn't let me go."[12]

Goodbye, Dragon Inn and these now closed or demolished theaters play a central role in Saw Tiong Guan's documentary *Past Present* (2013) regarding Tsai's poetics of space.[13] The documentary explores Tsai's relationship to movie theaters, especially those in Kuching (Sarawak, Malaysia) where Tsai was raised by grandparents who took him to the movies almost every day. Recalling the framed portrait of his maternal grandmother in *It's a Dream,* we learn that relatives will place such portraits in theater seats, as a kind of gift to their lost loved ones who can thus continue to watch films.[14] By paying melancholy homage to the cinematic past, Tsai thus suggests how private/public, personal/cultural cinema histories are deeply entangled.

It's a Dream was originally part of the metacinematic compilation film *Chacun son cinéma, ou, Ce petit coup au coeur quand la lumière s'éteint et que le film commence* ("To each his own cinema, or, That little thrill [literally: blow to the heart] when the light goes out and the film starts") featuring three-minute films by world cinema directors commissioned to celebrate the sixtieth anniversary of the Cannes film festival.[15] In *Chacun son cinéma,* something akin to a genuine cinema "fetish" emerges, beyond clichés of cinephilia, whether in the strictly Freudian formula of "I know cinema is dead, *but still* . . . [I love it]," or in the repeated motif of the motion-picture theater's intimate connection with sexuality, its dark atmosphere saturated with desire, arousal, and contact.[16] Roland Barthes's short essay "Leaving the Movie Theater" describes *the cinema*—which for Barthes connotes the hall itself—in precisely these *cruisy* terms.[17] But Barthes also describes the state of his body as it wakes from the dream/hypnosis of the movies, leaving the theater feeling *sleepy.*[18]

In this book, I will elaborate each of these affects and their interrelations: feeling cruisy, feeling sleepy, and feeling melancholy. Spaces like movie theaters induce such affective states or moods in the bodies of the audience members. Feeling cruisy suggests a mode of erotic availability, openness, and attentiveness within spaces that blur public and private.[19] Feeling sleepy suggests exhaustion from labor, chiefly, but also the work of being a subject: slipping into a soporific state or into a dream can feel like a relief or release from "individuation," what Jonathan Crary calls "the shallow subjectivities one inhabits and manages by day," or the routine coordinates of identity, time, and place.[20] Feeling melancholy suggests a different kind of loss, and has for the most part been understood in terms of temporality (being at odds with the present in a state of grief), but might also be understood in terms of place and space (for instance, the loss of the theaters Tsai continues to grieve in the quote above, suggesting they won't let him go). Each of these affects are linked in a kind of relay by Tsai's queering of cinematic space. The affective landscape of Tsai's body of work suggests new ways of understanding the way space and sexuality affect one another.

Tsai has revised and extended *It's a Dream* in "expanded cinema" installations using chairs from the movie theater in Malaysia—but installed facing each other, *mise en abyme,* and exhibited in Venice, Rotterdam, and Taipei[21]—a move to the museum that I return to in my conclusion on *Stray Dogs at the Museum: Tsai Ming-liang Solo Exhibition,* a "sleepover" at an art museum.[22] But Tsai's particular approach not only expands cinema beyond the screen, or, ambivalently, beyond the movie theater—suggesting Tsai's sense of melancholy for lost venues and audiences he hopes to regain, often selling tickets himself to students on the street[23]—but also expands the "other spaces" Tsai has worked to invest with wayward, cruisy, queer potential.

Feeling Melancholy, Cruisy, Sleepy

Tsai Ming-liang's films are remarkably queer. I argue that his films are "queer," not simply because the director is gay—Tsai "came out" on film in *Afternoon* (2015), or perhaps as far back as his early play, *The Wardrobe in the Room* (1983)[1]—but in the way they challenge the binary division between heterosexuality and homosexuality as supposedly fixed identity categories. As an auteur, Tsai produces a kind of queer metacinema. His hauntingly melancholy films are "metacinematic" in their self-reflexive approach to filmmaking and film viewing, including the prominence of cinema in the international perception of Taiwan.[2] Indeed, Tsai is one of the most celebrated of the "Second New Wave" film directors of Taiwan cinema (having won three Taipei Golden Horse awards and Venice Golden Lion and Grand Special Jury Prizes; he was also the first director commissioned to make a film for the permanent collection of the Musée du Louvre in Paris).[3] Tsai's cinema also plays a critical role in the perception of *tongzhi* (same-sex-oriented) identity within Taiwan.[4]

Cruisy, Sleepy, Melancholy: Sexual Disorientation in the Films of Tsai Ming-liang shows how Tsai expands and revises the notion of queerness by engaging with the local specificity and situated knowledge of the diasporic, migrant, tourist, or otherwise displaced characters in his films and their experiences of sexuality in Taiwan, Malaysia, and France.[5] Tsai's films are queer because they do not conceive of nationality and sexuality as essentialized identities or sexual orientations, but rather help us understand queerness in forms of spatial, temporal, and sexual *disorientation. Cruisy, Sleepy, Melancholy* engages queer film theory and approaches to queer diaspora, queer regionalism, and queer phenomenology to understand Tsai's queering of space.[6] Tsai's films help us think spatially about queerness, including the queerness of crossing borders (the border crossings of the director, the characters within the films, and the films themselves).

In their deliberately disorienting challenge to binary thinking, Tsai's films can "serve as illuminating examples for theorizing the cinema beyond a constricting Asia–West binary or an essentialized Asia," as Guo-Juin Hong suggests, noting the reasons are not merely biographical, "a Malaysia-born ethnic Chinese who began his filmic career in Taiwan and later become a transnational filmmaker par excellence beyond Asia and especially in France," but rather, Tsai's films are "emphatically, if also perversely, concerned with filmmaking itself, with how film cinematizes space and movement."[7] I also aim to expand on the way spatiality is employed by Zoran Lee Pecic to emphasize how queer Sinophone cinema is "neither exclusively queer nor inherently 'Chinese,' neither at the centre nor the periphery," excavating and interrogating "spaces that are caught between the local and the global, between 'China' and elsewhere" thus suggesting a "queer space that challenges identificatory mechanisms that 'fix' queerness in a particular position, in a particular place and at a particular time."[8] In the wake of Tsai's announcement of his retirement from commercial feature filmmaking, and based on interviews with the director, this book reappraises Tsai's body of work in order to advance a new theory of the relationships among queer sexuality, space, and our experience of cinema.[9]

Cruising the Corpus

Tsai has established himself as an auteur by the way in which he weaves specific motifs throughout his cinematic corpus, especially his symbolic use of water—flooding rain, broken water pipes, polluted rivers, hoarded bottled water, sudden drought compensated for by watermelons, or water vapor in bathhouses and clouds—nostalgic use of old-fashioned Mandarin popular music, and noticeably minimal spoken dialogue.[10] He also consistently uses the same set of actors, often playing similar familial roles, anchored by his "male muse" Lee Kang-sheng ("Hsiao Kang"),[11] with Miao Tien often cast as his father, Lu Yi-ching as his mother, and Yang Kuei-mei, Chen Shiang-chyi, Chen Chao-jung, and Norman bin Atun in erotically triangulated roles vis-à-vis Hsiao Kang. While sometimes psychologically opaque, Tsai's characters are often shown in intimate, embodied moments, in solitude, in underwear, masturbating, sleeping (or suffering from insomnia), crying, urinating, bathing, eating, and staring at fish tanks and television screens, or attempting to make contact in public and quasi-public spaces like movie theaters, urban streets, parks, and bathhouses, with an emphasis on nonnormative forms of sexuality.[12]

The *auteurist* approach thus seems the most amenable to examining Tsai's way of revising and reworking images, characters, metaphors, and scenarios. Such a practice creates an *intratextual* network between each of the films in his oeuvre, which rewards viewers familiar with his earlier films, and sometimes creates a sense of narrative continuity, but perhaps it is more accurate to say it creates *folds* of meaning and experience for the viewer.[13] This intratextual network is complemented and complicated by the frequent *intertextual* references Tsai makes to French New Wave cinema (specifically François Truffaut), 1950s–60s Hong Kong and Taiwan cinema (Grace Chang musicals and King Hu swordsman films), pornography, and very obliquely to Hollywood movies. Tsai also often "signs" his film credits, or includes handwritten notes, adding a *paratextual* signature by the queer auteur.[14]

The following introduction is intended to act as a thematic guide to the roles that feeling "melancholy," "cruisy," and "sleepy" play in Tsai Ming-liang's self-consciously auteurist oeuvre. Elaborating these affects also involves looking at the relays and resonances among them—for example, "cruisy" as a mood, mode, and affective potential that can be linked to feeling melancholy or sleepy—plus their cultural inflections.

I will also be *situating* keywords like "queer" (*ku'er*), "Sinophone,"[15] and "postcolonial"[16] in relation to Tsai's geopolitical position. A Chinese Malaysian who grew up in Kuching, Tsai arrived in Taiwan (Republic of China [ROC]) in 1977 at the age of twenty as a student of drama and cinema, during a time of major political transformation. As Agata A. Lisiak explains: "The beginning of Tsai's career coincided with massive political and social changes in Taiwan. After nearly four decades of strict censorship, prohibition of free assembly and association, arrests, torture and executions of dissidents, martial law was lifted in 1987. Already after Chiang Kai-shek's death in 1975, a modest relaxation of state restrictions allowed Taiwanese cinema to bloom."[17] Tracing Taiwan's complex colonial history and "unevenly postcolonial present" in relation to the categories of *tongxinglian* (homosexuality) and *tongzhi* (gay/lesbian; literally, "comrade"), Fran Martin argues compellingly that Taiwanese modernity must be thought of as "a highly syncretic formation" shaped by "Japanese colonialism, Chinese Republican culture, the US military presence and economic aid, and KMT [Kuomintang] Cold War political and cultural practice" complicated by more recent attempts to redefine Taiwan's modernity through appeals to "values of democracy, liberalism, and pluralism" and Taiwan's independence from the People's Republic of China (PRC).[18]

Being sensitive to Taiwan's complex colonial and Cold War history thus also calls for me to foreground my own positionality, engaging primarily with English-language publications on Tsai's films that foreground issues of Chinese translation and transnational reception.[19] I will also elaborate upon nuances in translating his film titles. Arguably, problems of language, translation, and communication may partially explain the notable lack of spoken dialogue in Tsai's films. But rather than representing a deficit, I will argue for the films' fruitful disorientation of our assumptions about speech and nationality (especially in chapter 4). Tsai's films suggest that the problems, queer gaps and slippages, and potentialities of cultural translation go beyond the linguistic and challenge the common belief that there can be no communication except in speech.[20] Instead, Tsai's films lend themselves to translation in a different way, through different cultural and theoretical traditions, and I hope here to provide one of many ways to read Tsai's multicultural corpus.

Melancholy

Many of the most significant publications on Tsai's films focus on questions of time—temporality and duration, but also nostalgia and melancholy—or what Song Hwee Lim has named "a cinema of slowness."[21]

Addressing melancholy, I situate my work within queer Sinophone film studies[22] like Shi-Yan Chao's *Queer Representations in Chinese-Language Film and the Cultural Landscape* and Jean Ma's *Melancholy Drift: Marking Time in Chinese Cinema.*[23] Chao contends that "gay melancholy in Chinese society . . . can be understood first and foremost as a structure of feeling constituted by a sense of loss that exists in immense tension with heteronormative family and social institutions."[24] Ma elaborates Tsai's "chronopolitics" of sexual identity, which "mounts a sharp-edged critique of heteronormativity, the patriarchal family, and the nation even as it eludes a representational politics based on visibility and the legibility of an unambiguous gay sexuality."[25] She foregrounds the temporal dimension of melancholy films by Tsai Ming-liang, Hou Hsiao-hsien, and Wong Kar-wai as a way of avoiding the spatial metaphor of Chinese "diaspora" that she notes might still center the idea of "home" or "nation."[26] However, I will contend that theorizing queer diaspora, queer regionalism, and queer sexual spaces can move beyond such limitations.

But I also hope to add to the "major"—and majorly theorized[27]—affect of melancholy within modernist, postmodern, and queer theory the more "minor" affects of feeling "cruisy" and "sleepy." These vernacular terms also suggest more capacious affects than the medicalized or anthropological categories of melancholia, cruising, and sleeping.[28] Time plays a significant role in each: the interminable grief of melancholia versus the "proper" and gradual time of mourning,[29] the way cruising entails "waiting" (calling for patience),[30] and sleep as a way of marking time with a pause.[31] However, I contend that we need a queer theory of space and spatial practices to understand Tsai's cinematic exploration of feeling melancholy, cruisy, and sleepy.[32] For example, I note the melancholy caused by urban "renewal"/disappearance, and real estate markets explored throughout his body of work. Tsai's films often feature characters falling asleep temporarily in spaces available for rent, as I will illustrate.[33]

What ties together Tsai's films most profoundly, I will argue, is his concern with space. Tsai and his cinematographer Liao Pen-Jung's typically static camera placement often highlights architectural space and the way it is utilized, navigated, and imbued with meaning by the inhabitants: postcolonial urban spaces that are labyrinthine, abandoned, under construction, squatted in, claustrophobic, hidden, domestic, liminal, rented, haunted, and, above all, cruisy—invested with surprising erotic potential. His first three major feature films are sometimes referred to as his "Taipei trilogy" (*Rebels of the Neon God* [1992], *Vive L'Amour* [1994], and *The River* [1997]), and Tsai's films, perhaps especially *The Hole* (1998), are often discussed as expressing a particular kind of urban malaise and alienation.[34] But I am especially interested in elaborating the co-implication of sexuality and space within Tsai's body of work, and how a phenomenology of space must attend to the affective charge of sexual, gendered, liminal spaces like movie theaters, bathhouses, parks, and hotels.[35]

While temporal and spatial thinking are "never really alternative to each other," as Eve Kosofsky Sedgwick reminds us in *Touching Feeling*, like Sedgwick I hope to push back against an occupational tendency in queer theory to "underattend to the rich dimension of space" (she singles out the work of Judith Butler and the way Esther Newton's pioneering discussion of the space of drag clubs in *Mother Camp* drops out in Butler's use of Newton's work to theorize gender performativity in more temporal terms as *repetition* in *Gender Trouble*).[36] Sexuality and affect are irreducibly phenomenological for Sedgwick, and she suggests conceiving of them in terms of relations that are "beside," noting how "beside" helps avoid dualistic or teleological thinking about identity.[37] My approach to affect and sexuality thus attends to queer phenomenology and film phenomenology, and spatial relations between bodies beside each other in space, and among bodies and places.[38]

Spatial and Sexual Disorientation

Tsai's films help us think spatially about queerness as a form of disorientation. The concept of "sexual disorientation" was first proposed by Michael Moon in his essay "A Small Boy and Others: Sexual Disorientation in Henry James, Kenneth Anger, and David Lynch."[39] Moon explains how these artists' works help the reader or viewer to see how "sexuality is not so much oriented by its object, by the perceived gender or age, race, social class, body type, style of dress, and so on, of its object, as it is *dis*oriented by mimesis."[40] He calls this *sexual disorientation* in order to denote "the position of reader- or viewer-subjects at least temporarily dislocated from what they consider their 'home' sexual orientation and 'disorientingly' circulated through a number of different positions on the wheel of 'perversions,' positions that render moot or irrelevant our current basic 'orienting' distinction, homo/heterosexual."[41] Moon is thus primarily concerned with how mimetic desire in cinema like that of Anger and Lynch (and here I add Tsai) disorients and temporarily dislocates sexuality from any "home" or "orienting" binary distinction.

In her book *Queer Phenomenology: Objects, Orientations, Others,* Sara Ahmed further elaborates the concept of sexual disorientation with regard to the experience of migration and queer relations to home, adding an important spatial dimension. Building on these two queer scholars' work, I will show how Tsai connects sexual disorientation to spatial disorientation specifically through his manipulation of cinematic space.[42] I will also foreground the role of "orientation"—including the connotations of "orient"—in Tsai's evolving relationship to Taiwan, Japan, Malaysia, and France, aiming to "dis-Orient-ate" an Orientalist and binary understanding of Asia versus the West.[43]

Cruisy

The concept of the spectator as cruisy and/or sleepy is particularly relevant to Tsai's films, notably his film about a *cruisy* movie theater on the night of its final screening, *Goodbye, Dragon Inn* (2003) (the subject of chapter 2). I draw on the work of Roland Barthes here for the way in which he queerly inflects these terms—via Marcel Proust for the term "sleepy," and via Renaud Camus for the term "cruisy."[44] Cruising has been a vital part of queer spatial practices, but Barthes also suggests it might describe the reader's relationship to the text.[45] Tsai's complex relationship to France, specifically his homages to French New Wave director François Truffaut, makes the intergenerational and transnational queer conversation I create with Barthes apropos.[46] In addition, both Barthes and Tsai have reflexively thematized their "retirement" in significant ways in relation to age, illness, and melancholy, but also to the spatial figure of "retreat," as Tsai discusses in *Afternoon.*[47]

That cruising as a *spatial* practice also has an *ethical* dimension has been an important topic in queer theory, especially in the work of John Paul Ricco *(The Logic of the Lure),* José Esteban Muñoz *(Cruising Utopia),* and Samuel R. Delany *(Times Square Red, Times Square Blue),* as well as the contemporary European research cluster "Cruising the Seventies," which explores cruising as a method for tracing the queer past and surviving in the present and future.[48] I extend such work via my consideration of cruising (in Chinese, "fishing"), queer ethics, and space in Tsai's films.[49] Specifically, I argue that Tsai's cinematic attention to preserving what are often fleeting queer spatial practices can help us to combat the amnesia wrought by gentrification and displacement.

I hope to bring out the queer spatial practices of cruising and the ethical role cruising plays within Tsai's exploration of urban "queer-scapes."[50] The spaces in Tsai's films elicit an affective atmosphere, mood, or potential for contact that I am calling *cruisy,* following the term's use in gay guides—those spatial maps that can reorient our understanding of the sexual landscape of cities.[51] Tsai also "disorients" space through juxtapositions of public/private (rented spaces), reality/fantasy (abrupt musical numbers), and waking/sleeping.

Sleepy

"Sleepy" is a third term, reminiscent of Proust's opening to *Swann's Way* quoted in the epigraph to this book.[52] The spectator of Tsai's films might feel sleepy ("dreamy") but is also remarkably alert to minute details of daily life, which links his filmic practice to Andy Warhol's.[53] Warhol and Tsai are queer filmmakers worth comparing, I suggest, so here I want to connect Warhol's *Sleep* (1963) with Tsai's *No No Sleep* (2015), a short film shot in Japan in a sauna and capsule hotel, another rented, "cruisy" space; and his film *I Don't Want to Sleep Alone* (2006), where I argue that Tsai explores both spatial and sexual disorientation (the subject of chapter 1).[54]

No No Sleep is one of Tsai's "postretirement" films, and the seventh installment in the "Walker" series of international site-specific, exhibition/platform-specific collaborations with his muse Lee Kang-sheng. In this series, based on the sixteenth-century Chinese story of the Tang dynasty monk Xuanzang's legendary pilgrimage to India, Lee is dressed as a Buddhist monk walking at a snail's pace.[55] But I will employ the film here as a way to catalogue the intertextual and intratextual motifs of homoeroticism, cruisy rented spaces, and sleepy affect pervading Tsai's entire body of work.[56]

According to Tsai, the "Walker" films are not just about Lee Kang-sheng walking very slowly but are also about the city and the people in the city where they are filmed. When I met Tsai at his studio in New Taipei City (with my colleague Jonathan Te-hsuan Yeh, who also helped translate our conversation),[57] I explained that I stayed at the Capsule Hotel Oasis in Ikebukuro, Tokyo, because I was interested in seeing the shooting location of No No Sleep (無無眠 Wú wú mián).[58] Tsai clarified the meaning of the title as a pun on a passage of the Heart Sutra, the best known and most popular Buddhist scripture (translated by Xuanzang), on the doctrine of emptiness: 無無明 wú wúmíng (明 = intelligence, 無明 = ignorance, hence 無無明 = no ignorance, but also 亦無無明盡 yì wú wúmíng jǐn = no end to ignorance, or, there is no ignorance, and no extinction of ignorance, 無無明，亦無無明盡).[59] Thus, the title of Tsai's short film connotes 無眠 no sleep (sleeplessness, insomnia), and 無無眠 (literally) no no sleep, no lack of sleep, no sleeplessness, no insomnia, but also implies no end to sleeplessness.

Prompted by my questions about the motif of rented spaces in his films, Tsai observed that in Tokyo people seem to live a "portable life"; they travel without settling, as can be seen in the ubiquitous phenomenon of capsule hotels and internet cafés.[60] He noticed a sense of instability in people seeking temporary shelter, also a major theme in his final feature film Stray Dogs (2013) about a homeless family squatting in Taipei (the subject of chapter 5).[61] This peculiar way of life results in anxiety and insomnia, restlessness. He also gets a kind of "science fiction" feeling from Tokyo, perhaps explaining the brightly overexposed lighting in the shots of Tokyo streets, pedestrian walkways, and JR train stations filmed from inside the train (with remarkably disorienting effect manipulating relative motion).[62] As Hou Hsiao-hsien did in Café Lumière (2003), Tsai filmed on the JR Line without a permit (a practice discussed in a documentary about Hou's film, Métro Lumière), since

filming on the train was a spur-of-the-moment decision.[63] Compared
to *Journey to the West* (2014), set in Marseille, France, where bystanders
stopped to observe Lee Kang-sheng as the walking monk, Tsai noted
that Japanese people walk faster and show less curiosity about other
pedestrians.[64] *No No Sleep* can be understood as engaging in a kind of
sensory ethnography of contemporary Tokyo.[65]

The actor Ando Masanobu, who appears alongside Lee in the sauna
and capsule hotel scenes, was familiar to Tsai from previous meetings
in Taiwan and Japan. Tsai decided to cast him intuitively since he felt
a film in Japan had to have a Japanese actor (the postcolonial significance of another Japanese man in *Goodbye, Dragon Inn* will be discussed in chapter 2). Ando expressed his interest straightaway without
knowing what he would be asked to do: lather soap and shower naked
sitting on a stool or standing before getting into a hot bath (in the traditional Japanese style). Tsai observed that the Japanese love bathing—
this is common knowledge in Taiwan since most of the hot spring
locations in Taiwan were developed during Japanese colonial rule (1895–
1945).[66] He explained that they shot the scene of Ando showering before
his bath twice because the first time he was clearly self-conscious about
his nudity, so it did not look natural, but the second time it did.[67]

A homoerotic relation between Ando and Lee is established when
the two men share the hot bath together, and the distortion of the
water's surface both warps and displaces their bodies so they appear to
be touching. This homoeroticism was noted by YouTube commenta-
tors asking, "Is this a gay film?" "They say gay porn is weird. But I
didnt' [sic] know it was this weird."[68] While Japanese people might be
quick to point out that public baths are not sexual, homo*eroticism* exceeds
homo*sexuality* per se, and the viewing experience clearly provokes a
kind of sexual disorientation.

Tsai employs his leitmotif of water to create a homoerotic "aesthetics of suspension" (akin to Barry Jenkins's *Moonlight* [2016]) that
implies both floating and tension,[69] in order to suggest the ambiguity
of both homoeroticism and water's symbolic meaning. We can observe
this indeterminacy in a shot of Lee in the sauna, with sweat streaming
slowly down his ruddy cheeks in a way that is indistinguishable from

tears flowing from his eyes, as he hovers halfway between sleep and waking (Figure 2). This is one of many close-up shots of Lee's face in Tsai's body of work, and one of many ambiguous shots of tears in Tsai's oeuvre (like Yang Kuei-mei's long crying jag at the end of *Vive L'Amour*), but here any narrative meaning that might be attributed to crying is suspended. The face as affective landscape par excellence indicates the point of indeterminacy among the affects under examination here: melancholy, sleepy, and cruisy/tears, steam, and sweat.

No No Sleep ends with the two men sleeping in apparently adjacent capsules. Their proximity is an effect created by the editing technique of cutting between each capsule. In this montage we perceive, paradoxically, an even more complexly disorienting homoerotic relation than seeing two men naked in a bath together, despite their spatial separation. The montage prompts the viewer to create the homoerotic meaning. This particular editing pattern goes all the way back to Tsai's treatment of the two young men in adjacent hotel rooms in his first feature film *Rebels of the Neon God*. Tsai frequently uses parallel editing to create narrative relations between characters, and this device can be

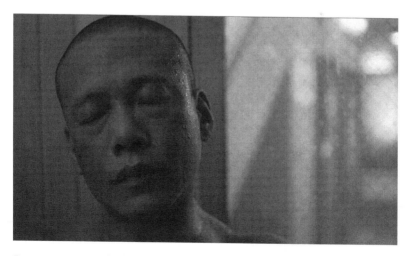

FIGURE 2. *No No Sleep* (Tsai Ming-liang, 2015). Lee Kang-sheng (as the Buddhist monk Xuanzang) sweating in the sauna room of the Ikebukuro Sauna and Capsule Oasis.

seen in other earlier films like *What Time Is It There?* (2001) and *The Wayward Cloud* (2005) (discussed in chapters 3 and 4).

However, Tsai's most recent films are moving further away from plot-driven narrative cinema toward a different mode of experiencing temporality and cinematic images *as images*, which leads me to connect his recent films, like *No No Sleep*, to Andy Warhol's filmmaking. Andy Warhol's *Sleep* consists of shots of the poet John Giorno (Warhol's lover at the time) sleeping nude. The completed film is not actually a linear, continuous recording of Giorno's sleeping body, but a collage of looped footage lasting five hours and twenty-one minutes.[70] (Tsai admitted that he had not seen Warhol's film, though he had heard of it, so it is left to me to make the cross-cultural and cinema-historical comparison here. Tsai's recent film *Your Face* [2018] is also worth comparing to Warhol's durational close-up Screen Tests.[71])

Like Warhol's "slow" durational cinematic collage of shots of Giorno sleeping naked, Tsai's shots of Ando's almost naked body—looking angelic with his long curly hair, lying in various positions with a towel draped across his waist but not completely covering his genitalia—and Lee's supine, blanket-covered slumber are patient, eroticizing temporal duration itself, like a lover watching someone sleep (Figures 3 and 4).[72] This erotic observation of sleep is in fact a recurring motif in Tsai's films, especially between the men sharing a mattress in *Vive L'Amour* (when Hsiao Kang [Lee] climbs into bed with the sleeping Ah-jung [Chen Chao-jung]) and between women in *What Time Is It There?* (Chen Shiang-chyi and a woman from Hong Kong she meets at a café in Paris who takes her home for the night). But we notice here that Ando is tossing and turning, unable to sleep, illuminated by the glow of a small television in the capsule (that I learned is playing pixelated heterosexual pornography). For this reason, I would describe *No No Sleep* as a "sleepy" film rather than a film about sleep, per se. And like Proust's narrator, feeling sleepy has profoundly disorienting and re-orienting effects on the body, on our experience of time, and on our understanding and perception of this rented space.

Tsai's short *No No Sleep* can be placed in dialogue and in tension with Warhol's monosyllabic *Sleep* and Tsai's feature film *I Don't Want to Sleep*

FIGURE 3. *No No Sleep* (Tsai Ming-liang, 2015). Ando Masanobu embodying the multiple meanings of the title: sleeplessness/sleepiness. He is illuminated by the glow of a small television in the capsule (playing pixelated porn).

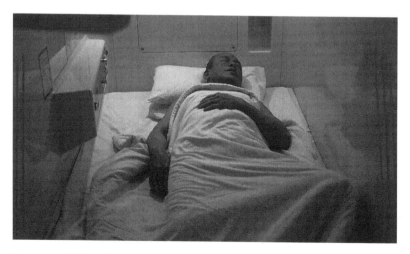

FIGURE 4. *No No Sleep* (Tsai Ming-liang, 2015). Lee Kang-sheng (as the monk Xuanzang) asleep in the capsule with a composition reminiscent of Andy Warhol's *Sleep* (1963).

Alone.[73] As chapter 1 explores in more detail, *I Don't Want to Sleep Alone* (Chinese title: *Black Circles under the Eyes*) represents Tsai's return to his "home" of Malaysia, but he ironically chooses to focus on migrants in the capital of Kuala Lumpur: intimate strangers Rawang (Norman bin Atun) and Lee as an unnamed man whom Rawang is nursing back to health after finding him beaten in the street (Lee also plays a paralyzed man cared for by his mother [Pearlly Chua] and her long-suffering servant [Chen Shiang-chyi]).[74] The two men share a dumpster-rescued mattress together, scrubbed down and tented with mosquito netting. *I Don't Want to Sleep Alone* resonates with Warhol's sleeping muse John Giorno's compassionate declaration: "My intention is to treat a complete stranger as a lover or a close friend."[75]

In one scene, late at night, the two men drag the mattress to a construction site where Rawang works, hoping for some relief from heat and bedbugs, and each man appears to take turns watching the other sleep. Homoerotic longing or curiosity is suspended between them in the air, as if in water, and both the characters and the viewer experience sexual disorientation. We do not know their "home" sexual orientations, and the basic orienting distinction Moon notes between homo/heterosexual is potentially rendered irrelevant, for characters and viewers alike. This scene takes place in a queerly dislocated and reoriented space: the apparent privacy of a shared mattress, but in a cavernous unfinished construction site.[76] Here we have a perfect emblem of Tsai's imbrication of sexuality and space, in one of many queer cinematic meditations on feeling disoriented, melancholy, cruisy, and sleepy. The next chapter will look at *I Don't Want to Sleep Alone* in terms of recurring motifs of temporal, spatial, and sexual disorientation in Tsai's oeuvre, and how the film explores themes and practices of border crossing, queer diaspora, and queer uses of space (relations "beside" like sharing a mattress)[77] explored throughout this book.

I conceive of Tsai's creative and critical agency and position in terms of queer tactics:[78] the queerness of Tsai's films, his characters, and his relationship with Lee Kang-sheng challenges easy classification (as gay) but "cruises" a queer erotic experience of rented spaces. While showing how Tsai is in conversation with French cinema, and participating in an ongoing conversation regarding Western queer theory and Taiwanese translations and transformations,[79] I will also be engaging with "queer Asia as method," enabling us to see Tsai's place within the wider circulatory and interlocutory networks of queer East and Southeast Asian cinemas.[80] The following chapters intervene in a number of debates: (1) Tsai's critical approach to nostalgia and multiple forms of disorientation; (2) queer film phenomenology and theories of (meta) cinematic experience; (3) queer approaches to camp and porn, challenging other critics' readings of Tsai as antiporn, or camp and sex as antithetical; (4) Tsai's evolving relationship to France and French commissioning institutions; (5) the question of home and homelessness in Tsai's career and films, and what his relationship with Lee Kang-sheng might teach us about "how to live together";[81] and (6) new approaches to embodied spectatorship, nontheatrical exhibition, and sleepy cinema.

1

Spatial and Sexual Disorientation

Vive L'Amour and I Don't Want to Sleep Alone

[T]his body of [Chinese-language] films is considered a "queer cinema" not only, or even primarily, because they portray lesbian, gay, bisexual, and/or transgender characters, but more often because they unsettle the parameters of heterosexuality and its kinship structure; confound expectations of coherence between gender identity, gender expression, and the sexed body; expand the possible configurations of sexual and emotional bonds; and subvert the aesthetic conventions and heterocentric presuppositions of mainstream cinema.

—Helen Hok-Sze Leung, "Homosexuality and Queer Aesthetics"

Tsai Ming-liang is known for films tinged with nostalgia and a sense of temporal and spatial disorientation in the modern world, often featuring encounters between strangers in liminal urban environments. Tsai's short film *The Skywalk Is Gone* (2002) functions as a coda to his feature film *What Time Is It There?* (2001). In the earlier film, Hsiao Kang (Lee Kang-sheng) and Shiang-chyi (Chen Shiang-chyi) meet briefly at Hsiao Kang's stall where he is selling watches on a skywalk connected to the central train hub Taipei Main Station, and she buys the double time-zone watch he is wearing before she leaves for a vacation trip to

Paris (even though he says it is "bad luck" since his father has just passed away; he is in a state of mourning and misrecognized haunting established at the start of the film). In *The Skywalk Is Gone*, Shiang-chyi has returned to Taiwan and the audience expects that she will finally rendezvous with Hsiao Kang after each has undergone a similar sort of melancholy temporal and spatial dislocation shown through the parallel storytelling between Taipei and Paris in *What Time Is It There?* Our expectations are frustrated along with Shiang-chyi, however, as she finds that the skywalk is now "missing" (it has been torn down), and she is ticketed for jaywalking as she tries to cross the street where the skywalk once was.

This sense of absence and longing reflects a kind of nostalgia in Tsai's work that is both spatial and temporal, and results in a unique form of disorientation and dislocation, as Brian Hu explains: "The two objects of nostalgia are the city of Taipei, which transforms so continually that Shiang-chyi does not even recognize it after returning from vacation, and the cinema itself, particularly the culturally Chinese cinema of the past and the local Taiwanese cinema of the present."[1] Nostalgia literally means homesickness and thus suggests longing for a lost place.[2] Hu argues that the nostalgia for any urban landmark is in some senses interminable:

> We realise that in an era of continuous dislocation through urban construction, the disappearance of a landmark leads to a search that cannot end: if a skywalk is gone, how does one possibly look for it? Shiang-chyi travels to where she thinks it ought to be, only to be led around it, in front of it, or on the other side of it altogether. The nostalgia for an industrialising city is thus by definition never ending.[3]

Hu thus suggests that the hopeless search for a place that is gone results in a feeling of dislocation that is also stretched out in time. Like the character Hsiao Kang—who in *What Time Is It There?* is constantly adjusting clocks all over Taipei to read Paris time instead—Tsai himself is hyperaware of his own temporal dislocation. Indeed, nostalgia is more commonly defined as a wistful affection for a time period in the past.

Hu's reading of Tsai's "retro" desire emphasizes how the past is mediated through film and music. Cinematic nostalgia and temporal dislocation are activated by the seemingly kitsch or camp Mandarin pop song from the 1960s, "Nanping Bell," Tsai ends the film with (I will argue that Tsai's relation to such songs should be understood in terms of queer camp).[4] Hu explains the historical significance of these now unpopular forms of popular musical songs, which were earlier used in Tsai's near-future dystopian musical film *The Hole* (1998):[5]

> As in *The Hole* (1998), *The Skywalk Is Gone* communicates with 1960s Chinese cinema through popular song. Famous outside of Asia for its martial arts films, 1960s Hong Kong cinema also saw a flourishing musical genre. Among its most popular stars were Lin Dai and Grace Chang, the latter's songs appearing prominently in *The Hole*. Tsai has cited these early musical films as direct influences on his own filmmaking.[6]

The Hole ends with a nostalgic *paratextual* epilogue looking both forward and backward: "In the year 2000, we are grateful that we still have Grace Chang's songs to comfort us."[7] Tsai has declared a great fondness for this sort of song in opposition to the American-influenced pop music currently predominant in Asia, which he sees as a result of what he calls the "terrifying phenomenon" of globalism.[8]

While globalism represents a kind of homogenizing effect for Tsai, certainly his films treat transnational and cross-cultural relations as a way of reflecting on the contingencies of both place and time. Issues of postcolonial temporality and spatiality are foregrounded by the fact that *What Time Is It There?* is a French/Taiwanese coproduction that critically reflects on Asian tourism in France, French *nouvelle vague* film, and the significance of "time zones."[9] In an interview with Michael Berry titled "Tsai Ming-liang: Trapped in the Past," Tsai clarifies how the past figures in his films: "It is not that I am setting out to introduce sixties culture to a new generation; it is just that my own life, or at least my ability to accept popular culture, is stuck in that era. And it is only natural that my films are a reflection of what's going on in my life."[10] This notion of being stuck or trapped in the past is also one of the defining features of melancholia.[11]

In this chapter, I will compare Tsai's early film *Vive L'Amour* (1994) with *The Hole* and his later *I Don't Want to Sleep Alone* (2006), drawing out these themes of disorientation, both in the spatial and temporal sense, and adding another dimension that I am calling "sexual disorientation." I draw from Michael Moon's application of this concept to David Lynch's *Blue Velvet* (1986) in my argument that sexual disorientation unsettles our assumptions, our "knowingness," about sexual identity, resulting in uncanny and queer effects on our reading of desire in cinematic narratives.[12]

Queer in the sense used in this book challenges the fixity implied by the logic of sexual orientation. The sexual orientation model understands desire as a sort of compass with a magnetic north aligned according to gender polarity, with sexual difference therefore determining whether "opposites attract" or whether homosexuality is thought of as same-sex attraction or gender inversion (where a man desiring another man must do so "as" a woman). Moe Meyer argues that unlike the identities labeled "gay and lesbian," "Queer sexualities become, then, a series of improvised performances whose threat lies in the denial of any social identity derived from participation in those performances. As a refusal of sexually defined identity, this must also include a denial of the difference upon which such identities have been founded."[13] In other words, queer involves the "deconstruction of the homo/hetero binary."[14] My reading of Tsai's films as having *queer effects* is in part a way of understanding why he has insisted that he is "sick of people labeling my films as 'gay films.'"[15] This may have to do with trying to avoid, early on, the ghettoization of LGBT film festivals, although Tsai has also stated that he has evolved on this issue.[16] I will argue that *Vive L'Amour, The Hole,* and *I Don't Want to Sleep Alone* perform a deconstruction of sexual identity in that they treat sexuality and desire as performed without cohering in an identity, but also in the way that they understand how bodies are oriented in space, in other words, how they "queer" space.

In her book *Queer Phenomenology*, Sara Ahmed extends Moon's concept of sexual disorientation—subjects "at least temporarily dislocated from what they consider their 'home' sexual orientation"[17]—to think about what happens when space itself is made queer. I will quote a passage at length here (excerpting her discussion of Maurice Merleau-Ponty) so that I may return to particular aspects of her argument in my readings of the films in this chapter.

What does it mean to think about the "nonresidence" of queer? We can consider the "affect" of disorientation. As I have suggested, for bodies that are out of place, in the spaces in which they gather, the experience can be disorientating. You can feel oblique, after all. You can feel odd, even disturbed. Experiences of migration, of becoming estranged from the contours of life at home, can take this form. . . . At the same time, it is the proximity of bodies that produces disorientating effects, which, as it were, "disturb" the picture . . . queer moments happen when things fail to cohere. In such moments of failure, when things do not stay in place or cohere as place, disorientation happens. The question becomes how we "face" or approach such moments of disorientation. . . . Queer would become a matter of how one approaches the object that slips away—as a way of inhabiting the world at the point in which things fleet.[18]

Ahmed's remark here about "the object that slips away" would certainly apply to Hu's understanding of nostalgia in Tsai's *The Skywalk Is Gone*. Furthermore, Tsai's love of songs considered camp might be thought of as a queer way of inhabiting the world in which things are fleeting. But I would first like to consider her very promising connection between the "nonresidence" of queer and the affect of disorientation (which is considered a hallmark of Taiwan New Cinema).[19]

Vive L'Amour, Vive la Différance

In a familiar plot pattern of "synchronous monadic simultaneity" identified by Fredric Jameson in relation to urban Taiwanese cinema,[20] Tsai's *Vive L'Amour* observes the convergence or coincidence of three individuals: a young realtor May Lin (played by Yang Kuei-mei), a street vendor

Ah-jung (Chen Chao-jung), and a columbarium salesman Hsiao Kang (Lee Kang-sheng). May Lin repeatedly fails to rent a large upscale apartment, and the three characters are shown variously occupying the vacant apartment like squatters: Hsiao Kang steals the key to the apartment and surreptitiously uses it as a sort of experimental space like a child might "play house": he unsuccessfully attempts suicide, takes a bath, washes clothes in the bathtub, tries on women's clothing, does cartwheels in the hallways, and makes out with a watermelon with holes cut in it, which he then uses as a bowling ball in one of the hallways (and this watermelon motif will recur in Tsai's "porn musical" *The Wayward Cloud* [2005]). While he is bowling, he is caught by Ah-jung who demands to know how he got in, despite the fact that he also has a dubious right to be there since he was merely brought there for a one-night stand by May Lin (after a remarkable scene of May Lin and Ah-jung cruising each other on the streets of Taipei). Ah-jung and Hsiao Kang form a sort of "buddy" relationship, however, and Ah-jung offers to drive Hsiao Kang anywhere he wishes. They go to the columbarium Hsiao Kang distributes flyers for, where people purchase niches for funerary urns, in a darkly comic parallel with the real estate theme of the film (also foreshadowing a recurrent motif of Taiwanese rituals of mourning for the deceased first seen in *What Time Is It There?*).

In another rather childlike or "adolescent" moment, Hsiao Kang masturbates in the empty apartment but is interrupted by the sound of Ah-jung and May Lin once again coming back to the apartment for a quick tryst, so he quickly hides under the bed, and proceeds to masturbate as they have sex on the bed above him. Once May Lin leaves and Ah-jung falls asleep, Hsiao Kang silently joins Ah-jung in bed, and watches him sleep with a look of intense and melancholy longing, finally giving him a rather timid kiss on the lips (Figure 5).

It is for this reason that Hsiao Kang is identified as "gay" in the promotional literature for the film, but I would agree with Angelo Restivo's demurral: Restivo finds the film "to be ambiguous on this point."[21] This is where I think the concept of sexual disorientation is helpful, not only for making sense of a romantic triangle established by the film, but for understanding that Hsiao Kang's "performances" in the apartment

FIGURE 5. *Vive L'Amour* (Tsai Ming-liang, 1994). Hsiao Kang longingly watching Ah-jung as he sleeps.

have a destabilizing effect on how we read his gender and sexual identity. As Ahmed argues, "queer moments happen when things fail to cohere" and Tsai manages to challenge the coherence of the audience's perception of the sexual identities of his characters. This disorientation-effect also helps explain a shy lesbian kiss in *What Time Is It There?* after Shiang-chyi meets a woman in Paris who is visiting from Hong Kong, and spends the night at her apartment, but their potential sexual encounter, as in most of Tsai's films, is missed or cut short at a kiss. In both of these examples, the idiom "sleeping together" is more literal than figural or, especially, consummated. Through these ambiguous cinematic encounters and moments of both contact and failure, Tsai thus highlights multiple forms of spatial, cultural, and sexual disorientation.

Ahmed's framework is also useful for how she draws attention to the sense of being "oblique," which she identifies in relation to the contours of "life at home." In her reading of emptied-out space and homosexuality in "*Vive L'Amour*: Eloquent Emptiness," Fran Martin argues that the film "references the homophobic cultural logic that opposes *jia* [family home] to *tongxinglian* [homosexuality] and relegates the latter to the realm of ghostliness, emptiness, and unreality. But it cites that system only to destabilise it by suggesting, at the last moment, that love between men might, on the contrary, occasion a hitherto unimagined fullness and connection."[22] I would like to expand Martin's reading slightly by arguing that domestic space is not only destabilized but also *disoriented* by Tsai's film in the ways *each* character is shown temporarily appropriating real estate. Examples include Ah-jung quickly rolling up the clothing he is selling without a permit on a blanket in the streets of Taipei, May Lin futilely waiting around in various vacant buildings for potential buyers, her active participation in the game of cruising in a food court and outside a movie theater with Ah-jung, and Hsiao Kang "playing house" in a queer fashion. As Ahmed suggests, Tsai depicts bodies that are out of place even as he emphasizes the idiosyncratic ways in which they use the space of the empty apartment. In this way, his film is "queer" in both its treatment of space and its treatment of sexual desire and behavior (including female sexual dominance and "gender inversion" in scenes between May and Ah-jung, who cruised each other in a quasi-gay fashion).[23] I agree with both Martin and Ahmed that it is the proximity of bodies that produces disorienting effects, and that contact, even if only fleeting, creates the dialectic between emptiness and queer plenitude in Tsai's films.[24]

The Hole: Disorienting Genre

Tsai's foray into the dystopia or disaster film genre, *The Hole,* originally commissioned as part of a 2000, *Seen By* series for French television, refines Tsai's concern for the uses of domestic space and his disorienting approach to sexual desire.[25] It is both the sense of estrangement and the proximity of bodies that can result in an oblique or queer relation to space, as Ahmed notes. Tsai constructs a situation in which proximity and social communication are rendered anxious and suspicious through a vague but omnipresent fear of viral infection, in this case by the Kafkaesque "Taiwan fever"[26] that causes people to act like cockroaches. The interactions between characters in the film are thus mostly oblique and phobic. In an interview with David Walsh, Tsai explains the concept behind this film that he was commissioned to make as a vision of the new millennium: "I thought the end of the century was too close to describe a future predicament, so it's actually a reflection of contemporary society. And being so dark, and full of disease, I think it's my observation of people also being so lonely, existing in their own solitude."[27] The interviewer remarks that this alienation is fairly universal at this point. Tsai agrees:

> I think that although I invented a disease called "Taiwan fever," there are similar situations happening in many parts of Asia. There are a lot of strange diseases developing. Ever since AIDS there are all sorts of unprecedented diseases. In terms of the cockroach symptoms . . . a lot of people live in poverty, and try to adapt to the role, to the living environment they have, and acquire the characteristics of a cockroach. Being adaptable to a bad situation. Living purely on survival instinct, with a lack of any dignity.[28]

Like another "contagious allegory" and uncanny genre obsessed with infection and survival, namely the modern zombie film (such as George Romero's *Dawn of the Dead* [1978], set in a shopping mall), Tsai uses the established genre of the disaster film to throw the realities of modern life into stark relief.[29] Tsai's approach to the ecocritical disaster film emphasizes "living on" (in the words of Lauren Berlant's *Cruel Optimism*)[30] under negligent neoliberal conditions, rather than typically patriarchal ideologies of "survivalism" that try to restore the Family (seen in AMC's *The Walking Dead* [2010–2022], Japan's *Survival Family* [2016], or South Korea's *Train to Busan* [2016]).[31] This approach can again be contrasted to Romero's "progressive" politics of race and gender in his original "living dead" trilogy.[32]

Through the character of the woman in the downstairs apartment (Yang Kuei-mei), Tsai highlights the interconnection of germ phobia and social phobia. As a counterpoint, Tsai reveals her fantasies of contact through rather disjunctive musical sequences, using the songs of Grace Chang mentioned earlier in connection with 1960s Hong Kong musicals. It could be argued that the conventions of the song-and-dance musical are now not only camp but also uncanny to modern audiences. Their appearance is increasingly highlighted as a moment that breaks with the diegesis. Examples include Lars von Trier's tragic meta-musical *Dancer in the Dark* (2000); Royston Tan's *15* (2003), with its homoerotic music video pastiche moments of the boys singing violent Singapore gang anthems; and Joshua Oppenheimer's *The Act of Killing* (2012), a documentary in which former Indonesian militia death squad killers reenact their mass killings in whichever movie genre they wish, including lavish musical numbers.[33] In *The Hole,* Tsai hybridizes two genres—the disaster film and the musical—in a way that is deliberately disorienting.

Reading the desire expressed by *The Hole*'s musical sequences might seem straightforward in that they are about the desire of a woman for a man (Lee Kang-sheng).[34] But the Brechtian "alienation effect" that Tsai achieves through such a jarring aesthetic juxtaposition renders the scenes all the more "queer."[35] Certainly, the film is structured by sexual difference, but this sexual difference is problematized and rendered uncanny along with the conventions of romance. For example, the interactions between the man and woman take place around a gaping hole in the floor, with the man above the woman, but if the hole is a sexual metaphor, as Kai-man Chang has suggested,[36] it is complicated by the fact that both parties "penetrate" it: he through dangling his leg and vomiting through it; she with bug spray that floods his apartment.

The man and the woman also interact on two levels of a courtyard, another hole in the middle of a building, in a way that highlights their missed encounters and renders them each oblique to the other. This is echoed by a scene in *The Skywalk Is Gone* in which Shiang-chyi and Hsiao Kang pass each other by on the escalators below the Shin Kong Mitsukoshi department store across from the Taipei Main Station (revising a scene from the start of *The River* [1997]).[37] In chapter 3, I will explore the possibility that *The Hole* demonstrates Jacques Lacan's assertion that "there is no sexual relation," in other words that fantasies of overcoming sexual difference and lack are illusory.[38] But, rather than Lacan's transcendentalization of heterosexual sexual difference, this obliqueness of gender and sex is potentially both feminist and queer.

Here I diverge from Chang's suggestion that *The Hole* represents Tsai's shift from exploring gay issues to feminist concerns like gender equality. Following Chang's argument about female fantasy in the film, I would suggest the film is capable of doing *both*.[39] Reading the film in terms of an aesthetic of "*tongzhi* camp," Shi-Yan Chao argues that "Tsai's camp sensibility is manifested in and through his five musical numbers, and his refusal to subordinate them to the narrative also highlights the performative aspect of heteronormative eagerness for musical integration. While there are no gay characters in *The Hole*, the film's heightened camp aesthetic epitomizes the director's unspoken (if not unspeakable) homosexual desire, and poignantly demonstrates the gay auteur's insistent negotiation with compulsory heterosexuality."[40] Tsai's queer take on heterosexuality and his critique of heteronormativity can be compared to New Queer Cinema director Todd Haynes's AIDS-allegory film *Safe* (1995), which also hybridizes the genres of plague cinema and domestic melodrama.[41]

My queer reading of Tsai follows Eve Kosofsky Sedgwick's suggestion that queer refers to the "gaps" of meaning where elements of gender, sex, sexual orientation, sexual preference, and sexual identity refuse to line up monolithically.[42] The camp musical sequences help highlight this nonstraight understanding of sexual differentiation and disorientation, and Tsai takes this up again in his "porn musical" *The Wayward Cloud*, which features the same characters as *What Time Is It There?* and *The Skywalk Is Gone*. Tsai's *askew* or queer handling of genres (romance, comedy, *nouvelle vague*, disaster, musical, pornography) is also disorienting for his critics, perhaps especially with *The Wayward Cloud*, but that is precisely what makes his films so ripe for queer reading: they challenge our orientation to normative plots about heterosexual difference and to normative rules of genre (as Leung suggests in the epigraph to this chapter).[43]

Once Upon a Mattress: *I Don't Want to Sleep Alone*

Tsai's *I Don't Want to Sleep Alone* is in some ways a continuation of the kind of queer love triangle explored in *Vive L'Amour*.[44] In this case, the triangulation is between a migrant Bangladeshi laborer Rawang

(Norman bin Atun), a battered Chinese homeless man he rescues and nurses back to health, Hsiao-Kang (Lee Kang-sheng), and a domestic servant, Chyi (Chen Shiang-chyi). They all share the same building with a *kopitiam* (coffee shop) on the ground floor operated by Chyi's older woman boss (Pearlly Chua) who is looking after her apparently unconscious paralyzed son (also played by Lee Kang-sheng) in Kuala Lumpur's Chinatown area (near the now-demolished Pudu Prison, whose long mural painted by prisoners is visible in Tsai's film).[45] In this film's mimetic erotic triangle there is much more overt expression of jealousy by the man who so lovingly cared for Hsiao Kang's bruised and frail body, but while he threatens to cut his throat near the end of the film, he is unable to carry out further violence to this body, and Lee strokes away his tears in a moment pregnant with both possibility and loss.

This film marks Tsai's return to his native Malaysia (though he was born in the Chinese community of Kuching, Sarawak, not Kuala Lumpur). However, like Ahmed's remarks about feeling oblique and queer through the disorienting effects of migration, Tsai's relationship to his "home" is quite complicated. Ian Johnston notes that

> the personal roots of this disconnectedness are broader than simply those of Tsai's sexuality. In Taiwan, he is a *huaqiao*, an overseas-born Chinese, someone simultaneously of the culture and outside it; which is a reflection of and variation on his shifting outsider status, growing up in Malaysia, as a Chinese in an officially-sanctioned/mandated majority Malay culture. So, in this return to his country of birth, his identification with migrant labourers—the most despised and discriminated-against portion of the population in wealthier Asian countries (Filipina maids in Hong Kong, Thai labourers in Taiwan etc)—is most appropriate.[46]

Tsai uses his ambivalent or oblique relationship with his homeland to critically comment in his film on both environmental and political aspects of contemporary Malaysian culture.[47] In terms of the environment, in *I Don't Want to Sleep Alone* "a smoky haze settles on the world of the film, just like the apocalyptic rain of *The Hole* and the drought of *The Wayward Sky [Cloud]*, enveloping the characters in a cocoon that is frustrating and then finally embracing." Johnston notes, "This haze has a realistic basis in the annual forest fires in Indonesia that cause such havoc to the air quality in Malaysia. But in a radio broadcast we hear the blame for this shifted onto migrant workers and the supposed illegal fires that they light in Kuala Lumpur."[48] Along with moments of nudity, this radio broadcast was censored in the cut of *I Don't Want to Sleep Alone* that was finally approved for viewing in Malaysia due to its perceived political volatility and negative depiction of Malaysia.[49] Like *The Hole*'s environmental disaster/disease that is introduced and politicized through radio announcements, television news, and interviews with distrustful civilians about garbage and how to sterilize tap water—echoing news transmissions and media skepticism in Romero's zombie genre—Tsai uses an environmental problem to comment on the political problems of xenophobia and racism.

It is therefore important to my discussion of Tsai's sense of dislocation that the film's most tender relationship is between a Bangladeshi laborer and a Chinese homeless man without a passport. Johnston notes how "there's no overt sexuality to Rawang's care for Hsiao Kang. It's a tender act of love, a selfless giving of himself to another."[50] Instead, we can understand their relationship as demonstrating a "queer" ethics of care and intimacy.[51] This is in contrast to the forced care Chen Shiang-chyi's servant character must give to the paralyzed son. In a shockingly uncomfortable scene, Chyi is physically forced by her boss to use her own hand to masturbate the boss's son in his incontinence diaper. This scene completes a vaguely incestuous action begun in an earlier scene where the boss massages her son's stomach with ointment, moving closer and closer to his crotch. These ambiguities between sexuality and care, these contrasts between forced and freely given care, and shocking scenarios reminiscent of sadomasochistic scenes from Lynch's *Blue Velvet* and their effects on the voyeur/viewer as described by Moon,[52] underscore the significance and ambivalence of sexual disorientation in Tsai's films.

Rawang's lost-and-found mattress is also *polysemic* in Tsai's film. It is the place where Rawang nurses Hsiao Kang back to health (with a poster stating "I Love You" above it). Rawang's roommate Shiva complains that he is "always bringing strangers here to sleep," an ambiguous statement but one that suggests a kind of queer erotic generosity. Seeking respite from the heat and bedbugs, Rawang and Hsiao Kang drag the mattress to the construction site where Rawang works.[53] The two potential pairs—Rawang and Hsiao Kang; Hsiao Kang and Chyi—each use this mattress. The latter two using the mattress is the original cause of Rawang's jealousy, after he finds them asleep on it together. However, the audience knows that Chyi and Hsiao Kang could not sexually consummate their relationship because they were choked by the smoke, further postponing consummation after an earlier scene where, following Chyi's refusal to have sex outdoors under a bridge by the Klang River, they are not able to get a hotel room because Hsiao Kang does not have a passport.[54] The lady boss, whom Hsiao Kang has previously masturbated in the alley behind her restaurant, also seems jealous as she too stalks the couple to the construction site, but is humorously foiled by walking down the M. C. Escher–like stairs into a pool of water in the dark—literally completely disoriented.

But Moon argues that sexual disorientation is not only a matter of triangulations of desire. Rather, he follows Mikkel Borch-Jacobsen's re-reading of René Girard's hypothesis about mimesis as primary in the formation of desire: rather than focusing on "simple triangulations of desire among persons, as he criticizes Girard for doing," Borch-Jacobsen "attempts to theorize the thoroughly *dis*orienting effects mimesis has on desire ('[D]esire is not oriented by pleasure, it is (dis)oriented by mimesis . . .')."[55] Moon thus argues that "sexuality is not so much oriented by its object . . . as it is *dis*oriented by mimesis."[56] I would suggest that *Vive L'Amour* and *I Don't Want to Sleep Alone* are also not simply about triangulations of desire among persons.[57] Rather, they are studies in the disorienting effects of mimesis, specifically in the way characters are shown imitating and initiating each other: Hsiao Kang holding on to porn magazines for Ah-jung, or Rawang helping the injured Hsiao Kang locate the toilet and urinate by supporting his half-naked body from behind, or teaching Hsiao Kang how to tie a sarong around his waist after he gives him a sponge bath and carefully removes his underwear (the scene of Rawang washing Hsiao Kang's underwear was also censored in the Malaysian version).[58] When they have to deal with bedbugs, Hsiao Kang scratches Rawang's back, literalizing the expression "I'll scratch your back if you scratch mine," and suggesting how one mirrors the other.

The musical numbers mimicked and ventriloquized in *The Hole* also illustrate Moon's claim that "*no* desire is our own—that is, originates with us; if desire is indeed primarily induced by imitation, mimed and ventriloquized, then it is impossible to maintain our ordinary 'orienting' notions of which desire we are at home with and which ones we are not."[59] Mimesis is the primary way in which we register *queer* eroticism in these films, but in ways that are disorienting rather than confirming of our sense of any "home" orientation of these characters, hetero/homosexual. But this is not, Moon cautions, "in order to try to efface this distinction, which on the gay side has been so murderously enforced" but rather "to extend our thinking about the dependence of both so called high and popular culture . . . on the sexually 'perverse' for their energies and often their representational programs."[60] This is especially urgent for Tsai's Malaysian film in the way it addresses homophobia.

Tsai uses *I Don't Want to Sleep Alone* to comment on the role of homophobia within Malaysian politics, specifically through the Chinese title of the film and the prop of the discarded mattress. The political aspect of Tsai's film is not only in the "allusions to the xenophobia and discrimination that the migrant workers suffer," Johnston points out, but also in the Chinese title of the film: *Hei yan quan* translates to "black circles under the eyes" which can mean both shadows under the eyes from lack of sleep and "a black eye" and

Tsai has himself stated how through both this title and the mattress of the story he is referring to the case of Anwar Ibrahim, the former Deputy Prime Minister and Minister of Finance, whose political downfall was orchestrated by Malaysian Prime Minister Mahathir Mohammad in a patently faked court case. One aspect of the court case was an accusation of sodomy (a crime in Malaysia [based on a British colonial era law]) where a stained mattress was brought as evidence into the courtroom and where Anwar appeared nursing a black eye. Yet Tsai's own take on

this is not so politically orientated but rather developed in a more gener-
alised statement that fits in with his own concerns in the film, namely that
"you could really be somebody and be brought down to being nobody"—
down, in other words, to the level of I Don't Want to Sleep Alone's three
main protagonists, Hsiao Kang, Rawang, and Chyi.[61]

Johnston's suggestion that Tsai's film is less politically "orientated"
might be productively complicated by an attention not only to homophobia as a political problem (and legacy of colonialism), but also how
queerness and sexual disorientation factor into Tsai's intervention in
local political problems of xenophobia and racism as well as that of
South–South migration and labor.[62] Tsai's concerns are both general
and local, and his characters figure in problems that are both romantic
and political. By calling attention to his own sense of spatial and temporal disorientation in relation to the globalization that is also experienced by his migrant characters, Tsai demonstrates the political and
critical value of queer diasporic and queer regional lenses.[63]

Like Wong Kar-wai's Happy Together (1997), about two gay men
from Hong Kong living in Argentina at the time of Hong Kong's
"handover" from Britain to China, Tsai focuses on queer transnational
migration and labor, and like Wong, Tsai manages to make a cheap
color-changing fiber-optic toy into a kind of poetic yet ironic image
of romantic fantasy and longing.[64] The final shot of the film shows
a dream-sequence image of the three main protagonists sleeping on
the mattress (or we could follow Rey Chow in reading the mattress as
the fourth character).[65] We have already seen a more "realist" scene of
Chyi in the attic crawling, exhausted, into the bed with Hsiao Kang,
noticing that he was not alone but sleeping next to Rawang (embodying the film's English title: I Don't Want to Sleep Alone). Now this shared
mattress floats very slowly down into frame in the dark pool of water
in the middle of the vacant unfinished construction site. The fiber-optic
toy almost comically floats by as another bittersweet nostalgic Mandarin song (by Hong Kong singer Lee Hsiang-lan, a cover of "Eternally"
set to the theme music of Charlie Chaplin's Limelight[66]) accompanies
the fade to black and credits rolling (Figure 6).

FIGURE 6. *I Don't Want to Sleep Alone* (Tsai Ming-liang, 2006). Chyi, Hsiao Kang, and Rawang sharing a mattress that is floating in a dark pool in an unfinished construction site in the dreamlike fantasy ending of the film.

The way these slumbering bodies share the mattress might imply queerness in the form of bisexuality or polyamory,[67] but it also emblematizes a more diffuse form of eroticism associated with being sleepy and dreamy, which Barthes associates with the collective bodily experience of the urban cinema in "Leaving the Movie Theater":

> Not only is the dark the very substance of reverie . . . it is also the "color" of a diffused eroticism; by its human condensation, by its absence of wordliness . . . by the relaxation of postures (how many members of the cinema audience slide down into their seats as if into a bed . . .) the movie house . . . is a site of availability (even more than cruising), the inoccupation of bodies, which best defines modern eroticism—not that of advertising or striptease, but that of the big city.[68]

In this remarkable passage, Barthes seems to suggest that seeing these characters "sleeping together" or "going to bed together" might return these idioms from the figural to the literal in a way that does not diminish but actually defines "modern" eroticism, precisely this kind of relaxation of postures and inoccupation of bodies makes them sites of erotic availability to each other (and the spectator).

But we cannot forget that the characters we see here are also, emphatically, bodies exhausted from labor.[69] Yet this points to one of the other comforts of the cinema. Like *The Hole*, Tsai also juxtaposes the rather destitute reality of urban labor in Malaysia with the Tamil musicals that entertain the migrant workers, and he uses the romantic fantasy elements of the lyrics to these musicals to comment ironically on the rather less idealized vision of sexuality and desire his film depicts.

The final disorienting shot of the bed floating on black water in the midst of ambiguous urban demolition/construction signifies—to twist a phrase from another text by Barthes—the "drift far from that all-too-pure pair" hetero-homo.[70] Tsai's films and characters thus depict both disturbing experiences of dislocation and productive forms of spatial, temporal, and sexual disorientation that ultimately encourage in his audiences a queer way of inhabiting a fleeting and shifting world.

2

Leaving the Cinema

Metacinematic Cruising in
Goodbye, Dragon Inn

Trick becomes the metaphor for many adventures which are not
sexual; the encounter of a glance, a gaze, an idea, an image,
ephemeral and forceful association, which consents to dissolve
so lightly, a faithless benevolence: a way of not getting stuck in
desire, though without evading it; all in all, a kind of wisdom.

—Roland Barthes, Preface to Renaud Camus's *Tricks*

In his evocative essay "Leaving the Movie Theater," Roland Barthes
proposes a particular way of going to the movies: "by letting oneself
be fascinated *twice over,* by the image and its surroundings—as if I had
two bodies at the same time: a narcissistic body which gazes, lost, into
the engulfing mirror, and a perverse body, ready to fetishize not the
image but precisely what exceeds it: the texture of the sound, the hall,
the darkness, the obscure mass of the other bodies."[1] This urban eroticism in the dark of the movie theater, the bodies sliding down in their
seats as if in a bed, is crucial as a way to reinsert "queer" eroticism into
movie-going.[2] Barthes enjoys the anonymity and availability of the dark
mass of the bodies in the movie house in opposition to the foreclosed
eroticization of the place in the well-lit domestic scene of the television,
noting how "television doomed us to the Family."[3]

That gay/queer[4] men in particular have made use of theaters for the
purpose of cruising has a long history, which shows up in *Midnight*

Cowboy (1969), *Happy Together* (1997), *Far from Heaven* (2002), and in Samuel R. Delany's *Times Square Red, Times Square Blue*.[5] But Barthes's works suggest that "cruising" might also be thought of as a more general type of experience: the reader's relation to the text, which at the same time "cruises" him or her.[6] Tsai Ming-liang's *Goodbye, Dragon Inn* (2003) connects both these aspects: the situation of the movie theater as a place of the anonymous multitude cruising each other in the dark, and the *drifting* relation of the spectator to the cinematic image.[7] Tsai simultaneously provokes fascination and distance, which best captures Barthes's sense that "I am hypnotized by a distance; and this distance is not critical (intellectual); it is, one might say, an amorous distance."[8] Both Barthes and Tsai emphasize the place and spatial conditions of the cinema itself—the shadowy box, the "big screen"—but also temporality—both in the sense of "duration" and "history." They ask: what does it mean to leave or say goodbye to "the cinema"? Barthes clarifies the pun: "Whenever I hear the word *cinema*, I can't help thinking *hall*, rather than *film*."[9]

Tsai's film fits into the longstanding genre of "metacinema" (from *Sunset Boulevard* [1950] to *Scream* [1996], or from *An Amorous History of the Silver Screen* [1931] to *Electric Shadows* [2004]),[10] but it also takes on a particular local significance: Tsai's choice of King Hu's 1967 *Dragon Inn* (aka *Dragon Gate Inn*)—as the final film screened at a movie theater that is closing its doors indefinitely—indexes the rise and fall of Taiwanese cinema, thereby invoking the industry's history in a wistful manner.[11] Such a description of the historic place of cinema can also be found in Barthes and Delany, but this is not simply nostalgia for a lost era, as Delany insists.[12] Instead, it laments the loss of the social contact that movie houses fostered—social contact that is cross-class and queer, thus feared by social conservatives.[13] Like José Esteban Muñoz in his discussion of the "Ghosts of Public Sex," I believe that rather than being simply hopelessly nostalgic, the present is haunted by the virtual potential of queer ways of occupying space, as in parks, public restrooms, arcades, and movie theaters.[14] Before directly engaging with *Goodbye, Dragon Inn,* however, I will consider the problem of *how* to read Tsai's work, foremost in relation to his entire oeuvre, since Tsai sees himself as an auteur; next in relation to critical debates about East–West aesthetic differences and influences; and lastly in relation to questions of modernism/postmodernism and globalization.

Beyond the auteurist repetition of certain motifs—pouring rain, a notable lack of dialogue, the same Taipei locations and actors/roles— Tsai's work is pervaded by the overall theme of urban alienation yet potential contact with strangers. Regarding *The Hole* (1998), Tsai has explained: "I think it's my observation of people also being so lonely, existing in their own solitude. It's what I've observed about Taipei."[15]

Some examples of intratextual links between Tsai's films (working backward) include:

- *What Time Is It There?* (2001)—which features scenes in the same movie theater used in *Goodbye, Dragon Inn,* and a hilarious gag about public restroom sex (Figure 7), and is explicit about heterosexual, gay, and lesbian cruising in Taipei and Paris.[16]
- *The River* (1997)—his most explicit treatment of another anonymous liminal queer erotic space: the bathhouse, and the possibility of accidental incest therein.[17]
- *Vive L'Amour* (1994)—a film about real estate, cruising, and a kind of "sexual disorientation" in the triangulated and mimetic relation between Hsiao Kang (Lee Kang-sheng), Ah-jung (Chen Chao-jung), and May Lin (Yang Kuei-mei).[18]
- *Rebels of the Neon God* (1992), where the recurring character of Hsiao Kang is first introduced in an ambivalent homosocial (homoerotic and homophobic) "stalking" relation with Ah Tse (Chen Chao-jung).[19] Hsiao Kang spends a great deal of time hanging around in arcades in the Ximending youth entertainment district of Taipei, which is where Tsai "discovered" the young actor.[20]
- *All Corners of the World* (1989)—Tsai's early television drama focuses on a family of movie ticket scalpers (who argue over Hollywood versus Asian films like Hou Hsiao-hsien's *A City of Sadness* [1989]) and features clandestine sex in movie theaters and love hotels in Ximending.[21]

Lee Kang-sheng (as the character Hsiao Kang) acts as a kind of muse within Tsai's oeuvre, representing a version of the sexually ambiguous "rebel without a cause" icon James Dean (who appears in poster-form in *Rebels of the Neon God*, another metacinematic gesture).[22]

These themes are in some ways a continuation of the concerns of the "New" Taiwan and Hong Kong cinemas, as Nick Browne has characterized them: "The contemporary, one might almost say 'modernist,' mode of Taiwan and Hong Kong cinemas adapts the art film format to the underlying and fundamental cultural trope of the period [the 1980s]—cultural and psychological dislocation."[23] In Taiwan cinema, "its central emblem is the aleatory form of metropolitan simultaneity and contingency."[24] Browne cites Fredric Jameson's argument in "Remapping Taipei" to explain how Edward Yang's *The Terrorizers* (1986)[25] "adopts a European form—a sustained formal reflexivity . . . [which] gives us a kind of modernist picture of total dissolution of the traditional social and ethical complex."[26] Regardless of whether this traditional social and ethical complex is "mourned" in Tsai's works (a case could be made

FIGURE 7. *What Time Is It There?* (Tsai Ming-liang, 2001). A gag about gay public restroom cruising in the same movie theater toilet featured in *Goodbye, Dragon Inn* (Tsai Ming-liang, 2003)—the man in the stall had stolen Hsiao Kang's (stolen) clock in the auditorium.

either way), Browne's emphasis on the emblematic metropolis is crucial for thinking about Tsai's films.[27]

Jameson goes into more detail regarding what he calls the "providential" plot of interwoven character destinies, or "the narrative of synchronous monadic simultaneity (henceforth, SMS)," which he finds essentially modernist. However, he notes that

> the return, therefore, of what looks like a Western modernist narrative paradigm (the SMS) in the work of a Third World filmmaker (in the thick of postmodernity as a global tendency, if not a global cultural and social reality) can be expected to raise new questions, which do not include the relatively idle one, debated by critics and journalists at the film's [The Terrorizers] first showing in its native Taiwan, as to whether the director had sold out to essentially Westernizing methods or style.[28]

It could be debated whether Tsai's work, like Yang's, should be seen as "Westernized"—a label Rey Chow has interrogated for all its ambivalence in relation to Chinese-language films that receive Western accolades, such as Zhang Yimou's or Tsai's.[29] Certainly, What Time Is It There? stands in dialogue with the history of the French nouvelle vague, with its metacinematic incorporation of Truffaut's The 400 Blows (1959).[30] But Fran Martin has argued that this retrospective transcultural citation needs a more complicated explanation than Eurocentric notions of "influence."[31] She says that "an adequate understanding of Tsai's cinema cannot be gained from simply observing stylistic resemblances between Tsai's style and those of particular European directors" but rather that we need to look "to the historical and cultural specificities of the local context of these films' production, conditions that determine, to a great degree, the cultural meanings of the films' emphatic European citations."[32] Brian Hu has also noted a shift in Tsai's work starting with The Hole, and discusses Tsai's short film The Skywalk Is Gone (2002) in terms of Taiwanese and Chinese rather than Western cinema traditions.[33] Hu argues that Tsai's films reflect nostalgia for Chinese and Taiwanese cinema history, and for the constantly transforming city of Taipei. I will return to the question of nostalgia, but would like to consider the role of the city itself first.

Rented Spaces

Setting a film in Taipei has specific effects on the basic SMS paradigm according to Jameson: "the novel as a multiplicity of plot strands," what Jameson calls the "Gidean project," persists in *The Terrorizers*, but with the difference that the urban framework is "here intensified and becomes something like a primary message of the narrative form itself."[34] The city frees up character and plot construction because "its chance meetings and coincidences allow for a far greater variety of character-destinies, and thereby a web of relationships that can be spread out and unfolded in a dazzling array of distinct ideological effects."[35] If the city intensifies the problematic of chance encounters, as we see in Tsai's early "Taipei Trilogy" (*Rebels of the Neon God, Vive L'Amour,* and *The River*), what are the distinct ideological effects of the urban setting of the movie theater itself? Echoing Michel de Certeau's work on "walking in the city," Tsai stresses the aleatory and oneiric aspects to how people make use of this place, a space that is simultaneously literal and metaphoric, actual and virtual.[36] De Certeau describes the utopia of the city in terms of "the relationships and intersections of these exoduses that intertwine and create an urban fabric . . . a universe of rented spaces haunted by a nowhere or by dreamed-of places."[37] The movie theater is precisely such a rented, dreamed, and haunted space for Tsai.

Tsai's *Goodbye, Dragon Inn* essentially works as a form of "ethnomethodology" for thinking about this space and how it is used (in other words, "spatial practices"). In the tradition of ethnomethodology, Tsai makes use of various "breaching experiments" in the movie theater and the men's restroom in order to reveal tensions and desire circulating among strangers in the theater.[38] Many of these are demonstrated through the character identified only as "the Japanese tourist" (Mitamura Kiyonobu). In the theater during the screening of *Dragon Inn*, the first rule breached is the rule of "silence": the young man glares over at a couple loudly smacking their lips while eating. The second rule governs proximity: as the Japanese tourist attempts to get a light for his cigarette from an older man in a leather jacket (Shih Chun, who was in fact an actor in the original *Dragon Inn*) sitting one row in front of him, another man swings his bare feet over the seat behind him, close to his face. Then another older man sits directly next to the Japanese tourist, despite the fact that we can see the rest of the theater is empty. This crowded composition of men is full of an ambivalent tension of desire/repulsion.

What follows is a game of "musical chairs," which finally ends with Mitamura sitting down next to Shih, once again trying to get a light for his cigarette, getting close and turning directly toward Shih, who continues staring ahead at the screen. Shih only looks over after the young man walks away, unsuccessful in this first attempt at contact (with the cigarette as well-known tool and signifier of "cruising"). Meanwhile, the soundtrack of *Dragon Inn* comments ironically on the scene through dialogue of two men meeting for the first time in a more classical providential plot:

"What name do you go by?"
"Hsiao Shao-Tze"
"Brother Hsiao. Where do you make your living?"
"I don't work. Anyplace where someone will spare some food, I'll stay awhile. I don't really think about what I do."
"I don't mean to be rude, but may I ask you a question? You come to this wilderness . . . for what purpose?"

So, we are in fact presented with an ironic juxtaposition of classical and newer forms of the chance encounter. Jameson explains how, in its earliest forms (the Byzantine novel), the "providential plot, based on the coincidence of multiple destinies interweaving, was not particularly urban in its spatial requirements."[39] If the urban comes to predominate in films like *The Terrorizers* and Tsai's films set in Taipei and Kuala Lumpur, it is because "the inns and highroads in which the protagonists of the older novel meet by accident and rectify their mistaken identities necessarily require such characters to be travelers with destinies of a specific type—exiles, runaways, pursued or pursuers, so that the plot itself is always molded according to a distinct subgenre of narrative type. The city frees all this up."[40] The homoeroticism of such encounters remains implicit or "virtual" in the classical novel or *wu xia pian* (chivalrous combat film) narrative, but here it is given a new dimension by the scene that follows: the Japanese tourist in the men's restroom.[41] Lee Edelman has argued that this particular space is densely loaded with "coded" homoeroticism, including fraught distinctions between public and private—urinals and stalls.[42]

For the entire restroom scene, the Japanese tourist stands at a urinal next to another man who is smoking, and they are joined by another— again in close proximity despite the long row of urinals. Meanwhile, we see a man leave one of the stalls to wash his hands, and a few moments later, a man's hand inside the stall closes the door shut. The Japanese tourist notices this, and the tension is maintained for the remainder of the scene as the first man to leave the stall continues to wash his hands for over a minute. The "breaching experiment" recurs when yet another man reaches through the men at the urinal to grab

FIGURE 8. *Goodbye, Dragon Inn* (Tsai Ming-liang, 2003). The Japanese tourist in the men's restroom of the theater at the start of the ethnomethodological "breaching experiment" involving personal space and the occupants of the stalls behind them.

his cigarettes left on the top of the wall, revealing the fraught arrangement of "personal space" at the urinal. In total, the restroom scene lasts three minutes without the men at the urinals finishing, which builds the tension and results in an oddly comic effect, uncovering the sink or urinal as an alibi for cruising. This is one of many scenes in Tsai's film that frustrate the audience's desire to see more explicit (gay) sexuality. But as a filmmaker Tsai is clearly interested in frustrating audience expectations, especially about shot duration, desired narrative, and clearly assignable sexual identity.[43]

The restroom scene foreshadows a later scene in which it seems like the storage hallways of the theater have been transformed into an expressionistic cruise park, with several men, including the Japanese tourist, wandering around as if in a maze and pressing past each other in tight quarters, like "shadows in the shade."[44] All of the young man's unsuccessful attempts at making contact (cruising in the most general sense) culminate in a scene in a dark upper hallway where he finally manages to get someone to light his cigarette (as in Kenneth Anger's oneiric cruising film *Fireworks* [1947]).[45] The man who lights his cigarette says to him, "Do you know this theater is haunted? This theater is haunted. Ghosts." The young man attempts to move closer to him, practically pressing his cheek to the man's face, but the man finishes his cigarette and walks away. As he leaves the frame, the young man says, "I'm Japanese" (in Mandarin Chinese), to which the man responds, "Sayonara."[46] The young man is left standing alone for a full minute, and it is unclear what effect the declaration of his nationality/ethnicity is supposed to have. In relation to Taiwan, a Japanese identity is certainly freighted with historical meaning (as colonizer) that is residual in the identity of "tourist."[47] This scene is therefore "haunted" by colonial history and by homoerotic sexual tension at the same time—John Whittier Treat has argued that it can be difficult to untangle the two in international queer relationships in Asia.[48] When the young man returns to the auditorium, he notices a glamorous woman loudly eating watermelon seeds (Yang Kuei-mei).[49] She languorously drops her shoe, bends down to pick it up, and moves up close behind the young man. He looks back at her and, after a pause, leaves the theater in a panic, perhaps thinking she is a ghost. His motives are ambiguous, but his behavior fits the general pattern of missed/failed encounters.

In another missed heterosexual encounter, the ticket woman (Chen Shiang-chyi) spends much of the film trying to make contact with the projectionist (Lee Kang-sheng). She steams a large pink birthday bun and attempts to leave him half, laboriously climbing up to his projectionist's booth with one leg in a brace, which gives her a distinct gait that underscores the long duration of these shots, filmed in deep focus to "describe" the distance she traverses. When she returns after attempts to spy on him, she finds the gift untouched where she left it, and she sits down for a while before finally picking it up (she lingers watching a lit cigarette left behind by the projectionist as it slowly burns). Tsai records over two minutes of her sitting still in profile, with nothing else but the discordant soundtrack of *Dragon Inn*. Tsai's emphasis on the duration of the almost totally still shot causes the audience to pay more attention to the soundtrack. Indeed, his film is not just about watching but also about *listening* to film. Often, what may appear to be mere background noise is in fact a complex ambient "soundscape" including rain and footsteps (recall Barthes's invocation of the "texture of the sound, the hall").

In Saw Tiong Guan's documentary *Past Present*, actress Chen Shiang-chyi is interviewed on the topic of space in Tsai's films, and the way space seems to "speak."[50] She explains: "The space breathes in his films. It's what makes the strongest impression on me." Chen describes the way Tsai's camera placement and filming style create "such great atmosphere" and in the many fine details "so many parts breathe and speak, I think that's so interesting. Like when I worked with him on *Goodbye, Dragon Inn*, even the leg brace my character wore, making that sound in the space, 'click, click, click,' they are speaking, so the actor doesn't need to speak." Commenting on the perception that Tsai's films contain little character dialogue, Chen suggests that "the actor doesn't have any lines, doesn't have anything to say, but the space all around him, or the sound that I just mentioned, or the objects or building, I think those things themselves can speak." Chen's perceptive remarks on what makes Tsai's films unique underscore the importance of space to Tsai's treatment of sound as well as time.

In comparison with the dynamic swordplay of the action film being projected, which is part of the classical cinema of the "movement-image" as Gilles Deleuze has characterized it, this scene of the ticket taker waiting in the booth depicts the pure passage of time. It develops into a purely optical and sound situation. Deleuze explains that in the modern cinema of the "time-image," time is presented in its pure state: "The time-image does not imply the absence of movement (even though it often includes its increased scarcity) but it implies the reversal of the subordination; it is no longer time which is subordinate to movement; it is movement which subordinates itself to time."[51] Thus, Deleuze argues, the time-image has become direct: "This is no longer a sensory-motor situation, but a purely optical and sound situation, where the seer [voyant] has replaced the agent [actant]: a 'description.'"[52] Deleuze finds this exemplified in the cinema of Ozu Yasujiro, in which appear "opsigns, empty or disconnected spaces, [which] open on to still lifes as the pure form of time."[53] The scene from Tsai's film acts as just such a still life, where we can only guess about the character's thoughts or emotions as she hesitates before a situation to which she cannot properly react. Her expression is something like a vague "resignation." But at the end of the film the potential contact or relation between the ticket woman and the projectionist is left open. We see him leave, taking the electric steamer with the half bun she left in it, and she watches him leaving but does not stop him. This same sense of "resignation" coupled with open-endedness can be found in the sign on the theater itself that says: "Temporarily Closed."

Specters of Cinema

Exemplifying Deleuze's account of the shift from the classical (movement-image) to modern (time-image) cinema, the fate of the cinema itself in postmodernity is put into question in Tsai's film. As the original actors from *Dragon Inn*, Shih Chun and Miao Tien (accompanied by a little boy)[54] recognize each other in the lobby after the show, they seem to have become the living "ghosts" of this cinema. They wistfully remark, "I haven't seen a movie in a long time." "No one goes to the movies anymore, and no one remembers us anymore."

The history of Taiwan's film industry has involved several ups and downs, and *Dragon Inn* marks a particular moment in this story. In his account of Taiwanese cinema history, John Lent has explained the impact that changes of thematic content had upon the industry:

> About the time Grand [Movie Company] was going bankrupt, another Shaw Brothers Studio director, Hu Chin-Chuan, migrated from Hong Kong, bringing with him another genre of film that has endured since 1967—swordsman. Hu's first Taiwan-produced swordsman picture, *Dragon Inn*, came out of Union Film Company Studios, which, with its associated companies International Film Company and China Arts Motion Picture Company, then went on to build the largest civilian studio in Taipei—International Motion Picture Studio. Swordsman movies poured out of these and other studios at a blistering rate between 1967 and the mid-1970s.[55]

This history clearly determined Tsai's choice of the film (we might also consider the fact that both directors are part of the Chinese diaspora: Tsai was born in Kuching, Malaysia, Hu in Beijing).[56] In the beginning shots of *Goodbye, Dragon Inn*, which might represent the theater's "golden age," Hu's film plays to a full house, but at the close of Tsai's film there remain only two old men and a child watching. Tsai's homage is underscored in an ironic way by the fact that Tsui Hark produced a remake of *Dragon Inn* in 1992 (directed by Raymond Lee, starring Brigitte Lin and Maggie Cheung).[57] But one could argue that remakes are also sometimes a form of *amnesia,* and do not work the way Tsai intends his homage to work.

Lent explains (circa 1990), "Besides home video, game parlours, more restaurants and parks and more mobility with the growth of the automobile industry, improved television fare is hurting the movie industry."[58] In other words, shifts in urban real estate, changes in youth culture, and multiplexing mean that it is especially unlikely that this

FIGURE 9. *Goodbye, Dragon Inn* (Tsai Ming-liang, 2003). Tsai's long take lingers on the empty theater after the final screening (*mise en abyme* for those watching Tsai's film in an auditorium).

sort of movie theater would ever again be full of people as in the opening scene. It is then particularly ironic that I first watched *Goodbye, Dragon Inn* at home on DVD, the format David Bordwell and others have indexed as one of the reasons (along with piracy) for the decline of movie-going in East Asia and elsewhere.[59] Only later, when teaching the film in a large auditorium, was I able to fully sense the recursive effect of *mise en abyme* that inevitably results when watching the film in a movie theater. The penultimate scene of Tsai's film shows the lights come up on an empty theater, and after the ticket woman cleans up the trash and exits the frame Tsai lingers on the empty hall for what seems like an intensely long "moment of silence" (Figure 9).[60] These few minutes also resemble shots of the empty theater from Dziga Vertov's *Man with a Movie Camera* (1929), both reflexive films acting like "bookends" of a particular historical era of a particular type of theater.[61] Kenneth Chan explains:

> The Fu Ho Theatre represents a pre-video, pre-multiplex cinema, one that often occupies a single building, has a huge screen for Cinemascope

movies, and has a large audience sitting capacity. As an instance of these "grand old dames of yore," the theatre offers a singular cinematic experience, where everyone gathers to enjoy *one* movie, simply because there is only *one* giant screen. The singularity of the filmic experience, of course, implies that there is a greater imagined sense of cultural and social connectivity. . . . The pleasure (and there is pleasure in lamentation) in Tsai's use of the theatre, therefore, is a nostalgic one.[62]

We can also find this feeling in Tsai's three-minute film *It's a Dream*—his contribution to the sixtieth anniversary Cannes anthology film *Chacun son cinema* (2007), wherein Tsai's voice-over recounts a dream of his family occupying the space of a movie theater in Malaysia.[63] We watch them sharing durian fruit (a notoriously culturally specific taste/aroma), while a woman shares pears on a skewer with the man sitting behind her, echoing the eating motif in *Goodbye*. This sort of memorialization is even more apparent in Hou Hsiao-hsien's contribution to the anthology, *The Electric Princess Picture House*, which like *Goodbye, Dragon Inn* juxtaposes the glory days of a theater with its spectral and decrepit present.[64]

Like the almost still shot of the ticket woman sitting in the projectionist's booth, the long take of the theater presents a pure time-image, which is both empty and full of virtual tension or affect. We also experience this when Shih—the original actor from *Dragon Inn*—chokes up watching the final scenes of the film. Tsai singles him out in medium close-up as we watch his eyes well up with tears. It is in fact one of the only moments in Tsai's film when someone seems glued to the screen. Other characters have a purely discretionary attitude toward the film, or a mix of distance and fascination, such as when the ticket woman stares through the back of the silver screen, her face beautifully lit with pinpoints of light, and Tsai intercuts the action onscreen, creating an odd shot/reverse shot "dialogue" between the woman and *Dragon Inn's* characters. This full range of responses once again recalls Barthes's division between the "narcissistic body" glued to the image, and the "perverse body" that fetishizes the dark theater itself.[65] The "sliding down" bodies Barthes describes perhaps represent a different kind of spectator as well, one more attuned to duration, the prolongation of long takes (or what Chan identifies as an aesthetics of "lingering"), and less to narrative suspense and the visual pleasures of identificatory projection.

Tsai's unique approach to narrative and his juxtaposition of his own type of cinematic text alongside that of Hu's classical swordsman film might also be thought of in terms of another division and "doubling" in Barthes—between the text of pleasure and the text of bliss (*jouissance*):

> Text of pleasure: the text that contents, fills, grants euphoria; the text that comes from culture and does not break with it, is linked to a *comfortable* practice of reading. Text of bliss: the text that imposes a state of loss, the text that discomforts (perhaps to the point of a certain boredom), unsettles the reader's historical, cultural, psychological assumptions, the consistency of his tastes, values, memories, brings to a crisis his relation with language.[66]

According to Barthes, the subject who can keep these two texts in his[67] field—who can keep "the reins of pleasure and bliss" in his hands—is an anachronistic subject, who "simultaneously and contradictorily participates in the profound hedonism of all culture" *and* participates in "the destruction of that culture: he enjoys the consistency of his selfhood (that is his pleasure) and seeks its loss (that is his bliss). He is a subject split twice over, doubly perverse."[68] Hu's film *Dragon Inn* is a text of pleasure that does not necessarily break with the patriarchal ideology of its culture (as Chan points out), whereas Tsai and his viewers are in the position of Barthes's anachronistic subject. Tsai's film simultaneously pays homage to the pleasure of Hu's film and brings the audience to a crisis that unsettles our assumptions (about sexuality, cultural tradition, narrative, etc.). Even if Tsai's long takes cause boredom, Barthes points out that this is a common response to such disorientation: "Boredom is not far from bliss: it is bliss seen from the shores of pleasure."[69]

Tsai closes *Goodbye, Dragon Inn* similarly to his use of the romantic musical numbers in *The Hole,* with a melancholy song by Yao Lee with the lyrics:

I remember
Under the moon
I remember
Before the flowers
So much of the past
Lingers in my heart
Half is bitter
Half is sweet
Year after year
I can't let go
Can't let go
Can't let go
Under the moon
Before the flowers
Can't let go
Can't let go
I'll remember with longing forever[70]

Tsai has explained the function of old songs by Grace Chang in *The Hole* in a way that also fits *Goodbye, Dragon Inn:* "On another level, the musical numbers are weapons that I use to confront the environment at the end of the millennium. Because I think that toward the end of the century a lot of qualities—such as passionate desire, naive simplicity—have been suppressed. The musicals contain those qualities. It's something that I use psychologically to confront that world."[71]

But are we then only talking about nostalgia? Many critics responding to Tsai's film seem confident in this reading.[72] But Jameson in particular is suspicious of postmodern forms of nostalgia for an ungraspable past.[73] And certainly, the death knell of cinema has been heard a few times already, so much so that people speak of the "deaths of cinema" in the plural. However, Deleuze takes a slightly different approach to metacinematic reflection and argues:

It was inevitable that the cinema, in the crises of the action-image, went through melancholic Hegelian reflections on its own death: having no more stories to tell, it would take itself as object and would be able to tell only its own story (Wenders). But, in fact, the work in the mirror and the work in the seed have always accompanied art without ever exhausting it. . . . By the same token, the film within the film does not signal an end of history, and is no more self-sufficient than is the flashback or the dream: it is just a method of working. . . . In fact, it is a mode of the crystal-image.[74]

Deleuze explains what he means by the crystal-image: "the point of indiscernibility of the two distinct images, the actual and the virtual, while what we see in the crystal is time itself, a bit of time in the pure state."[75] These terms provide us with a better approach to Tsai's film, which presents us with a direct image of time and emphasizes the mutual implication of the actual and the virtual. What Tsai seems to be presenting us with is the actual death of cinema, but in his rather tongue-in-cheek invocation of "ghosts"—such as the intertextual reference of featuring the poster for the Hong Kong ghost film *The Eye* (2002)—he makes it clear that the virtual possibilities of contact that the cinema facilitated do not completely vanish.[76] It is a cliché to call images "haunting," but what Tsai seems to provide us with in the long final take of the empty theater is a form of what Jacques Derrida called "hauntology."[77] Tsai dwells on the specters of the cinema.[78]

This is also true of accounts of public sexuality in Muñoz's "Ghosts of Public Sex: Utopian Longings, Queer Memories" and Delany's book, as we are asked to remember queer ways of using space to facilitate cross-class and cross-generational contact between strangers in the city.[79] In defending his positive account of pre-"redevelopment" Times Square porn theaters, Delany plainly rejects those who accuse him, along with Rem Koolhaas and the photographer Langdon Clay, of nostalgia for "the pre-AIDS golden age of hustling."[80] He explains that the sexual contact he describes in area theaters was primarily not commercial (thus not about hustlers). In addition, "it is not nostalgia to ask questions such as the ones that inform the larger purpose of this meditation. How did what was there inform the quality of life for the rest of the city? How will what is there now inform that quality of life?"[81]

He explains that his account is "forward-looking, not nostalgic, however respectful it is of a past we may find useful for grounding future possibilities."[82] Tsai's previous explanation of the power of sentimental songs to confront the present likewise respects the past but interrogates the quality of life at the turn of the millennium. The death of cinema is not really the problem—as Deleuze says about metacinema in general—but rather the death of theaters like the Fu Ho Grand Theater depicted in *Goodbye, Dragon Inn*.[83]

Like Delany, I hope that *cruising* can be folded back into our thinking about the "promiscuous pleasures" of film, to use Paul Burston's phrase.[84] Let us return to Barthes's meditation on "Leaving the Movie Theater." Rather than calling for the destruction of pleasure, Barthes multiplies perversion and pleasure in favor of that which exceeds the image. Victor Burgin explains how Barthes "sliding down in his seat, adopts a posture toward the film that cannot be assigned to a simple position on a scale between enthrallment and vigilance."[85]

In order to distance himself from the image or "take off," Barthes complicates the "relation" between spectator and image by adding the "situation" of the movie theater.[86] Leaving the movie theater he feels sleepy, like he is coming out of hypnosis. And as we know from his diary, "Soirées de Paris," his relation to films and to the entire evening is pervaded by a sense of *drifting* and *cruising* (Barthes's experience of the cinema is also historically particular to a *cinephile* metropolis such as Paris).[87] Tsai's *Goodbye, Dragon Inn* also reflects on the practices of movie-going and cruising in a way that reveals their historical and cultural contingency and mutual implication, and its "goodbye" to the cinema is intensely bittersweet: "I'll remember with longing forever."

3

Queer Camp and Porn Musicals

The Hole and The Wayward Cloud

The opposition between the beauty and the camp may itself be an element internal to camp culture, a camp projection rather than a natural reality. . . . Much contemporary gay male culture represents a sustained effort to recombine the beauty and the camp.

—David Halperin, *How to Be Gay*

Tsai's cinema has always been, in a crucial sense, matter-of-factly pornographic. . . . A general air of muckiness and a fix on 'making do' with small, furtive possibilities for sexual communion (frequently perverse and indirect) are central to his work—indeed, they provide the ground for a very particular kind of Romanticism which marks him as a modern artist.

—Helen Bandis, Adrian Martin, and Grant McDonald, "The 400 Blow Jobs"

Tsai Ming-liang has directed two films that *explicitly* address the pornography industry in Taiwan, although porn has been featured in some form in most of his films. His short film *The Skywalk Is Gone* (2002, a coda to his 2001 film *What Time Is It There?*) ends with the character Hsiao Kang auditioning for a porn film in a doctor's white coat.[1] Hsiao Kang and Chen Shiang-chyi's characters return in his "pornographic musical" *The Wayward Cloud* (2005), set in an apartment complex in the south of Taiwan during a water shortage, where the first porn scene prior to any behind-the-scenes making-of framework features Hsiao Kang in the same doctor's coat with Sumomo Yozakura, an established Japanese adult video actress, using a watermelon as a fetishistic substitute for genitalia (to both humorous and disorienting effect, as Hsiao Kang also becomes a helmeted watermelon-head). Substituting watermelon juice for water during the shortage is also proposed on television. Ignorant of his work in porn for most of the film, Shiang-chyi offers Hsiao Kang glasses of watermelon juice to thank him for his efforts trying to break open the stuck lock on her luggage (from Paris), not knowing he negatively associates watermelon juice with the scene he just filmed. Some critics assume that the tragicomic or grotesque tone of *The Wayward Cloud* shows the auteur director's antipathy to pornography, but I will argue here that it is more productive to read the film in terms of the cinematic mode of queer camp.

I also want to question the received wisdom—best summarized in David Halperin's book *How to Be Gay*—that camp and sex are somehow antithetical.[2] The compatibility of camp and porn fandom has been corroborated by recent work in porn studies, in particular David Church's book on the archive and reception of vintage porn and stag films *Disposable Passions,* and the reemergence (and online remediation) of the archive of "feminist camp" videos by sex worker activist pioneers Annie Sprinkle and Carol Leigh, aka Scarlot Harlot.[3] Camp as a framework for understanding Tsai's approach to sexuality and pornography has also been suggested by Sinophone film scholars including Vivian Lee, Song Hwee Lim, and Shi-Yan Chao.[4]

I will therefore propose camp as a queer way of engaging with pornography, and reevaluating the relationship of camp, porn, and musical genre conventions in Tsai Ming-liang's oeuvre. I also draw here on my research as visiting scholar at Taiwan National Central University's Center for the Study of Sexualities on the translation and transformation of Western discourses of queerness and camp in the local context of Taiwan's art film and porn industries, and both the local and transnational reception of Tsai's films.[5]

When I screened *The Wayward Cloud* at National Central University to my graduate students, a woman passing by the classroom kicked open the door due to the amplified female orgasmic noises, to "check" that this was actually for a class.[6] The fortuitous and fortunate aspect of this experience was that the students then were put in the position of defending their right to watch the film (anticensorship), rather than blaming me for "making them watch it" (a familiar problem for anyone who teaches sexuality and media, or "sex media").[7]

This chapter will trace the evolution of Tsai's juxtaposition of musical genre conventions with other genres, beginning with his environmental disaster film *The Hole* (1998), featuring musical numbers presented as fantasy sequences, an intertextual and metatextual approach he returns to and revises in *The Wayward Cloud,* with song-and-dance numbers that critics note ironically recall *Les parapluies de Cherbourg* (1964).[8] I will also explain the intratextual relation of the two characters (Lee Kang-sheng and Chen Shiang-chyi) whose "romance" is traced, or, more accurately, *interrupted* and *postponed,* across three films: *What Time Is It There?*, *The Skywalk Is Gone,* and *The Wayward Cloud* (but which has also been suggested in *The River* [1997] and *Goodbye, Dragon Inn* [2003], and gets transformed into a love triangle in *I Don't Want to Sleep Alone* [2006]). This necessitates revisiting a few key points about sexual disorientation, allegory, and disorienting genres.

Contagious Allegories of Sexual Difference

The Hole envisions an environmental disaster at the turn of the millennium with the outbreak of the Kafkaesque "Taiwan fever" that makes people exhibit cockroach-like symptoms (aversion to light with the urge to crawl and hide) in a historically uncanny, contagious allegory.[9] The plot focuses on a man and a woman who refuse to evacuate: the "man upstairs" (Lee Kang-sheng) and the "woman downstairs" (Yang Kuei-mei) in a large public housing complex. Garbage collection has stopped in the quarantined area, and water will be cut off on the first day of the year 2000. Government workers spray disinfectant that seems more endangering than the disease (the man tries to rescue a cat from the food market stall where he continues to work).

In "Gender Hierarchy and Environmental Crisis in Tsai Ming-liang's *The Hole*," Kai-man Chang explains how, "Instead of having the man upstairs and the woman downstairs fall in love with each other as Hollywood filmmakers would often do, Tsai highlights their gendered differences and power relationships."[10] These gender differences and power relations are illustrated via their hierarchical positioning, spatial dynamics, and interactions around a hole that a plumber makes in the floor between their apartments.

The hole becomes a ludic object/space for the man upstairs (Figure 10): he comes home drunk and vomits into it, uses a hammer to widen it and insert his leg, which almost gets stuck, and uses it as a peephole to observe the woman downstairs, who fights back by spraying cockroach spray through it, or by plugging the hole with tape and with a mop. We thus observe a kind of "war of the sexes," but this is treated with campy humor, and Chang suggests a potential concluding message about gender equality, moving from the "ridiculous" sexualization of the hole (the man's leg getting stuck suggesting *vagina dentata*)

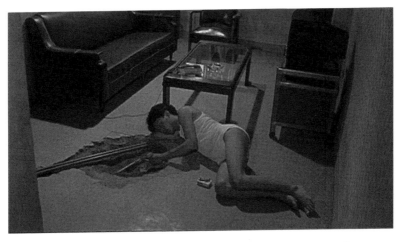

FIGURE 10. *The Hole* (Tsai Ming-liang, 1998). The "man upstairs" reclines in his underwear, smoking and tapping his cigarette ash into the hole made by the plumber (experienced as "ludic" by the man but as a violation by the woman).

to a sympathetic exploration of female fantasy and female agency, illustrated by a phone sex scene between the woman and the plumber, where she transforms the man upstairs' voyeurism into her own fantasy of exhibitionism.

Grace Chang (Ge Lan) musical numbers from 1950s and 1960s Hong Kong cinema with "liberated woman" lyrics are lip-synched in fantasy sequences by the woman downstairs. Tsai's musical sequences manage to "challenge the status quo of gender hierarchy by casting the past into the future, inserting fantasy into reality and turning margins into centers."[11] Chang suggests that, "despite its dystopian vision of the future, the film turns an environmental crisis into an opportunity for gender equality."[12] Tsai thus confronts us with "three urgent and yet seemingly unrelated issues" in fin-de-siècle Taiwan: environmental decay, social alienation, and gender inequality.[13]

Water is an important symbol in the film of both disease and destruction—the TV news warns people to boil water, suggesting that the virus is spread through cockroach excrement in water—and a means of dissolving social alienation and gender hierarchy: Tsai's montage between the apartments highlights their shared water supply between toilets and sinks. At the end of the film, the shared glass of water as the man lifts the woman up to his apartment after she has started showing signs of the fever suggests gender equality and "human solidarity in the face of environmental crisis."[14] The final fantasy sequence—its status as fantasy underscored not only by a costume change to ballroom dance clothes, but also by the fact that the furniture has disappeared from the man's apartment—features Grace Chang's "I Don't Care Who You Are" and the couple partnered in a slow dance.

Chang argues against reading the woman's fantasies in terms of a Freudian/Lacanian idea of "lack" (following Luce Irigaray's critique of "a hole in men's signifying economy").[15] However, I am cautious about this "hole" becoming "whole" reading of the ending because of the way it might *naturalize* ideas of heterosexual union that have been *denaturalized* through camp in the film. Jacques Lacan's insistence that "there is no sexual relation" has the potential to denaturalize heterosexuality (even though, in practice, Lacanian formulations often remystify and transcendentalize heterosexual sexual difference).[16] Elizabeth Grosz clarifies Lacan's assertion: "The subject demands a wholeness, unity, and completion which it imagines the other can bestow on it. The symbolic, on the other hand, requires a subject irrevocably split, divided by language, governed by the phallus and the Other. Love relations aspire to a union or unity that is strictly impossible. The two can never become *One*."[17] Grosz here uses terms that fit the fantastical and *fantasy* unifying ending of Tsai's *The Hole* quite well.

A productive comparison might be made between Tsai's *The Hole* and the near-future science fiction film by Spike Jonze, *Her* (2013), about a man falling in love with an A.I. (his phone OS), which has been read by Matthew Flisfeder and Clint Burnham in terms of "Capitalist Realism" and Lacan's theory of fantasy (as explained by Slavoj Žižek):

> Žižek explains how fantasy helps constitute our subjective experience of reality with reference to an English beer advertisement based on the fairy-tale motif of the woman who kisses a frog believing that he will turn into a prince . . . the woman kisses the frog, which then turns into a handsome prince. . . . The handsome prince then draws nearer to the woman, and as he kisses her, she turns into a bottle of beer. For Žižek, this asymmetry is a clear sign of the Lacanian thesis that "there is no sexual relationship." For the woman, her love and affection are tied to a "phallic" presence: the handsome man who was transformed from the frog. For the man, however, his affections are tied to an object: the bottle of beer—a partial object or the object-cause of his desire (the Lacanian *objet a*). The asymmetry here is that we have either a woman and a frog or a man and a bottle of beer but never the ideal couple as such.[18]

In contrast with Chang's "hopeful" reading of the ending of *The Hole*, the woman's fantasy of the man upstairs is presented as *a fantasy of sexual relation,* of coinciding, and equality, that Žižek and Lacan suggest is impossible due to the nonrelationship of sexual difference, and the way desire is tied to objects, especially under capitalism. As Flisfeder and Burnham clarify: "[W]hen we experience the non-relationship of the sexual difference, we should recall this example as a representation of the fact that the fantasies of each side . . . never overlap."[19] With a comic effect equal to the beer commercial, in *The Hole,* the woman "partner dances" with a fire extinguisher that the man hands her in the musical sequence set to Grace Chang's "Wo Yao Ni De Ai" (I want your love).

Yet, by emphasizing the woman's fantasy *over and against* the man's fantasy, perhaps Chang's reading and Tsai's film suggest that the Lacanian phallic, heterosexual paradigm wherein "there is no sexual relationship" is ultimately irrelevant. The ideal heterosexual couple *as such* is a fantasy, and the film underscores this, but that does not necessarily obviate questions of gender equality beyond the cinematic fantasy of the romantic couple. The problem of shared water during an environmental crisis supplants questions of sexual difference or the symmetry/asymmetry of phallic fantasy.

Is *The Hole* therefore about gender equality? What about gender fluidity? Perhaps we can follow the film's water metaphor further and suggest that it plays out the sexually disorienting effects of "leaky" gender and sexuality distinctions and genre distinctions. *The Hole* can be read as camp both for *hyperbolizing* sexual difference and the vulgar reduction of a woman's genitalia to a "hole"—contradicted by the film's emphasis on the woman's subjectivity and fantasy life—and for the gay connotation of a public restroom stall "glory hole," which might suspend homo/heterosexual difference ("a hole is a hole is a hole").[20] To address these issues, we can turn to Tsai's *The Wayward Cloud,* his second major experiment with juxtaposing genres: environmental disaster films, art films, musicals, and pornography.

Queering Pornography

The Wayward Cloud builds on scenarios involving Lee Kang-sheng and Chen Shiang-chyi first set up in *What Time Is It There?* and the short film *The Skywalk Is Gone:* themes of diaspora and postcolonial "trajectories of identification" between Taiwan and France or between Taiwan and Japan,[21] heterosexual and homosexual cruising, and fleeting contact between strangers. When Chen's character encounters Hsiao Kang sleeping on a swing, and briefly watches him sleep (Tsai's frequent sleepy motif), upon his waking she asks him, "Are you still selling watches?" She is unaware at this point that he now works in pornography. In addition to Tsai's intratextual stitching together of his films through this line of dialogue and recurring characters, *The Sky-walk Is Gone* and *The Wayward Cloud* thus also refer intertextually to other media and genres: specifically advertising and pornography.[22] Porn has also been featured as an object of homosocial/homoerotic exchange going back to his early films *Rebels of the Neon God* (1992) and *Vive L'Amour* (1994), and as an object of female desire in *The River*.[23]

In *The Wayward Cloud*, physical DVD and print magazine pornography represent objects of desire, curiosity, and repulsion for Lee and Chen's characters. Shiang-chyi remains unaware that Hsiao Kang works in porn until the denouement of the film. At first she is nervous about a man following her out of the porn section of a video rental store in her building, but later she assumes that Hsiao Kang is turned on when they visit this same porn section (she *assertively* caresses his chest with the physical porn DVD cases *from behind*), not realizing that he associates porn with work and his struggle with exhaustion and erectile dysfunction (in another scene he tries to rub porn magazines on himself after their images do not seem to work to arouse him). As in *The Hole*, Tsai punctuates their protracted courtship with fantasy musical numbers, but in a change from their function in *The Hole*, these musical numbers in *Wayward* hyperbolize the gender and sexuality (and fantasies) of several characters, especially those acting in the laborious and awkward porn shoot scenes that alternate with them in the film.

Despite what at first appears to be contrapuntal framework, the porn and musical genres actually have many similarities.[24] Like the musical, pornography can be considered an iterative "citation" of codified fantasies of hyperbolized sex, gender, and power roles.[25] In terms of their similar plot structures, Linda Williams proposes in *Hard Core* that "the hard-core feature film *is* a kind of musical, with sexual number taking the place of musical number."[26] But the musical privileges the exclusive couple form of the romantic duet.[27] Song Hwee Lim argues that "the musical's convention is, therefore, heteronormative, whereas the porn film, by its very nature, is more promiscuous and often disavows the reproductive imperative by ending with a shot of external penile ejaculation, as in the ending of *Wayward*."[28] The use of the term "wayward" in the English title is thus apt, akin to the way Sigmund Freud originally used the term "perverse" (for anything that veers away from what is presumed to be the properly heteronormative "sexual object" or reproductive "sexual aim").[29]

Musicals also have a historically important place in gay culture. In *How to Be Gay*, David Halperin turns to D. A. Miller's *Place for Us* to explain their significance. In that text, Miller focuses yet again on "Open Secrets": "It used to be a secret that, in its postwar heyday, the Broadway musical recruited a massive underground following of gay men. . . . If the postwar musical may be called a 'gay' genre . . . this is because its regular but unpublicized work has been to indulge men in the spectacular thrills of a femininity become their own."[30] Halperin insists that musicals are gayest when they don't *literally* represent gay people (unlike *Rent, Kinky Boots,* etc.). I will follow this line of thought in suggesting that Tsai's films *The Wayward Cloud* and *The Hole* are "queer" in their figural treatment of heterosexuality and sexual difference beyond heteronormativity. They have what can be called a "camp eye" (recalling Susan Sontag's suggestion that camp sees everything in quotation marks: it's "not a woman, but a 'woman.'")[31]

Here I will build on Vivian Lee's reading of the gender and sexual allegory in each of the musical sequences in *The Wayward Cloud* along with their intertextual references, in performances that offer theatrical, ironic, and camp readings that translate the originals' romantic sentimentalism "into a hyperbolic, and queer, mode of representation that disrupts the normative signification of the original text."[32] Briefly, these musical sequences feature:

- Hsiao Kang bathing in a rooftop water tank transformed into a sequined crocodile in a romantically lit pool (singing a song about "Half the Moon"). The crocodile invokes the famous Taiwanese novel *Notes of a Crocodile* by Qiu Miaojin, where the crocodile represents a genderless queer figure in the lesbian/queer coming-of-age story.[33]

- An older porn actress (played by Lu Yi-ching, who is frequently cast as Hsiao Kang's mother in other films, perhaps pointing to the genre of incest porn) who loses her false eyelashes in a faked shower sex scene where they run out of clean bottled water. She is transformed into a Spider Woman—referencing "singsong girls" in Hong Kong musicals, where the sex worker is seen as both victim and femme fatale, a figure of both "glamour and abjection" (as Halperin puts it), along with potentially referencing Manuel Puig's *Kiss of the Spider Woman*.[34]
- Flower girls seductively dancing around a statue of the former president/military dictator of the Republic of China (ROC), Chiang Kai-shek—a mockery of the phallic cult of the leader and his reproductive imperative.[35]
- A song-and-dance number about mistaken identity at the iconic Dragon & Tiger Pavilion in Kaohsiung, with each of the characters cross-dressed and carrying umbrellas with watermelon designs. Hsiao Kang is in "genderfuck" drag wearing a vintage dress with the front unbuttoned, and Yang Kuei-mei returns but in Charlie Chaplin–style male drag.[36]
- Hsiao Kang's impotence on set allegorized in a fantasy public toilet dance number with Hsiao Kang dressed like a penis with balloon testicles doing combat with marching women brandishing plungers and wearing safety-cone brassieres (perhaps evoking Madonna in her famous Jean Paul Gaultier cone bra).[37]

Many of these numbers can be understood within the idiom of drag performance and camp culture. Camp and gay male femininity often revels in excessive, staged, performed, active, undignified, and abject images of femininity.[38] Drag queens are particularly drawn to porn stars and other cisgender and transgender female sex workers for inspiration, but this can come across as "disidentification" (which is quite complex).[39]

Camp versus Sex or Camp Sex

Halperin also draws on Esther Newton's *Mother Camp: Female Impersonators in America*, where she argues that every good gay party needs two individuals: The Beauty and The Camp (for example: *The Boys in the Band* [1970]).[40] Halperin mostly sees "camp" as opposed to sex, following the "butch in the sheets, femme in the streets" model of gay sociability and hierarchy.[41] He argues that camp deflates the gay obsession with masculinity and male beauty, which can be quite exclusionary, in favor of a democratizing and leveling "bitchy" humor.[42] In addition to *The Boys in the Band,* we can watch the queen-versus-butch dynamic teased out in the men's bathhouse setting of *Vapors* (1965), directed by Andy Milligan.[43] But the presence of camping in the cruisy bathhouse suggests camp and sex are *not* mutually exclusive. I was delighted to read in Allan Bérubé's history of gay bathhouses that camp classic movies like *The Women* (George Cukor, 1939) were sometimes screened in the bathhouses.[44] More recent phenomena like the drag festivals *Wigstock, Bushwig,* and *Wigwood,* which are quite "cruisy," suggest to me that perhaps the opposition between sex and camp is changing or evolving.[45] Halperin admits, "The opposition between the beauty and the camp may itself be an element internal to camp culture, a camp projection rather than a natural reality. . . . Much contemporary gay male culture represents a sustained effort to recombine the beauty and the camp."[46] I will suggest that Tsai is part of this sustained effort.

Newton identifies camp as a way for gay people to laugh at their incongruous situation in heteronormative society instead of crying.[47] Halperin elaborates on how this violation of the generic boundary between comedy and tragedy is a central aspect of gay culture and aesthetic appreciation, especially drag queen humor and the gay love of dark comedies like *What Ever Happened to Baby Jane?* and *Mommie Dearest:* an "insistent, and persistent, violation of generic boundaries— a transgressive practice characteristic of gay male culture, which seems determined to teach us to laugh at situations that are horrifying or tragic."[48] Likewise, Jack Babuscio argues that "In order for an incongruous contrast to be ironic, it must, in addition to being comic, affect one as 'painful'—though not so painful as to neutralize the humor. It is sufficient that sympathy is aroused for the person, thing, or idea that constitutes the target of an incongruous contrast. To be affected in this way, one's feelings need to clash."[49]

Many observers of Tsai's films and their tragicomic scenarios note this clash of feelings (Adam Balz's review of *The Wayward Cloud*, for example, calls it "a comedic tragedy").[50] Camp irony thus "allows us to witness 'serious' issues with temporary detachment, so that only later, after the event, are we struck by the emotional and moral implications of what we have almost passively absorbed. The 'serious' is, in fact, crucial to camp. Though camp mocks the solemnities of our culture, it never totally discards the seriousness of a thing or individual."[51] So we see that camp creates both affective dissonance and potentially political dissidence. This may explain why the question of camp's relationship to homophobia/misogyny is so tricky to resolve.

But why has Halperin maintained the generic boundary between camp and sex?

Does camp cause erectile dysfunction? The political phallus is mocked, but is camp a solvent of both morality and sex? As Williams has noted, pornography is an "excessive" bodily genre.[52] But in keeping with Tsai's body of work—the work of bodies in his films—he avoids the convention Williams identifies in mainstream heterosexual pornography where sex always comes at the right time ("on time!") for the partners.[53] This explains why the sex between Hsiao Kang and Shiang-chyi is always at the wrong time, out of sync, and the "lip sync" musical numbers act as fantasies of escape or compensation, drawing on the convention of musicals first explored, but also exposed, in *The Hole*. Expanding on Richard Dyer's work on utopian feelings in film musicals in relation to capitalist deprivation and frustration, Shi-Yan Chao suggests that

in contrast to the prevailing inertia and the sense of desolation in Tsai's cinematic reality, the representational codes associated with the song-and-dance convey distinct non-representational qualities, particularly the utopian feelings of energy, abundance, and intensity. Unlike most musicals dealing with social inadequacies, which console the audience with this sense of utopia, *The Hole* exposes that mechanism. Within the song-and-dance, the representational rift between the songs and the lip-synching character/performer potentially undercuts the efficacy of the non-representational signs. This ironic representational discrepancy refers back to precisely the performative nature of the non-representational signs associated with the musical genre. Instead of serving as closed diegesis, the song-and-dance numbers in *The Hole* thereby subvert the musical's generic norms.[54]

Tsai's ironic and subversive approach to generic norms is indeed a recurring feature of his entire cinematic oeuvre, but with important variations due to the gendered cultural hierarchies of genres and the contexts of their reception.

Wayward Genres

In Tsai's films, what kind of "dialectic" is established between genres?

- between *wu xia pian* and Taiwan New Cinema in *Goodbye, Dragon Inn* (2003)[55]
- between musical and disaster film in *The Hole*
- between camp and porn, or camp and sex in *Wayward Cloud*
- between tragedy and comedy
- between hetero and homo?

Tsai can be seen as queering hetero tropes through *mise en abyme* and Brechtian estrangement,[56] for example the history of the *sex comedy* and the romantic comedy: *Wayward Cloud* potentially alludes to *Annie Hall*'s escaped lobster scene (here, escaped crabs).[57] This scene is followed by a shadow play of Hsiao Kang and Shiang-chyi ravenously eating the crabs (invoking the proto-cinematic history of Chinese shadow puppets, and the Chinese characters for film, 電影 *dianying*, meaning "electric shadows").[58]

In an Asia Society interview, Tsai was asked why in his films sex is not sexy, not satisfying, or connected to love, and he responded simply, "I don't make Hollywood films" (he then clarified that sex in real life is often awkward: the wrong timing, or wrong position).[59] Again we can see Tsai problematizing the fantasy of romantic "union" in the form of the couple. Multiple motifs of bridges, overpasses, and highways in these films suggest a desire for connection or transcendence, but it is so much more ironic that the "bridge" that connects the trilogy of *What Time Is It There?* and *The Wayward Cloud* is a film about a *missing* overpass and a missed connection: *The Skywalk Is Gone.*

As another challenge to cinematic heteronormativity and patriarchy, Tsai's films often emphasize female subjectivity: female sexuality, female fantasy, and the female gaze. Shiang-chyi takes over the solitary ludic treatment of watermelons from Hsiao Kang in *Vive L'Amour:* she tongue-kisses a watermelon in her fridge (Figure 11), and later acts out giving birth to a watermelon in the stairwell, scenes that revise and parody the opening porn scene between Hsiao Kang and Sumomo with the watermelon as fetish object (Sumomo's name means plum or sour peach, another fruit reference).[60] In fact, female porn vocalization is no more "fake" than actresses pretending to give birth on camera, typically seen as a measure of skill in authentic performance.[61] Shiang-chyi is actually the one aroused by the porn DVD packaging, and she seems fascinated as she watches a porn video featuring Sumomo, whom she recognizes after having dragged her to her apartment after finding her passed out from dehydration in the elevator.

FIGURE 11. *The Wayward Cloud* (Tsai Ming-liang, 2005). Shiang-chyi makes out with a watermelon, recalling Hsiao Kang's similar action in *Vive L'Amour* (1994).

After returning Sumomo's body to the porn set, and learning that Hsiao Kang performs in porn, her mixed feelings are expressed by her placement in a mirrored corner as she confronts Hsiao Kang.[62] She then watches the final porn scene being shot with the comatose (or dead?) Japanese porn star being manipulated like a puppet by three men and Hsiao Kang. She watches through a circular window with a wooden lattice, staring in shock but seemingly unable to walk away, and finally participating in the scene by vocalizing female porn noises, which sometimes sound like screams. The scene ends with Hsiao Kang jumping up to the window, inserting his penis in her mouth, and ejaculating. Tsai juxtaposes a shot of Hsiao Kang's buttocks dripping sweat with a profile shot of Shiang-chyi, mouth gagged by Hsiao Kang's penis, releasing a single tear from her eye (creating a parallel motif of liquid released from the body). Some have read this final "union" of the couple as a consummation, release of tension, or even as hopeful or utopian in contrast with the prior dystopian scenarios, but it also caused one woman at the Brisbane, Australia, premiere to stand up, point at the screen, and declare "fuck you," eliciting cheers from the audience as she walked out, with others following.[63]

In some sense, does Tsai here *literalize* feminist critiques of porn's objectification and degradation of women as formulated by Catharine MacKinnon and Andrea Dworkin (also provocatively literalized by David Cronenberg's *Videodrome* [1983])?[64] Does his film help illustrate feminist critiques of straight and gay male varieties of misogyny? Should the film be read in terms of a critique of male voyeurism/narcissism (with Hsiao Kang jerking off and ejaculating on a mirror in one scene)? But does this problem then eclipse female voyeurism? Following a rather orthodox feminist critique of heterosexual pornography, Vivian Lee observes how Shiang-chyi "gradually emerges as the active viewer while the Japanese woman is increasingly objectified and silenced, a fact that tellingly reveals her role *as* a porn star, an object and victim of the institution of pornography and the sexist visual regime that supports it."[65] Lim points out that, "the regime of pornography is not merely visual as Shiang-chyi's stand-in performance for Sumomo at the end of the film is purely on the vocal level."[66] But Lim also insists that, "Rather than seeing Tsai's use of a female comatose body that cannot grant consent as a form of misogyny, it can be argued that the film illustrates forcefully and critiques unequivocally the exploitation of the sexed-up female body in its various forms, at once consumable, disposable, and recyclable. It is clear in this climactic sequence that Shiang-chyi has a voice but not a body whereas Sumomo has a body but not a voice."[67] Yet Lim also points out that Tsai's use of a comatose body that cannot consent to sexual activity is not (female) gender-specific (hence inherently misogynistic) if we consider the treatment Hsiao Kang's comatose body in *I Don't Want to Sleep Alone*.[68]

I suggest that the whole film acts as an exploration of sex worker stigma: Why is Sumomo's consent treated as irrelevant? How will Shiang-chyi react when she finds out Hsiao Kang is a porn actor? But like another fictionalized story about the porn industry, *Boogie Nights* (1997), the film may actually only compound this stigma.[69] The film does, however, highlight the exhausting work of sex work (precisely what sex workers are not allowed to complain about for fear of giving opponents ammunition to justify depriving them of worker rights, unlike other forms of exploited work).[70] In *The Wayward Cloud*, Sumomo is comatose from dehydration. Hsiao Kang is exhausted, always napping between shots, and often struggles with erectile dysfunction on set and with his girlfriend.[71]

How should we make sense of the drought in the film? To briefly outline a potential *semiotics of thirst*—echoing the way one might now call a sexually desperate person "thirsty"—we see Tsai's water motif undergoing transformation here:

- Water = love?[72] (*The Hole* = wet; *Wayward Cloud* = dry)
- Watermelon = fetish, substitute? (echoes *Vive L'Amour*)
- Webs: Spider Woman, trapped in her web, semen as web
- 天邊一朵雲 *The Wayward Cloud* (*Tian bian yi duo yun,* literally: a cloud on the edge of the sky)
- Cloud (painted on Shiang-chyi's ceiling) = semen, but also euphemism for sex in classical Chinese literature (in *The Dream of the Red Chamber,*[73] cloud or "flipping the cloud" = sex)

Kai-man Chang suggests that "the lack of water in *The Wayward Cloud* signifies the lack of love in a porn-flooded city."[74]

Is *The Wayward Cloud* therefore an antiporn film (or an antiporn porn film, as one critic called it "Tsai's pornographic 2005 anti-porn musical")?[75] Ian Johnston has argued that *The Wayward Cloud* is "a minor work, a one-note vehicle to give expression to Tsai's distaste for pornography (although it's amazing how some critics were able to quite misread Tsai's frankly over-emphatic intentions)."[76] However, Tsai has frequently stated that he is not interested in making "social problem" films or taking a position on any controversial issue (migrant laborers, gay identity, or pornography).[77] Perhaps *The Wayward Cloud* is like seeing shapes in a cloud in the sky: you find what you make of it.

Are the "antiporn" readings of Tsai's film in fact *too literal* and insensitive to the *figural* work of camp? Certainly, Tsai can be very sincere (noted by Corrado Neri in his reading of *The Wayward Cloud*) but an overly earnest reading misses the "genre bending" and transgression of camp.[78] We might compare this problem to the "straight" responses to *Mommie Dearest* (child abuse is never funny!) discussed by Halperin in *How to Be Gay*—"Earnest, judgmental, sententious, moralistic, therapeutic, *literal*: How much straighter can you get? Could anyone doubt that these views, with their essentially documentary relation to the movie and its supposedly serious portrayal of important social and psychological problems, could spring from anything but a heterosexual culture . . . ?"[79] The musical numbers in Tsai's film denaturalize and "queer" heterosexual sexual difference through hyperbolic "drag" performance of gender but also through juxtapositions of sexual and cultural hierarchies: high art film versus low pornography seen as "trash."[80]

Camp thus also needs to be understood in relation to class: Tsai aestheticizes the indigenous working-class culture of Taiwan, what is known in Taiwanese dialect as *song*: "gaudy, vulgar, tawdry, saucy, loose, ersatz, smelling of the street if not the gutter"—*su* in Mandarin,[81] as Emilie Yueh-Yu Yeh and Darrel William Davis argue in "Camping Out with Tsai Ming-liang" in their discussion of *The Hole* and Tsai's approach to musical appropriation.[82]

The aesthetic categories of taste and class are clearly at stake in sexuality and pornography (note the [ironic?] names of many mainstream American porn magazines like *Penthouse* and *High Society*). But it is camp's connection to *affect* that draws it back into the sphere of the sexual. The Mandarin translation of "camp" proposed by Jonathan Yeh, 敢曝 *ganpu* "dare to expose," illuminates the provocative power of camp to transfigure shame.[83] However, in her critique of queer theorists' "faith in exposure," Eve Kosofsky Sedgwick points out the limitations of Judith Butler's "paranoid reading" of camp and drag as only serving to expose the social construction of gender normativity, a kind of x-ray vision of culture.[84] Sedgwick proposes a "reparative reading" of camp instead:

> The startling, juicy displays of excess erudition, for example; the passionate, often hilarious antiquarianism, the prodigal production of alternative historiographies; the "over"-attachment to fragmentary, marginal, waste or leftover products; the rich, highly interruptive affective variety; the irrepressible fascination with ventriloquistic experimentation; the disorienting juxtaposition of present with past, and popular with high culture.[85]

Each of these points might help us better appreciate the films by Tsai discussed here, especially his "over"-attachment to marginal, waste, and leftover products, as well as the sense of affective "interruption" and variety in Tsai's juxtapositions of genres and affects, along with the way past/present and high/popular culture are juxtaposed and disoriented in Tsai's films. In Saw Tiong Guan's documentary about Tsai, *Past Present*, queer Thai auteur Apichatpong Weerasethakul expresses his kinship and admiration for Tsai in terms of Tsai's films' rich and interruptive affective variety: "You shift your emotion so violently, during the course of the film. Some people say his films contain really void and nothingness but for me it's the opposite because the emotion there is very broad from comedy to something, it changes so quickly, like comedy it changes within the same shot, [it] change[s] with time."[86] He cites *Goodbye, Dragon Inn* as an example, but his point could also be applied to *The Hole* and *The Wayward Cloud*, especially scenes featuring almost slapstick humor.

Sedgwick mentions Jack Smith, who described his aesthetic as "moldy," drawing from the ruins of old Hollywood (especially the films of Maria Montez and their trappings of exoticism). José Esteban Muñoz suggests Smith reformulated these trappings through disidentificatory performance, whereby "glitter transformed hackneyed orientalisms and tropical fantasies, making them rich antinormative treasure troves of queer possibility."[87] We can compare Tsai's aestheticization of *song* (including porn as a "low" cultural form, but also outmoded popular musicals) and literal ruins (derelict buildings). Both Smith's *Flaming Creatures* (1963) and Tsai's *The Wayward Cloud* mix cross-dressed camp with staged rape, and both have confounded critics and censors alike, perhaps especially over how to classify the genre of their films.[88] Smith's original description of *Flaming Creatures* as a "comedy set in a haunted movie studio" that was nonetheless banned as pornography might also describe Tsai's films. *Flaming Creatures* was seized by the New York district attorney, with the exhibitor Jonas Mekas brought up on obscenity charges. But Smith refused to capitalize on the notoriety around *Flaming Creatures:* according to J. Hoberman, he was particularly bitter that the film he had designed as a comedy had been turned into "a sex issue of the Cocktail World."[89] This affective dissonance with regard to genre and reception is precisely what camp is known for.

Chao suggests that the musical numbers in *The Hole* should be read as drag performances that resist heteronormative narrative integration and thus critique heteronormativity, which could be called a paranoid reading of camp (likewise for the way Chao emphasizes the significance of "the closet" in Tsai's career and filmography after homophobic critical backlash to *The River*).[90] But Chao's reading of the utopian feelings and longings in Tsai's film and the aesthetic of *tongzhi* camp, where "it's being so camp as keeps us going" (citing Dyer again), also suggests a queer reparative impulse with regard to the musical genre versus the sense of desolation in Tsai's cinematic reality.[91]

The Hole and *The Wayward Cloud* therefore seem to be *both* exposing heteronormativity (and the exploitive and sexist practices of the low-budget Taiwanese porn industry) *and* holding out a utopian or reparative rereading and recoding of cultural refuse (old musicals and cheap porn films). Pornography and gay men's love of musicals are both subject to what Sedgwick (and Michael Moon) called privileged "knowingness" because they are "open secrets" to be presumed upon but also disavowed.[92] For many Taiwanese audiences, Japan equals porn,[93] so casting a Japanese actress triggers this knowingness (as someone once told me, *"yamete"* [stop it] is the Japanese word every Chinese man knows because of porn, also provoking questions of how nonconsent is staged and eroticized on film). However, Tsai refuses attempts at disavowal, while exploring these open secrets in the manner he also explores other open secret queer practices such as cruising.

Perhaps *The Wayward Cloud* does not feel like a musical because musicals are associated with escapism (for example, Warner Bros. musicals during the Great Depression), and that is generally how audiences respond to the musical sequences here and in *The Hole*, whereas the last scene of *The Wayward Cloud* makes us feel *trapped*.[94] One option is to walk out (like the woman in Brisbane).[95] Porn often conjures the phrase "can't unsee" (for example, shared online shock porn like "two girls one cup" discussed by Helen Hester in *Beyond Explicit*)[96] In a self-reflexive article in *Porn Studies*, Linda Williams notes the lie we tell when we click "OK" consenting to the common online porn entry paragraph certifying, in advance, that we do not find the contents offensive or obscene, when clearly, we seek out porn that might shock and offend our more polite sensibilities or transgress our personal limit to some degree in order for it to feel like *porn*.[97] Is Tsai doing the same to his (art film) audience?

As in David Lynch's *Blue Velvet* (1986), we feel violated by scenes of violation. But such voyeurism is also profoundly sexually disorienting, according to Michael Moon's reading of Lynch. The film itself seems *wayward, perverse, queer,* and its reader/viewer is "'disorientingly' circulated through a number of different positions on the wheel of 'perversions'" as outlined by Gayle Rubin (nonprocreative, nonmonogamous, for money, on camera).[98]

Finally, how might camp relate to Tsai's environmental messages about water supplies (sharing/hoarding/drought) and trash in *The Hole* and *The Wayward Cloud*? Recycling?[99] Conservation? Industrial critique? In "Queering Waste through Camp," Guy Schaffer explains how camp, queer theory, and discard studies are interrelated in their concern with the strange and imperfect construction of binaries, divisions, and categories—"in discard studies, that between waste and not-waste; in queer theory, those between hetero/homosexual, between male and female"—that "do violence to humans, cultures, and environments."[100] He proposes that "As a mode of thinking through and beyond and before binaries, or perhaps of thinking binaries promiscuously, queer theory is indispensable to the study of disposal."[101] Moreover, "While camp is a useful mode of reading for any field of study marked by questionable binaries, it is particularly relevant with regards to waste because camp is all about the reevaluation of a culture's trash. Camp offers a mode of celebrating, reappropriating, and rendering waste visible, without pretending that waste has stopped being waste."[102] We could also consider the connection between camp, feminism, and ecology in Tsai's films in terms of "eco-camp." Lauran Whitworth discusses the ecosexual activist art of Annie Sprinkle and Elizabeth Stephens, explaining how "eco-camp is a mode of florid performance, spectacle, and ostentatious sex-positivity that champions new forms of relationality between humans and other earthly inhabitants."[103] Whitworth suggests how "ecosexuality's campy ecological ethics provide an alternative to the didacticism and moralism that characterise much contemporary environmentalism. In the spirit of carnival, the tragi-comic, and, at times, parodic tone of ecosexuality generates an affective dissonance that spurs us to feel the full effects of our discordance with nature."[104] The florid performances of Tsai's films are equally "tragicomic," and eco-camp could indeed provide alternatives to didactic or moralistic interpretations of sexuality, porn, and ecology within the films.

We have seen the way disparate genres leak into one another in Tsai's ecocritical disaster/survival films, and the kinds of gender equality/fluidity/hyperbole he uses to critique the heteronormativity of such genres. This is what makes Tsai's films queer: their affective dissonance, camp way of rendering waste and excess visible (rather than disposable), "recycling" of cultural artifacts from the past, and promiscuous attitude toward binary divisions between high/low genres, waste and not-waste; human and nonhuman; hetero/homosexual; male and female "that do violence to humans, cultures, and environments."

4

Different Time Zones

What Time Is It There? and *Visage*

[*What Time Is It There?*] indexes a characteristically postcolonial relation to time that I call *temporal dysphoria*: a disorientation in relation to time rather than space. Designating something analogous to motion-sickness (time-sickness?) that is a subjective effect of the regime of cultural time-lag as experienced by postcolonial subjects, this temporal dysphoria underlines the enduring effects of the former, strongly hierarchized relations between centre and periphery; west and non-west; and, arguably, between European film and its "others."

—Fran Martin, "The European Undead:
Tsai Ming-liang's Temporal Dysphoria"

Arguably, some of the most compelling films about France, French ideology, and Parisian daily life have been made by "outsiders": Roman Polanski's *The Tenant* (1976); Krzysztof Kieślowski's *Trois Couleurs* trilogy (1993–94); and Michael Haneke's *Caché* (2005) and *Amour* (2012).[1] These European "auteur" directors have been embraced at the Cannes film festival by the French film establishment. Another set of directors from China, Hong Kong, and Taiwan have also been embraced at Cannes in part because of their self-consciously auteurist approach to film: Zhang Yimou, Wong Kar-wai, Hou Hsiao-hsien, and Tsai Ming-liang. While box-office popularity and domestic funding for these last three directors might have dried up in their home countries, their

popularity and funding opportunities have expanded in France, resulting in a series of films that overtly address what it means for a Chinese
director to make a film in France, and the "influence" of French auteurs,
especially the French New Wave directors Jean-Luc Godard and François
Truffaut, on their work, including complex "trajectories of identification" between East and West in the postcolonial context.[2]

This chapter will compare two French-Taiwanese Tsai Ming-liang
films, *Visage* (2009),[3] which was commissioned by the Musée du Louvre as the first film in its permanent collection, and his earlier film
What Time Is It There? (2001), in order to explore how intratextual
and intertextual auteurist references (especially to Truffaut) function
in Tsai's metacinematic films, and the significance of French-Taiwanese
coproduction.[4] I will also contextualize Tsai's films in relation to Hou
Hsiao-hsien's *Le Voyage du Ballon Rouge* (2007), sponsored by the Musée
d'Orsay as a tribute to Albert Lamorisse's *Le Ballon Rouge* (1956), and
Wong Kar-wai's short films *There Is Only One Sun* (2007) and *I Travelled 9000 Km to Give It to You* (from the sixtieth anniversary Cannes
film festival global auteur compilation *Chacun son cinéma* [2007]), which
reference Godard films and Wong's prior French coproductions *In the
Mood for Love* (2000) and *2046* (2004).[5]

Building on the exhaustive inventory of intertextual and intercultural
references already elaborated by Michelle Bloom in her book *Contemporary Sino-French Cinemas,* I will examine the shifting meanings of
"Chinese" and "French" in these reflexively auteurist films' modes of
transcultural citation, promotion, and distribution.[6] I will focus on
their casting decisions and recourse to a directorial "double" within the
films themselves. I will also suggest that Tsai's *Visage* should be understood as metacinematic in a way that extends beyond intertextual reference and involves making a film *about* the commission to make the
film: a "film of commission" that focuses on *the preparation of the film,*
the behind-the-scenes process itself, including dress rehearsals, de-
ferrals, delays, and interruptions (the actual process of making *Visage*
took three years including research and location scouting) becoming
the scenes of the actual film produced.[7]

Time Zones

Cross-cultural "flow" is literalized through a montage of shots at the start of *Visage*: the water flooding a Taipei apartment appears to drain into a Paris street. *What Time Is It There?* also uses parallel editing between Taiwan and France to reflect on transcultural citation, especially Truffaut's *The 400 Blows* (1959), and temporality: after Chen Shiang-chyi buys Hsiao Kang's (Lee Kang-sheng) dual time-zone watch from him in Taipei before her trip to Paris, Hsiao Kang and Shiang-chyi are shown in different "time zones" experiencing different relationships to France. Hsiao Kang obsessively watches *The 400 Blows* (Figure 12), drinks French wine, and changes clocks all over Taipei to Paris time, hoping to escape the difficulties of his home life left alone with his mother in her melancholy state after the loss of his father. Shiang-chyi, as a tourist, ironically experiences the rather alienating, chilly, and brusque "reality" of Paris (a kind of disappointment or subversion of "the tourist gaze" described by John Urry).[8] She is framed in scenarios depicting her as lonely, cold, and unable to communicate clearly. After sleepless nights from jetlag and noisy neighbors, she spends the night with a woman from Hong Kong who takes pity on her in a café after she finds her vomiting in the bathroom from too much coffee (the woman brings her a glass of hot water—common practice in Hong Kong).[9] But their potential sexual contact stops short at a late-night kiss in the woman's bed—Shiang-chyi initiates the kiss, and the woman reciprocates, but then turns her head away.

The kiss between the women is posited by Emily Barton as "a kind of queer intimacy, but also might be an intimacy of home. The two women share the same language in a place where it is not the primary one. In this way, they share the time and space of their home in a place that is geographically separate from it."[10] She argues that *What Time Is It There?* thus "uses space as a way to make time material. Concrete manifestations of the passage of time—wristwatches, films, languages, the presence of an actor's body—all become ways that Tsai presents time to the spectator. Time, then, becomes the method of (queer) desire and belonging."[11] While this aligns with Martin's reading of temporal dysphoria in Tsai's film (quoted in the epigraph to this chapter), I appreciate Barton's refusal to separate queer temporality from questions of space, specifically an experience of space and the problem of home that reflects queer diaspora, disorientation, and life in a queer time and place.[12]

Cruising is also woven into the plot of the film in other ways.[13] Through cross-cutting we observe that while Shiang-chyi experiences her queer encounter, Hsiao Kang is sleeping in his car and invites a street-based sex worker to join him to have sex in his car. She leaves while he is sleeping and steals his watch sample case, a rather stereotypical depiction of sex worker criminality, but one that matches his own comic law-breaking behaviors in the film, and literalizes a "stolen time" (watch, clock) recurring theme. He is also openly cruised by a man in a movie theater—the same theater as *Goodbye, Dragon Inn* (2003)— who steals his clock and takes it into the men's toilet, where he places it over his otherwise naked crotch and makes the hands of the clock appear to "throb." Hsiao Kang just shuts the stall door on him and

FIGURE 12. *What Time Is It There?* (Tsai Ming-liang, 2001). Hsiao Kang hugs a pillow while watching François Truffaut's *The 400 Blows* starring Jean-Pierre Léaud as the adorable delinquent Antoine Doinel (in a spatially disorienting scene in a Rotor).

walks out, which Robin Wood reads as "mildly homophobic," but I do not believe we need to read failed cruising that way, as *Goodbye, Dragon Inn* dilates upon failed cruising attempts in a remarkably queer way.[14] Along with her encounter with the woman from Hong Kong, Shiang-chyi is cruised by Jean-Pierre Léaud (lead actor from Truffaut's *The 400 Blows*), who tries to pick her up by giving her his phone number in a cemetery (the Cimetière de Montmartre, the location of François Truffaut's grave).

In "The European Undead: Tsai Ming-liang's Temporal Dysphoria," Fran Martin claims that the teleological developmentalist narrative implied by the notion of European "influence" on contemporary Taiwanese cinema needs to be rethought with a sensitivity to postcolonial time, suggesting that the signifier "Europe" works in contradictory ways in contemporary Taiwanese film and public culture: "On the one hand, 'Europe' may offer itself as an imaginative resource by means of which the specific regional history of American post-war cultural dominance is implicitly critiqued by Tsai and other Taiwan filmmakers. On the other hand, however, 'Europe' also functions as a mythologized cultural 'other' that is sometimes conflated with 'the west' in general."[15] Martin argues that this complex postcolonial relation is addressed in *What Time Is It There?* by "its structuring obsession with the temporal disjuncture between Taipei and Paris," using the term "postcolonial" in the relatively broad sense of "designating the relation of alterity self-perceived by Taiwanese intellectuals to 'Europe' as a mythic geo-cultural formation connoting modernity, a relation conditioned by the persistent modern division of the world into 'east' and 'west.'"[16] While Martin notes that this division is losing credibility in a polycentric and postcolonial world, it still haunts Tsai's films and those of his Taiwanese contemporaries.

Yet Martin also suggests that "the film can be seen as problematizing its own westward trajectory, as . . . Paris is also figured, precisely, as *the land of the dead.* . . . an association is made between France and the *nouvelle vague*—not with notions of futurity and progress, but on the contrary, with impressions of ghostliness and death."[17] Thus, while Tsai's film career and the order in which I discuss these films may appear to reaffirm a Eurocentric queer migration narrative, I will argue that his films also problematize and subvert such progress narratives of globalization.[18]

Films of Commission

In an interview with Tsai Ming-liang about *Visage*, he explains how the original concept for the film was having Léaud meet Lee Kang-sheng since they never met in *What Time Is It There?*[19] Thus, like the "sequel" quality discussed in the previous chapter linking *What Time Is It There?* to *The Skywalk Is Gone* (2002) and *The Wayward Cloud* (2005)— signaled by a line of dialogue in *Wayward*, "are you still selling watches?"— *Visage* creates a fascinating and somewhat disorienting or reorienting "loop" back to *What Time Is It There?* But Tsai also shifts positions and evolves, incorporating new actors, revising certain motifs, and putting a different twist on queer metacinema.

In *Visage*, Tsai's muse or "fetish actor" Lee Kang-sheng plays Kang, the director of a film commissioned by the Louvre about the myth of Salomé.[20] Lee playing the role of the director reflects the fact that he is also a film director in his own right.[21] *Visage* is also replete with inter-textual references to Truffaut's metacinematic *Day for Night* (1973)— featuring a film-within-a-film (the love triangle drama *Meet Pamela*), cinematic tricks like fake snow, both male and female actors on the verge of nervous breakdowns, and a film production interrupted by death (of a crew member's mother, and of a lead actor).[22] In *Visage*, during the preparation phase of the film-within-a-film's production, Kang is informed that his mother has died, necessitating a trip back to Taiwan to engage in religious rituals of mourning, accompanied by his French producer/handler (played by Fanny Ardant, one of Truffaut's actresses).

This trip home revisits a significant location of *What Time*: Hsiao Kang's mother's apartment, where she was engaged in the process of incomplete mourning (melancholy) for Hsiao Kang's father, who dies at the start of *What Time* (which is dedicated to both Tsai and Lee's fathers).[23] In that plot, the mother interprets a clock in the kitchen that Hsiao Kang had changed to Paris time (a sign of his own obsession) as a sign from her deceased husband that he wants to come back and that she needs to block out the light in the apartment in order to let his spirit return to be with her and eat the food she has prepared for him. She also speculates that his spirit might have come back in the form of the large fish in a tank in the apartment, suggested by a poignant shot of her gazing at the fish with profound sadness. We later see her dressed up for a dinner date with the spirit of her husband, and then masturbating with a rattan pillow, with his portrait photograph watching over her, a scene of virtual sexual consummation (and actual satisfaction) that is juxtaposed with the encounters between Shiang-chyi and the woman in Paris and Hsiao Kang with the sex worker in his car, through Tsai's parallel editing of these lonely sex scenes. The scenes are contrastingly juxtaposed but also subjected to a compassionate comparison through montage.

In *Visage*, Ardant's producer character is shown in the same apartment eating the food ceremonially offered to the now deceased mother, and through the fish tank we see the mother's spirit sharing the meal. Tsai has thus created an intratextual loop within his oeuvre, one that centers on domestic spaces rendered uncanny through melancholy. He also uses the French producer/handler to comment on cultural misunderstanding and the commission of his film (via the film-within-the-film). *Visage* might at first seem incomplete because it is so porous and unbounded, but it becomes a film about the interruptive and uneven process of making a film and the unfinished process of grief (mourning/melancholy).[24]

Visage being commissioned by the Musée du Louvre continues a pattern of French institutional funding also seen in Hou Hsiao-hsien's *Le Voyage du Ballon Rouge*, which was commissioned by the Musée d'Orsay. Critics in France who responded positively to *Le Voyage du Ballon Rouge* were surprised by how well a foreign director was able to capture the *je ne sais quoi* of Parisian everyday life. On a *Culture 8* broadcast dedicated to the film, Vincent Julé, a journalist with *Écran Large*, remarks how "I have never seen a film which captures the life of Paris so well, but above all the life of Parisians. It's not cliché, it's not a postcard, no, for me who lives in Paris, it's truly Paris—beautiful, gray, everything—and it's a foreign director who arrives at this."[25] On my reading, this is a result of Hou's unique approach to watching/listening to his characters and settings that is simultaneously distant and intimate, like his earlier film *Café Lumière* (2003), filmed in Tokyo and commissioned by Shochiku studios to commemorate the centenary of Ozu Yasujiro's birth, which was also hailed as remarkably "true" to Japanese daily life, along with reflecting the complex postcolonial position of a Taiwanese director vis-à-vis Japan.[26]

Ballon Rouge pays homage to both Albert Lamorisse's short film—about a lonely boy, played by Lamorisse's son, who befriends a magically personified red balloon—and a painting in the Orsay museum, Félix Vallotton's *The Balloon*. These two intertexts act as bookends for the film itself: it starts with its young boy protagonist Simon (Simon Iteanu) talking to the off-screen balloon, trying to convince it to come down from a Métro stop. The balloon follows him onto the subway and is pushed away by adults in the same manner seen in Lamorisse's original. But for the rest of the film, the balloon is more of a background character, a possible symbol of Simon's somewhat detached position within the "complicated" adult social world of his frazzled mother Suzanne (Juliette Binoche), a puppet vocalist who is recently separated from her husband and has hired an au pair named Song Fang (the actress's actual name) to look after Simon. Song Fang's character was a film student in Beijing and is currently working on a film about *Le Ballon Rouge* (Leo Goldsmith speculates that the opening segment of the film is perhaps supposed to be an excerpt from her film rather than Hou's).[27] She films everything she sees using her video camera, which Julé notes functions as a kind of *mise en abyme*.[28]

There are many similarities between Tsai and Hou's "French films": the use of a directorial double, filming at a museum location and paying homage to famous European filmmakers and paintings, working with mythological luminaries of French acting (Binoche, Léaud, Ardant, Jeanne Moreau, etc.). But this orients us toward established French cultural distinction and hegemony in a way that Martin cautions us against (along with Pierre Bourdieu).[29] I will go on to consider how Tsai's "film of commission" renegotiates his relation to the institution via a consideration of his casting choices, problems of linguistic communication in the film, and his insistence on returning to and revising his own auteurist themes and motifs, many of which are specific to the Chinese language and to Taiwanese culture. This includes something as minor as a plastic bowl of soft tofu in ginger syrup *(doufu hua)*, a night market staple, somehow appearing in a scene between Kang and his French actress (Laetitia Casta, costumed as Salomé) in the underground tunnels of the Louvre. Moreover, Tsai's cultural references and scenarios are profoundly queer, as I will show.

As noted, Lee Kang-sheng plays a directorial double for Tsai, and this semi-autobiographical casting is similar to Truffaut's use of Léaud as Antoine Doinel in his films. Here Léaud plays the aging actor "Antoine" playing King Herod in the myth of Salomé. The film is about the making of a film at the Louvre, and yet the scenes mostly take place in the underground tunnels and the surrounding park, the Jardin des Tuileries, with only one brief scene of Antoine emerging from a vent in the wall into one of the museum galleries (perhaps recalling the uncanny, communicating architectural spaces in *The Hole* [1998]). Tsai has thus already profoundly disoriented the space of the museum and our expectations about a film set in the Louvre.[30] As if following the Freudian logic of a crass joke made by Edina Monsoon (Jennifer Saunders) in the "Paris" episode of *Absolutely Fabulous*—"I'm going to the toilet. To the Louvre. No to the—it's a joke, sweetheart. Mummy's little joke. Quick Pompipoo in the Louvre," punning on the near homonym loo/Louvre and the Centre Pompidou[31]—Tsai's cinematic approach to the architectural space of the museum is to literally descend into its bowels and the water-filled old sewer tunnels beneath, in the same way his films often linger in cinema toilets.[32]

One scene features self-consciously auteurist dialogue in a conversation between Lee and Léaud sitting near a video monitor in the park that has been transformed into an artificial snow- and mirror-filled set (here we have multiple metacinematic layers already). They do not share a common language but can list the names of great World Cinema auteurs: Pasolini, Fellini, Antonioni, Murnau, Dreyer, Truffaut, Mizoguchi, Welles's *The Lady from Shanghai* (which features a hall of mirrors).[33] These references combine auteurism and Orientalism, which we also see in Tsai's use of the Orientalist story of Salomé.[34] Song Hwee Lim and Michelle Bloom suggest that Lee and Léaud's director name-dropping conversation refers intertextually to a similar director name-dropping scene in Truffaut's metacinematic *Day for Night*, and allows Tsai to join the pantheon of great directors listed.[35] But their conversation in the park might also be linked to Godard's short film *All the Boys Are Called Patrick* (1957), closer to the era of *The 400 Blows*, where a pickup artist "accosts" a girl in a public park in Paris and tries to guess her nationality by saying all the phrases he knows in English, Swedish, German, and finally Japanese, which is just "Mizoguchi Kurosawa?"[36] Tsai's potential citation and appropriation of this early French New Wave film and its cinematic Orientalist dialogue thus reconfigures it to suggest a queer public encounter between the men akin to cruising in a foreign language, literalized later when Lee cruises and makes interrupted sexual contact with another French man (Mathieu Amalric) in the Tuileries brush. Their encounter is interrupted by a call informing Lee that his mother has died, bringing cruising and mourning/melancholy into abrupt and intense contact—the French man tries to check if he is all right when he appears visibly shaken by the call.[37]

Tsai also incorporates references to *The 400 Blows* when the producer (Ardant) peruses a *400 Blows* flipbook and some Truffaut monographs saying, "you are here too." Tsai has said in interviews that he sees himself as having the opportunity to follow Lee and Léaud as their faces (and bodies) age, and also to continue the work of Truffaut beyond the grave, as it were.[38] I will go on to explain how crucial the idea of the "face" is within this intercultural dialogue. The other autobiographical element is Tsai reflecting on the loss of his mother, just as *What Time Is It There?* was about the loss of a father (Lee Kang-sheng lost his father prior to the filming), and thus these films are haunted both by paternal and maternal figures and by directorial ghosts.[39]

The film is also haunted by ghosts of Tsai's previous films, in a thoroughly auteurist mode (consistent actors, roles, themes, etc.). Tsai has suggested that the film is a kind of "self-portrait" containing themes, symbols, and imagery seen across his body of work.[40] In a sense he was hired to do "more of the same" as one often is with a commission, but of course each time there will also be variation on methods and materials, and potential new discoveries. Rachel Sagner Buurma and Laura Heffernan have suggested there is a contemporary genre of "novels of commission" that focus on the process of writing rather than the finished, canonical work, an approach I will connect to Tsai's approach to the "film of commission."[41] Buurma and Heffernan examine Roland Barthes's Collège de France course "The Preparation of the Novel" where Barthes proceeds "as if" he were going to write a novel, with his wanting-to-write entailing his *reorientation* from literary critic to writer and a *renegotiation* of his institutional position (rather than viewing the course as an obstacle to dedicating himself to writing, the course becomes part of the preparation process itself, with the course finally taking the place of the novel).[42]

Like Barthes's *Preparation,* Buurma and Heffernan suggest that in novels of commission (such as Sheila Heti's *How Should a Person Be?*), "successfully writing the commissioned work . . . involves a similar renegotiation of the terms of novelistic realism in order to reconfigure their imagined relations to literature's commissioning and canonizing institutions" thus considering the institution's presence in the writing process.[43] While commissioning institutions can seem to require "an impossibly pre-canonized work," in the novel of commission, "the preparation for writing the work in fact slowly and over time comes to constitute the work," reimagining its relations to the institution that initiates it and offering a different preparatory work in place of the more canonical one originally imagined.[44]

I propose that Tsai's *Visage* can be considered a "film of commission" in which the process of making the film, commissioned by a prestigious institution that obviously represents the canonization of art and artists (the Louvre), and the preparation of the film (within the film) comes to constitute the work, renegotiating Tsai's relationship to the commissioning institution in a way that moves from originally being inspired by specific, already-canonized artworks within the museum (or the Criterion Collection), to making a film about the process, including the interruption of unforeseen events (death, makeup and wardrobe malfunctions, and difficulty communicating between French, English, and Chinese speakers).[45] Buurma and Heffernan highlight how for Heti's character (also named Sheila), what she perceives as a block to her ability to create the work is actually the obstacle of her "romantic notion of creation," which divides life ("living") from the "whole cloth production of an already-canonized, expressive work of literature."[46]

Likewise, the metacinematic plot of Tsai's *Visage* might at first seem to oppose the interruption of "reality"—death or mourning/melancholy—to the already-canonized film the director (Kang/Lee, but also Tsai) is supposed to finish. But slowly that very process of unfinished mourning and the delayed, interrupted, slowed-down process of making the commissioned film becomes the actual film Tsai has created for the Louvre's permanent collection. Lee's inability to control the animal actors—stags in the artificial-snow-filled park who charge at the series of mirrors on the set, or who slowly wander around the Jardin des Tuileries at the end of the film where Tsai also makes a brief appearance on camera—perfectly illustrates how the integration of life into the work is actually the real work, thereby substituting a porous process for a closed-off product.[47]

Folding Meaning, Folding Space-Time

Tsai's own film is replete with references not just to Truffaut's films and well-known actresses, but to his own queer cinematic universe, itself in a continual state of revision and redrafting as we will see.[48] Like Barthes's reorientation toward writing in *The Preparation of the Novel*, I find Tsai's *Visage* to be remarkably reorienting: from French to Taiwanese cultural references, and from heteronormative to queer cultural forms and practices, or forms of sexual disorientation.

Here I will briefly catalogue some recurring elements—following the notion of Tsai's auteurist intratextuality proposed by Song Hwee Lim[49]—from Tsai's impressive and very queer body of work, which find new iterations in *Visage:*

- *Rebels of the Neon God* (1992): An early, almost slapstick scene in *Visage* features a broken sink flooding a Taipei apartment, echoing the flooded apartment in Tsai's first film (establishing Tsai's leitmotif of water; the motif of a mattress in a flooded room also appears in the father's room in *The River* [1997] and the woman downstairs' flooded apartment in *The Hole*).[50]

- *Vive L'Amour* (1994): The producer (Ardant) crawls into bed with Lee and watches him sleep, trying to make intimate contact by "spooning" him, echoing Hsiao Kang crawling into bed with Ah-jung.
- *What Time Is It There?*: Once more we see the ghost of a parent, syncretic Taoist-Buddhist funeral ceremonies, food offerings and framed photos of the deceased, blackened/taped-up windows (in *Visage*, the actress Laetitia Casta becomes obsessed with blocking out windows and mirrors with black tape, as if trying to block out her own image). We also see the same park's reflecting pools at the end of both films (Chen's suitcase is floating in one at the end of *What Time*, and is retrieved by the ghost of Hsiao Kang's father [Miao Tien], who appears to have traveled to Paris—perhaps haunting her via the dual time-zone watch given to her by Hsiao Kang, who cautioned her it was bad luck because he was in mourning).[51]
- *The Skywalk Is Gone*: Along with the ability to continue and follow up on *What Time Is It There?* we observe Taiwan New Cinema clichés of framing and composition in reflections in glass in a café at the start of the film,[52] where Lee and Léaud fail to meet, reflecting a real missed first encounter between Tsai and Léaud: "My first appointment with Jean-Pierre Léaud in Paris was in a café that he frequents. However, he got the time wrong and thought that I was late. He left without waiting, and I only found his empty cup."[53]
- *Goodbye, Dragon Inn*: Gay public and anonymous cruising in a liminal space: Lee and a French man (Mathieu Amalric) start to engage in oral sex in the Tuileries brush before they are interrupted by Tsai's phone ringing (with the news about his mother). *Visage* also features reunions between famous actors (Truffaut's signature actresses Fanny Ardant, Nathalie Baye, and Jeanne Moreau at a banquet, but the host never arrives—yet another missed encounter).
- *The Hole* and *The Wayward Cloud*: Mandarin popular music in musical fantasy sequences featuring lip-syncing: in *Visage*, Laetitia Casta

lip-syncs to Zhang Lu's 1940s hit song "You're So Pretty" ("*Ni zhen meili*"), which expresses active female sexual desire and fantasy.[54]

- *I Don't Want to Sleep Alone* (2006): in *Visage*, Tsai returns to the visual motif of a mattress floating on water. He also revises scenes of mother-son intimacy caused by illness, with the almost-incestuous contact here reversed by Lee's character rubbing his mother's stomach with ointment on a mattress in a flooded apartment, thus establishing that she is ill at the start of the film. Tsai's Malaysian actor Norman bin Atun also reappears, naked and in intimate scenes with Laetitia Casta, who kisses him all over in the dark, lit only by a cigarette lighter (again her active sexuality and male "objectification" are emphasized). This is just one of many scenes of cross-cultural intimacy, beyond language and heteronormative codes, in Tsai's body of work.

What is worth noting about the above list of intratextual references is not just Tsai's practice of creating loops and folds of meaning (or folds of space-time) within his oeuvre, but also how Tsai reorients spatial and temporal trajectories of identification between Taiwan/Malaysia and France, and disorients our assumptions about cultural boundaries and divisions between heterosexuality and homosexuality.[55] Bloom argues that Tsai's earlier films "feature alienation and unsatisfying or one-sided sexual encounters. By contrast, *Face* depicts more fruitful Sino-French connections. Rather than existing in parallel, cross-cut universes, the characters (Kang and Antoine, Kang and the Man in the Bushes, St. John and Salomé) connect, at least temporarily, through diminished distance."[56] Moreover, as Sara Ahmed has argued, it is the proximity of bodies that produces disorienting and queer effects.[57]

Reparative Reading

With this sense of the additive and accretive in mind, we can now revisit Eve Kosofsky Sedgwick's reparative reading of camp in order to consider the ways Tsai's *Visage* also features "startling, juicy displays of excess erudition" (Tsai's art historical "homework" and scouting in the museum);[58] "passionate, often hilarious antiquarianism" (reviving Oscar Wilde's *Salomé*);[59] "production of alternative historiographies" (revising the artistic and cinematic canon, and his own oeuvre); "'over'-attachment to fragmentary, marginal, waste or leftover products" (old Mandarin musicals, the Louvre's basement); "rich, highly interruptive affective variety" (slapstick/eroticism/grieving); "irrepressible fascination with ventriloquistic experimentation" (Laetitia Casta lip-syncing to Zhang Lu's "You're So Pretty" in Mandarin and the song "Historia de un amor" in Spanish); and "the disorienting juxtaposition of present with past, and popular with high culture" (French *nouvelle vague* with the Taiwan New Wave, popular with art cinema, Taiwanese night market food with a formal banquet in the Louvre).[60]

We might compare this inventory with film phenomenologist Vivian Sobchack's discussion of disorientation in cinema, specifically her discussion of Stendhal Syndrome: "In the cinema, too, we can find similar, if scarce, examples of losing one's orientational moorings in a vertically elongated and polyphonic space-time that collapses and conflates past and future in and with what becomes a vertiginous and all-consuming present."[61] But note that Sobchack's examples of disorientation in cinema are primarily heterocentric[62] and emphasize negative forms of panic at being lost, whereas Sedgwick and I hope to draw out queer forms of pleasure and bliss associated with queer disorientation in space-time and art history.[63]

Sedgwick's foundational work in queer theory insisted that gay/queer culture is hardly marginal, but is in fact central to much "high culture" in the West, although it is often closeted and disavowed, noting sarcastically how "[i]n the very first of the big 'political correctness' scare pieces in the mainstream press, *Newsweek* pontificated that under the reign of multiculturalism in colleges, 'it would not be enough for a student to refrain from insulting homosexuals . . . He or she would be expected to . . . study their literature and culture alongside that of Plato, Shakespeare, and Locke.' *Alongside?* Read any of the Sonnets lately? You dip into the *Phaedrus* often?"[64] Likewise, with *Visage*, not only is Tsai inserting himself into the canon of Great Artists in the Louvre, and great (straight) World Cinema auteurs, he is engaged in a queer reparative and "cruisy" reading of the canon of Western art and the space/place of the French museum itself. This includes Leonardo da Vinci, as Tsai features his painting of *St. John the Baptist* (but this also evokes Freud's androgynous interpretation of "pretty boys of feminine tenderness with feminine forms" in da Vinci's paintings),[65] Oscar Wilde's French-language play *Salomé* (which was also turned into a silent film in 1923 with an allegedly all-queer cast; cemetery scenes of Léaud refer back to his cemetery cruising in *What Time*[66] but also remind us that Wilde's lipstick-covered grave is located in Paris),[67] and the men continuing to cruise the Jardin des Tuileries brush, still an "open secret" place for queer cruising.[68]

What is new to Tsai's filmmaking and typically French "haute bourgeois" is the use of a French top model Laetitia Casta who wears couture gowns designed by Christian Lacroix (also beloved by Edina Monsoon in *Absolutely Fabulous*). Tsai told Casta not to worry about good acting, and that he was influenced by Robert Bresson's idea of actors as models.[69] This modeling/commercial aspect is comparable to Wong Kar-wai's long-form commercial for Philips Aurea, *There Is Only One Sun*, which revises many of the themes and visual elements of the science fiction sequence of his earlier French-Chinese coproduction *2046* but with a French model (and a Russian spy and Cuban music), along with the clear influence of Godard's *Alphaville* (1965).[70] *Alphaville* is also incorporated intertextually in *I Travelled 9000 Km to Give It to You*, Wong's contribution to the Cannes compilation of short films by world cinema auteurs about the movie theater, *Chacun son cinéma*: we hear the *Alphaville* dialogue soundtrack playing in the movie theater as we watch a Chinese man and woman petting in the dark with Wong's trademark fetishistic sensuality and vivid use of color and adjusted film speed.

So, the question remains: What gets lost in translation? Let us return to Tsai's film and the meanings of the title according to different cultural codes: *Visage/Face/Lian/*臉.

Visage

Tsai is not known as a director of the close-up, per se (until his recent "postretirement" film *Your Face* [2018]),[71] but *Visage* lingers over the faces of his famous, aging cast of French stars (especially the scarred face of Léaud), yet also, like Wong Kar-wai's *There Is Only One Sun*, lingers over the unblemished face of his female model lead Laetitia Casta (who in 1999, was chosen as the new model for Marianne, an allegorical symbol of the French Republic, following earlier models Brigitte Bardot and Catherine Deneuve).[72] In his discussion of "The Affection-Image: Face and Close-up," Gilles Deleuze notes that one imagines "a face is suited to one particular type of affect or entity rather than others. The close-up makes the face the pure building material of the affect" leading to "strange cinematic nuptials in which the actress provides her face and the material capacity of her parts, whist the director invents the affect or the form of the expressible which borrows and puts them to work."[73] In fact, *Visage* emphasizes the rather sadomasochistic element of this relationship, where Casta has ice cubes held against her face to get just the right blush *director* Kang is looking for. But this orthodox idea of the feminine muse is somewhat counterbalanced by Tsai's homoerotic attention to his male muse *actor* Lee Kang-sheng's face as he plays John the Baptist symbolically beheaded and kissed by Casta as Salomé. In this scene, she pours a can of tomatoes on him while he sits wrapped in plastic in a bathtub in a freezing cold

FIGURE 13. *Visage* (Tsai Ming-liang, 2009). Lee Kang-sheng playing John the Baptist symbolically beheaded—covered with tomato sauce and surrounded by ice in a meat freezer—and kissed by Laetitia Casta as Salomé.

meat cooler after she has performed the famous Dance of the Seven Veils (Figure 13)—another moment where flesh and fruit intermingle or act as substitutes.

Deleuze notes that ordinarily, three roles of the face are recognizable: it is individuating; it is socializing; it is relational or communicating. But according to Deleuze, "the face, which effectively presents these aspects in cinema as elsewhere, loses all three in the case of the close-up."[74] He cites Ingmar Bergman as undoubtedly "the director who has been the most insistent on the fundamental link which unites the cinema, the face, and the close-up: 'Our work begins with the human face . . . the possibility of drawing near to the human face is the primary originality and the distinctive quality of the cinema.'"[75] Deleuze argues that in Bergman, the affection-image dissolves the character's profession, social role, desire to communicate, and individuation (here he invokes Bergman's *Persona* [1966]).[76] According to Deleuze, "There is no close-up of the face. The close-up is the face, but the face precisely in so far as it has destroyed its triple function."[77] We can also see this operation in Kieślowski's *Trois Couleurs: Bleu,* which features multiple close-ups of Juliette Binoche's face, but in the context of a story about her loss of identity, sociality, and desire to communicate. Deleuze suggests that the facial close-up is "both the face and its effacement."[78] The actress/model Casta is shown in *Visage* trying to obliterate her reflection via covering up a mirror with black tape, quite literally attempting to efface her face, but perhaps also her identity or social role. Similarly, Lee as Kang the director faces into an artificial snow machine to cover or blast away his face.

Ahmed points out how the French phenomenologist Maurice Merleau-Ponty describes the face "as oriented," and she suggests therefore "the significance of the face is not simply 'in' or 'on' the face, but a question of *how we face the face,* or *how we are faced.*"[79] With this in mind, we can turn to the meaning of face in Chinese.

Face/*Lian*

Both Chinese and English use a related expression for the social function of the face: "losing face" or "saving face" as in maintaining one's reputation: "The English semantic field for 'face' words meaning 'prestige; honor' is smaller than the corresponding Chinese field, but historical dictionaries more accurately record its history. The *Oxford English Dictionary* (2nd ed., 1989) documents how the English community in China originated *lose face* and *save face* in the late 19th century."[80] Unlike Chinese, in English it is not possible to "give face" except in the idiomatic fashion/ballroom expression reflected in a line from Madonna's "Vogue": "Rita Hayworth gave good face," which is closer to Deleuze's concept of the actress's "work."[81]

A Western guide to doing business in China called the *China Culture Corner* summarizes the importance of face: "In China and much of Asia, Face represents a person's reputation and feelings of prestige within multiple circles, including the workplace, the family, personal friends, and society at large."[82] The article refers to 面子 (*mianzi*), though Tsai uses another character for face: *lian* 臉 = "face; countenance; respect; reputation; prestige," which is seen in several "face" words:

- *lianshang* 臉上 (lit. "face on/above") "one's face; honor; respect"
- *lianmian* 臉面 (lit. "face face") "face; self-respect; prestige; influence"
- *lianpi* 臉皮 (lit. "face skin") "face; sensitivity; compassion"[83]

These Taiwanese and Hong Kong directors who have a "reputation" at Cannes and are commissioned by museums and electronics brands to "reface" their images may be especially attuned to what it means to "give" or "maintain" face in these high-stakes arenas.

Shi-Yan Chao also notes that for "a gay subject to have his or her identity exposed as homosexual is, in many cases, 'to lose face *(lian)*, to have one's claim on a social position radically destabilized.' To save one's *lian* and to avoid shame, then, means that the gay subject often has to subjugate him/herself to the heteronormative public gaze by passing, or symbolically putting on a straight mask. Aided by techniques of shaming and dissimulation, the Chinese concept of *lian* helps foster the queer sensibility gravitating toward the surface, role-playing, and theatricality" within the aesthetic of *tongzhi* camp Chao outlines.[84] We can certainly see this camp aesthetic of the surface and the metaphor of life as theater elaborated in Tsai's *Visage (Lian)*, though I have also suggested ways of reparatively reading queer camp and queer intertextuality beyond the "paranoid lenses" of the closet.[85]

Finally, there is the more "literal" understanding of the value and meaning assigned to faces: if the "Asian" versus "Caucasian" face is stereotyped as phenotypical marker of racial difference (as we see explored in Roland Barthes's *Empire of Signs*)[86] to what degree might these transnational coproductions *deface* or *efface* national differences between "Chinese" and "French"? How might we understand these films as staging a complex negotiation of the triple function of the face: individuation, socialization, and communication? Certainly, Hou and Tsai's films are about the social professions of the filmmaker and actor, and relational communication and miscommunication. But each of their films pose the question of what it means to make a film with a "mixed" (racial, national, linguistic) cast, or for a director to transition to making films with primarily European faces. Casta's role was originally going to be played by Hong Kong actress Maggie Cheung, which would have created an intertextual web with Wong Kar-wai's *In the Mood for Love* and Cheung's films in France, including the metacinematic *Irma Vep* (1996) with Jean-Pierre Léaud,[87] and would have profoundly disorienting and reorienting effects on our interpretation.[88] Are the faces in front of or behind the camera the marker of a film's cultural "face" as it circulates transnationally? Is the Chinese directorial double a way of maintaining ethnically Chinese "presence" in the work? We might want to follow Buurma and Heffernan's suggestion that "relatedness is the antidote to representativeness" in artwork as a social object of meaning and value, therefore reading *Visage* as not necessarily about representation, but about the way Taiwan and France are placed in relation by the film.[89]

Postcolonial temporal, spatial, and sexual disorientation are in fact complexly intertwined by Tsai's transcultural, intertextual, metatextual, and intratextual modes of citation. While I agree with Bloom's argument that "intertextuality facilitates boundary crossing, reflecting the fluidity of the contemporary age of globalization," with *Visage* epitomizing "Sino-Frenchness" for her[90]—I also find Fran Martin's careful postcolonial contextualization of such strategic citations to be crucial. Where I have diverged from Martin is from her contention that Tsai's postcolonial temporal dysphoria is not equally about spatial disorientation. The notion of being in different "time zones" affects how we perceive both space and time. Like Sara Ahmed's work in *Queer Phenomenology*, such divisions also affect how we perceive "The Orient and Other Others":[91] how we are oriented toward certain cultural objects, entailing how we are oriented in relation to certain bodies and faces, thus involving both sexual orientation and disorientation.

5

Haunted, Rented, Queer Spaces

From *Vive L'Amour* to *Stray Dogs*

The gay men in the Fu Ho Theatre are ultimately ghostly not
only because of their abject status in Taiwan, but also in terms
of their appropriation of liminal spaces abandoned by
mainstream culture and society. They "haunt" the theatre.

—Kenneth Chan, "*Goodbye, Dragon Inn:*
Tsai Ming-liang's Political Aesthetics of Nostalgia,
Place, and Lingering"

Tsai's body of work is in fact Lee's body; one could interpret
Tsai's cinema as an exploration of the yearnings, fragility, and
power of Lee Kang-sheng's body. . . . In each film, Lee's bodily
functions, be they ingesting water, urinating, ejaculating, or
bathing, become important motifs, with Lee's exposed figure a
key image throughout.

—Brian Hu, "The Unprofessional: An Interview
with Lee Kang-sheng"

In *The Practice of Everyday Life,* Michel de Certeau describes the City
as "a universe of rented spaces haunted by a nowhere or by dreamed-
of places."[1] Tsai Ming-liang's body of work portrays the cities of Taipei,
Kaohsiung, Taichung, Paris, Kuala Lumpur, Hong Kong, Marseille,
and Tokyo[2] in similar terms through his emphasis on rented spaces

as haunted by "cruising" figures: a nearly abandoned movie theater (*Goodbye, Dragon Inn* [2003]), bathhouses (*The River* [1997], *No No Sleep* [2015]), public toilets (*What Time Is It There?* [2001], *The Wayward Cloud* [2005]), and real estate that is crumbling and abandoned or part of rapid construction and yet to be rented (*Vive L'Amour* [1994], *The Skywalk Is Gone* [2002], *I Don't Want to Sleep Alone* [2006]). Tsai's allegedly "final" feature film *Stray Dogs* (2013) depicts the survival tactics of a homeless family in Taichung: a distressed father (Lee Kang-sheng) earns only enough to feed his young son and daughter by holding up signs by the highway as a human billboard for new luxury real estate—into which he sneaks for a long nap, after creeping up a spiral staircase shot in an unusual canted angle that renders the space even more surreal as it twists diagonally (Figure 14).[3]

Tsai's scenarios of urban survival recall de Certeau's opposition between the "tactics" of the marginalized and the "strategies" of those with economic power and property.[4] As Agata A. Lisiak underscores, "Tsai's

FIGURE 14. *Stray Dogs* (Tsai Ming-liang, 2013). A disorienting canted-angle long shot of the homeless father climbing up a spiral staircase in a hall of mirrors in the luxury real estate for which he works as a human billboard (he has sneaked in to take a nap).

characters find pockets of opportunity in the otherwise hostile city: they develop elaborate structures and devices to deal with insufficient infrastructure."[5] The real estate theme and sleeping scene in *Stray Dogs* hark back to Tsai's early film *Vive L'Amour* in which a real estate agent (Yang Kuei-mei) tries to rent several apartments, but these apartments are mostly used for brief sexual encounters and by a lonely queer figure who uses the apartment as a ludic space. But in *Stray Dogs,* Lee's embodied performance emphasizes endurance of the elements—holding up the sign against the force of the wind and rain, singing to himself—and the need to seek shelter. The homeless family members in *Stray Dogs* squat in abandoned buildings, bathe in public toilets, and depend on the maternal kindness of a Carrefour supermarket employee, who also feeds stale meals to stray dogs.[6] In a surreal casting decision, this maternal character is embodied by all three of Tsai's favorite actresses: Yang Kuei-mei in the prologue, Lu Yi-ching in the supermarket, and Chen Shiang-chyi in the closing scenes.[7] *Stray Dogs* brings to the fore questions of home and homelessness in Tsai's films and in his own life.

In this final chapter, I inventory the ways in which space functions as a crucial dimension of queerness in Tsai's filmmaking practice. Tsai's films, via the spatial practices of his characters, suggest the value of rethinking sexual orientation in terms of sexual disorientation.[8] Tsai's practice of revising characters, relationships, themes, and locations from his previous films achieves a similar effect of disorientation and reorientation within his oeuvre. This chapter ends with a coda on the queer, *idiorrhythmic* relationship between Tsai and his muse Lee Kang-sheng (aka Hsiao Kang) as discussed in Tsai's filmed conversation with Lee, *Afternoon* (2015).[9] *Afternoon* was screened alongside *Stray Dogs* during an overnight event at the Museum of National Taipei University of Education (MoNTUE), which was transformed into a forest where the audience members could camp out and watch the films projected on the walls (looped but out of sync), and documented in *Stray Dogs at the Museum,* a "sleepover" and move to the museum I will return to in my conclusion.[10]

Haunted Spaces

In José Esteban Muñoz's "Ghosts of Public Sex," he discusses New York poet and artist John Giorno's memoirs about his utopian experiences of public sex (pre-AIDS crisis) alongside a 1994 photography project by Tony Just that attempted to capture what Muñoz calls the ghosts of public sex: "The project began with just selecting run-down public men's rooms in New York City, the kind that were most certainly tea rooms before they, like the Prince Street toilets that Giorno describes, were shut down because of the AIDS/HIV public health crisis. Just then proceeded to do the labor of scrubbing and sanitizing sections of the public men's rooms. . . . Just's labor exists only as a ghostly trace in a sparkling men's room."[11] Moreover, Muñoz employs Jacques Derrida's concept of "hauntology" to suggest that the ghostly aura and luminous halos in the work are one aspect of the ghosts of public sex, and that we see in Just's work a surpassing of the binary between ideality and actuality in favor of the "eventness" of the space.[12]

Some sense of the "eventness" of such spaces is also conveyed in Fred Barney Taylor's documentary portrait, *The Polymath, or, The Life and Opinions of Samuel R. Delany, Gentleman* (2007), where science fiction author and black gay cultural critic Delany acts as a "guide" who retrospectively describes in detail *how* exactly queer sexual spaces (baths, piers, trucks, theaters) were used.[13] Delany thus tries to account for what de Certeau identified as "spatial practices" that subvert attempts at panoptic surveillance: "these multiform, resistan[t], tricky and stubborn procedures that elude discipline without being outside the field in which it is exercised, and which should lead us to a theory of everyday practices, of lived space, of the disquieting familiarity of the city."[14] Tsai's cinematic body of work also manages to capture this disquieting familiarity of the city through his careful attention to everyday practices in the lived space of the urban environment.

Questions of nostalgia, loss, and haunting preoccupy Tsai, whose films frequently feature scenes of queer cruising in bathhouses, ambiguous urban spaces, and movie theaters. As we have seen, Tsai's *Goodbye, Dragon Inn* is about gay/queer men cruising for sex in an allegedly haunted old movie theater on its last night (a theater which Tsai rented to make his film as soon as he learned of its inevitable closure).[15] The theater patrons include two older men who starred in original the King Hu film being screened *(Dragon Gate Inn)* who muse that no one goes to the movies anymore, so they are like "ghosts," as well as a Japanese tourist who mingles among the men cruising each other in the theater's hallways and bathrooms.[16] This scenario is based on Tsai's observation of such cruising in the theater before it closed.[17] Like Delany's *Times Square Red, Times Square Blue,* Tsai's film laments the loss of the cross-class and queer social contact that movie houses fostered.[18] Like Muñoz's reading of the ghosts of public sex in Giorno's memoirs and Just's photographs, Tsai's films go beyond nostalgia to reveal the way the present is haunted by the virtual potential of queer ways of occupying space: parks, bathhouses, public restrooms, arcades, and movie theaters.

Goodbye, Dragon Inn hybridizes and overlays the genres of the *wu xia pian* (like the old King Hu swordsman film *Dragon Gate Inn* being screened as the last showing in the theater), the Chinese ghost story, and a kind of pseudo-documentary realism observing spatial practices. These spatial practices include the "backstage" operations of a movie theater, playing out in real time: the various activities of the ticket taker, the projectionist, and the patrons within the rather labyrinthine space of the Fu Ho (aka Fuhe) Grand Theater in the Yonghe district in the southern part of New Taipei. *The Wayward Cloud* also mixes realist de- pictions of the behind-the-scenes action of low-budget pornography— suggesting that porn is the only thriving cinematic industry in con- temporary Taiwan[19]—with extravagant musical sequences, including a sex comedy number set in a men's room where Hsiao Kang is cos- tumed as male genitalia, with a phallus helmet and inflated balloon testicles, and is pushed around by female janitors wielding plungers. Critics were polarized over whether Tsai's film was meant as a straight- forward indictment of pornography,[20] but I have argued that it makes more sense to consider *The Wayward Cloud* in the queer idiom of camp, which allows us to laugh at the open secrets of porn and sex in public toilets (here parodically heterosexualized as a means of hyperbolizing sexual difference and sex segregation).

From *Vive L'Amour* to *Stray Dogs*

In his review of Tsai's final commercial feature film *Stray Dogs*, Tony Rayns concedes that some critics may feel that Tsai "plows one furrow a little too often."[21] He notes how no other contemporary director "has returned so compulsively to the same themes, the same images, the same actors, the same tragicomic tone."[22] As I have traced in my previous chapters, Tsai's films tend to loop back on each other. Rayns points out how

> in *Stray Dogs*, the shots of Lee Kang-sheng struggling in driving rain and wind to hold up a signboard advertising expensive real-estate inevitably bring to mind the shots in *Vive l'Amour* ([19]94) of Yang Kuei-mei trying to put up her "For Sale or Rent" posters under similarly adverse weather conditions. The shots of vagrants settling in the shells of derelict buildings likewise recall the central motif in *I Don't Want to Sleep Alone* ([20]06), while Lee's invasion of a luxury furnished apartment for a good night's rest alone takes us back to *Vive l'Amour* again.[23]

But one could argue that rather than mere redundancy, the effect of this repetition—we could even call it a *repetition compulsion*—is to render these motifs and spaces "uncanny." The uncanny involves defamiliarizing the familiar, including the notions of family and home connoted by the term *familiar* (the German *unheimlich* literally translates as unhomelike), capturing how the city feels disquietingly familiar, to borrow de Certeau's phrase, but also perhaps disquieting our familiarity with the city and with Tsai's themes regarding domestic and liminal spaces.[24]

I argue that the notion of "rented space" is what ties all of these films together (since movie theaters are also rented spaces). In *Stray Dogs*, Tsai also spotlights acute contradictions between speculative urban real estate and the reality of homelessness.[25] The ambivalent motif of home/homelessness even carries over into the non-movie-theater screenings of Tsai's most recent film and video work, work that some have suggested is more "at home" in museums and gallery spaces.[26]

Rayns notes how there is indeed something new here in that *"Stray Dogs* is in fact unlike Tsai's nine previous features in one crucial respect: it does away almost completely with continuity editing. Most of its scenes are single shots, and there's no causal link between one and the next."[27] He juxtaposes some shots that are "so realist that they could have been taken with a hidden camera,"[28] namely digital video shots of Lee braving the elements at his job, or eating boxed lunches with his children or in vacant city lots, outdoor shots suggested by the film's Chinese title meaning "Excursion" (in Japan, the film was given the ironic title *Picnic,* though Tsai provocatively parallels their box lunch meals with those of the literal stray dogs in the film, making the film's English and French titles—*Stray Dogs, Les Chiens errants*—both literal and figurative).[29] But Rayns notes how other shots in the film "are so stylized that they might well represent dreams."[30] We have already seen this stylization and meditation on cinema as a dream in Tsai's *The Hole* (1998), *The Wayward Cloud, It's a Dream* (2007), and *Visage* (2009).[31] This dreamlike stylization can also be seen in several of Tsai's recent commissioned "expanded cinema" projects that sometimes also involve the audience sleeping in the museum. Like Muñoz on Just, Tsai's mixture of stark realism and surrealism suggests an attempt to surpass the binary between actuality and ideality in favor of the "eventness" of the space.[32]

The final part of *Stray Dogs* shifts into the dreamlike space of a partially burned house with black scorched walls that is now inhabited by the family we saw in the first part of the film. Prior to this, we observe the father and children subsisting in the cracks of the city and on the kindness of a supermarket employee, a plot that is worth comparing to Kore-eda Hirokazu's films *Nobody Knows* (2004) and *Shoplifters* (2018), which also expose the scandal of postrecession survival tactics of near-homeless families in another major metropolis, Tokyo, or to the queer kinship of three homeless people in Kon Satoshi's *anime* film *Tokyo Godfathers* (2003).[33] It is not entirely clear whether the final section of *Stray Dogs* represents a dream, alcoholic delirium, or fantasy of the family reunited in a different space, a place where the father can take a bath, and his family celebrates his birthday with a cake. The children are told a kind of bedtime story about the strange house they are in, which is said to be "crying," with the marks from the rainwater streaming down the scorched wallpaper described as "the tracks of its tears" (echoing the wallpaper peeling from flooding that the woman downstairs finally gives up on reapplying in *The Hole*). This scene epitomizes Tsai's approach to *affectively charged spaces,* and his recurring water motif.

Stray Dogs is Tsai's most searing critique of uneven urban real estate development, although it has been a theme since *Vive L'Amour* and his interview with the *World Socialist Web Site* about *The Hole*.[34] *Stray Dogs* confronts the audience with the negligent neoliberal city's treatment of the homeless family *like waste,* barely hidden in the urban environment, surviving on scraps.[35] As critic J. Hoberman describes the homeless family, "They do not live in the metropolis so much as haunt its ruins."[36] While *Stray Dogs* resembles more traditional disaster/survivalist films by focusing on a patriarchal figure (Lee) and a fantasy reunion of a dysfunctional or broken family,[37] it can be aligned with the queer (and proporn) critique of gentrification launched by Delany in *Times Square Red, Times Square Blue* and read aloud by him in *The Polymath:*

> Were the porn theaters romantic? Not at all. But because of the people who used them, they were humane and functional, fulfilling needs that most of our society does not yet know how to acknowledge. The easy argument already in place to catch up these anecdotes is that social institutions such the porn movies take up, then, a certain social excess—are even, perhaps, socially beneficial to some small part of it (a margin outside the margin). But that is the same argument that allows them to be dismissed—and physically smashed and flattened.[38]

As I have argued, Delany's trenchant account of Times Square "redevelopment"—as destruction rather than "cleaning up"—helps us to make sense of Tsai's unwillingness to "dismiss" the cruisy movie theater in *Goodbye, Dragon Inn*. Tsai's critique of the way luxury urban real estate redevelopment reinforces social inequality goes back to *Vive L'Amour*, and the disorienting effects of the rapidly changing city land-scape are once again emphasized by Shiang-chyi's bewilderment in *The Skywalk Is Gone*, finally culminating in *Stray Dogs's* assessment of those who have fallen through the cracks and are surviving by squat-ting in abandoned buildings.

Ruins

As part of the screening of *Stray Dogs* at the "Taiwan, the View from the South" conference at Australian National University (ANU),[39] Tsai's public conversation with Linda Jaivin before and after the film ad-dressed several important issues that have occupied my previous chap-ters: sleepiness in the cinema, disorientation, home/homelessness, and the inter-implication of time and space in his body of work.

Tsai starts the screening by joking about whether the audience is mentally prepared or prepared to have a little nap. He notes "and if you do fall asleep, do not feel guilty. You know a theater is a pretty good place to have a nap." However, he also jokes that, "The type of film where I fall asleep is usually the action pictures. But my films are—it's really easy to fall asleep in them, if you're not moving with it, you're out, 'oh my god, I'm not there anymore.'" As this phrasing suggests, sleepiness can cause a sense of both temporal and spatial disorienta-tion ("I'm not there anymore"). I have suggested that both time and space are deliberately disoriented in Tsai's filmmaking practice as well. Tsai explains to the audience that *Stray Dogs* "is a film about time, but you can't have time without place" and notes that "I've been making films for twenty years, and I've discovered that really what I'm talking about is time and place."

As noted regarding the critical debate over *The Wayward Cloud*, Tsai does not see himself as making "social problem" films, intentionally making films about pornography as a social problem, migrant labor-ers, the "dysfunctional family," or homelessness. He tells his audi-ence he is "not really interested in making films about *society*, about *topics*—people think of this film as about people on the margins, on the lower strata of society, but really what I'm interested in is the face of my lead actor Lee Kang-sheng" (Tsai has worked with Lee from the age of twenty-five to forty-five, he explains). While his comments may sound dismissive of these sociopolitical issues, I would argue that Tsai's focus on Lee's aging face still raises issues of time and place that cannot be separated from the sphere of the social—reputation, support, compassion—as we saw in the previous chapter regarding the French and Chinese meanings of "face."

Tsai laments, "People in Asia are often arguing about the face of cities: Why is it so ugly?" This anthropomorphizing phrase, the "face" of the city, reorients Tsai's focus on the face in his films.[40] He notes that in Asia, people are "constant tearing down and building up," which "leaves a lot of wastelands." He suggests that what he says about Taipei is true of really any city in Taiwan. In the press kit for *Stray Dogs*, Tsai explains:

> The fast paced and Western influenced development of Asian cities gives me the feeling that we are in a state of constant anxiety and un-certainty, as if we were drifting without any solid foundation beneath us. We seem to be living inside a huge construction site, with houses and roads and the subway constantly being refurbished or demolished and rebuilt. And the more development there is, the more things there are which get discarded. . . . I have never shied away from . . . showing construction sites where the concrete is rising up, or older buildings abandoned and left in ruins.[41]

Indeed, we can see this concern—and the corresponding "affects" of uncertainty, anxiety, and drifting—going back to *The Skywalk Is Gone* and centrally figured in the unfinished construction site in *I Don't Want to Sleep Alone* (Tsai seems to be invoking the latter in his figures of speech).

Yet, on the topic of urban wastelands, he tells the ANU *Stray Dogs* audience, "I love wastelands and ruins." Important ethical objections have been raised to the phenomenon of so-called "ruin porn," specifi-cally the much-documented postindustrial ruins of cities like Detroit (in the United States), and the way the capitalist and racist sociopolitical causes of such destruction get abstracted by superficial images of "beautiful decay," or by romanticizing the apparent inevitability of decline and neglect.[42] The suffix "porn" here is used as rather lazy moralistic shorthand for exploitation, and does not really help to clarify the question of how filmmakers like Tsai specifically approach such "ruins."[43] While Tsai arguably does aestheticize them in his films, noting how "these wastelands and ruined places are very beautiful" to him,[44] he also returns to a theme from his interview with the *World Socialist Web Site* about the allegory in *The Hole*: the specific sociopolitical and economic effects of rapid urban development, including destruction of the environment and worsening of class inequality. "While they want to improve their economic situation, you don't see the quality of life being improved. One of the most prominent problems is the difference between the poor and the rich, the uneven distribution of wealth. And under those conditions a lot of people live in poverty, and try to adapt to the role, to the living environment they have, and acquire the characteristics of a cockroach."[45] Like *The Hole, Stray Dogs* is hardly a straightforward "social problem" film, but it is a powerful artistic allegory about the contemporary urban environment and its marginal spaces and populations.

The final segment of *Stray Dogs* takes place in an apartment building from the 1970s that was destroyed by fire. Tsai notes that it was "fashionable at the time to have wallpaper" but the water-damaged remains of the wallpaper make it look like a painting. This comparison of artistic mediums had begun in *Visage,* and as he did for that film Tsai did a great deal of location scouting for *Stray Dogs*. Specifically, he found a mural, made with charcoal, "in a place where nobody went," of a mountain in the south of Taiwan, based on a photograph by a Scottish journalist from 1871. Tsai was curious who the artist was, noting how it is a very "charismatic mural, you can't tear yourself away." He found out the name of the artist, Kao Jun-Honn, and discovering this mural changed the conclusion to his film.[46] Chen Shiang-chyi stares at the mural, late at night, saturated with slate blue light (Tsai notes that he "never realized you could see this at night"). Tears start to stream down her face. Lee, quite drunk, walks up and then embraces her from behind, as they stare with intense melancholy at the mural. Metacine-matically, we stare at them on the illuminated screen as they stare at an illuminated panorama on the wall, a *mise en abyme* reminiscent of the ending of *Goodbye, Dragon Inn*.

Tsai informs the ANU screening audience that this place was knocked down, and does not exist anymore.[47] The cinema therefore functions as a crucial archive of space and place and of memory in the face of the amnesia wrought by urban demolition and redevelopment.[48] In this, Tsai joins some of the most politically engaged filmmakers like Taylor in *The Polymath* interviewing Delany about the old porn the-aters in Times Square; or like Jia Zhangke's *Still Life* (2006) about the effects of China's massive Three Gorges Dam project on the in-habitants of the area; or Huang Weikei's *Disorder* (2009), assembling disturbing amateur digital footage of urban social dysfunction and dis-ruptions in Guangzhou's infrastructure.[49] I have suggested that film can function as a form of "anamnesis" (unlosing, unforgetting) in the face of such destruction, and that this constitutes a form of queer ethics, like Delany refusing to allow queer sexual and spatial urban practices to be forgotten, thus perhaps complicating the ethical questions posed about "ruin porn."[50]

A similarly reparative impulse is revealed in Tsai's discussion of the relationship between sound and place in *Stray Dogs,* and, by exten-sion, the rest of his films. Tsai notes how in postproduction, or in a studio, the goal is typically to reduce "noise," but he says, "I like what is considered unnecessary," noting how the ambient sound "reminds me of where this space was." He notes an early scene with the home-less children in *Stray Dogs* where they are by a tree in the city, "near a primary school, so you can hear the kids, and this space seems so sep-arate but is so close."[51]

Tsai is asked by an audience member at the screening about the theme of home/homelessness in his film, and asked what place or coun-try he feels at home in: Taiwan, Malaysia, or France? He suggests that, "before I made this film, I really didn't have a sense of where I be-longed." We know that Tsai is designated *huaqiao,* "overseas Chinese."[52]

He explains that he has lived in Taiwan for thirty years, and has chosen to stay. In his work, he has also considered this question of home, specifically looking at homeless and migrant workers in Malaysia or Taiwan. He intends the ending of *Stray Dogs* to get the audience thinking about the meaning of "home," whether it is a recollection or memory, and to stimulate people to think afresh about the concept of home.

He tells his audience that recently, "Lee Kang-sheng and I moved into a place together, in the hills, and suddenly I have a feeling of 'I don't want to go any other place,'" and he feels like he has "found a lost world I love" reminding him of his youth "in a mountain, outside the city." This revelation prompts me to place *Stray Dogs* in dialogue with Tsai's film *Afternoon*, an over-two-hour-long filmed conversation with his muse Lee Kang-sheng in an abandoned-looking building connected to the house they share in the mountains, outside the city, another place that Tsai likens to beautiful ruins (with trees coming in the empty window frame). This location is also the setting of Tsai's VR (virtual reality) film *The Deserted* (2017), which brings together many of Tsai's recurring themes of haunting, aging bodies, and what Elena Gorfinkel calls "the affective life of ruins."[53] In a long poem included in the brochure for the Venice Biennale installation of *The Deserted* titled "Living Where No One Lives" (dated July 31, 2017), Tsai describes the location (filled with water and nature imagery) and the inspiration for *The Deserted* in terms of cohabitation (with Lee and with ghosts):

I was ill at that time.
Hsiao Kang and I went up the mountain
at the city outskirts
and found some abandoned houses.
We decided to live there.
Not long after,
Hsiao Kang's old ailment came back.
It was even more serious than mine.
Neither of us could find the cause
of our illnesses.

[. . .]
Later on, I was told that
someone had committed suicide
in one of the houses.
But no one knows which one.
Since then,
Everytime I entered one of the houses
I'd whisper softly, "Sorry to disturb."
Sometimes I get the feeling that
it's not that we have no neighbors.
It's just that we can't see them.

One day,
while Hsiao Kang was watering the plants,
he suddenly broke down in tears.
He said he will never recover from his illness
and that he doesn't want to suffer anymore.
He wished I could let him go.
Let him decide for himself.
I was stunned
And didn't know how to console him.
I waited for him to finish crying and told him
I never thought of giving you up.
Even if your neck were twisted for life,
you will still be the male lead in my films.
Let's continue making films.[54]

This poem also touches on several of the topics of conversation in *Afternoon*. In the coda that follows, I will suggest that *Afternoon* can also be placed in conversation with Roland Barthes's course *How to Live Together*, in which Barthes proposes the notion of *idiorrhythmy*, the (sometimes) difficult work of respecting people's different rhythms or pacing in the way they live, alongside Barthes's strangely *untimely* text, *A Lover's Discourse*.[55]

Coda: *Afternoon*, Ideorrythmy, and *A Lover's Discourse*

In "Unlovely Spectacle," David Greven responds to D. A. Miller's snide review of the film *Call Me by Your Name* (2017), noting how Foucauldian queer critics like Miller, David Halperin, and Michael Warner show disdain for the idea of letting gay sex "degenerate into love" (Halperin's phrase; also see Jane Ward's "Against Gay Love").[56] In this coda, I suggest that this situation may be the consequence of Roland Barthes's relative marginalization in queer theory compared to Foucault (with Miller playing an ironic part in this).[57] What might the "amicable return" of Barthes, specifically *A Lover's Discourse: Fragments,* help teach us about this predicament?[58] Writing in the sex-radical 1970s, Barthes suggested that the sentimental had become more obscene than sex. To lovingly revive Barthes's text, I want to bring it into conversation with Tsai's *Afternoon.*

Afternoon consists only of a static medium long shot in an almost-continuous take (137 minutes in four locked shots) of a career-retrospective conversation between director Tsai and Lee Kang-sheng sitting together in an empty building open to the elements with foliage creeping in and lush mountains in the background visible through the window frames.[59] While I have continually referred to Lee as Tsai's "male muse," I want to defamiliarize the term here in order to capture the queerness of their relationship and our struggle to name it. When compared to the open and crumbling architecture of this setting, the spatial metaphor of "the closet" appears inadequate.[60] In some ways, *Afternoon* feels like an "exit interview" upon Tsai's announcement of his retirement from making commercial feature films (after completing ten, all with Lee). And yet, they continue to work and produce films together—as the previous poem explains, and the queer Teddy Award–winning feature film *Days* [2020] demonstrates[61]—and they live together in a nearby house up in the mountains in New Taipei City. Thus, the interview touches on both their working relationship and careers, and how they live together (Figure 15).

Their conversation, staged for the camera yet also clearly improvised, involves a complicated working through of positions not unlike

I encounter people who don't understand how we work together.

FIGURE 15. *Afternoon* (Tsai Ming-liang, 2015). Tsai Ming-liang in conversation with Lee Kang-sheng—in a crumbling building open to the elements—explaining the premise of this filmed discussion of their relationship and how they work and live together.

those in Barthes's *A Lover's Discourse,* where the lover is alternately mother and son, oscillating between possessive jealousy and an ideal of non-possession. In terms of familial roles, Lee jokes that Tsai is "like a second mom who nags at me all day," and Tsai explains that Lee does feel "more like my child, I'm always looking out for you." In their conversation, Tsai and Lee's positions are described as: maternal, paternal, fraternal, and/or grandparental; director-actor, employer-employee, artist-muse, and/or lover-beloved; friends, fellow travelers, and/or telephone companions. They also speculate about whether they knew each other in a past life, and if they meet again in another life, whether perhaps their director-actor roles will be reversed.[62] Tsai asks Lee, "Do you want to meet me again in your next life?" He then jokes that he is such a romantic, believing they have a predestined relationship, and asks, "Am I declaring my love for him?" But he insists, "This is definitely not a romantic relationship"; rather "it feels closer, like family." In an even more bizarre metaphor, Tsai describes Lee as "like a tumor in my body. It's benign, but if you cut it, I will bleed and feel pain."

Some of their conversation addresses the question of how to live together, their cohabitation suggesting Barthesian *idiorrhythmy*, that is, respecting the other's pace of living.[63] Tsai has also said this problem was a revelation to him early on in trying to direct Lee on film, where Lee refused to speed up an action, thus forcing Tsai to respect his pace, profoundly affecting his approach to "slow cinema."[64] We could also compare their conversation about their relationship to Michel Foucault's interview "Friendship as a Way of Life," where Foucault considers relations between men not necessarily in the form of a couple but "as a matter of existence: how is it possible for men to be together? To live together, to share their time, their meals, their room, their leisure, their grief, their knowledge, their confidences? What is it to be 'naked' among men, outside of institutional relations, family, profession, and obligatory camaraderie? It's a desire, an uneasiness, a desire-in-uneasiness that exists among a lot of people."[65] But even when Tsai and Lee do talk about family and profession, they suggest a kind of queer kinship that exceeds the family, or that *queers* notions of friendship and family, expressing desire-in-uneasiness.

Theirs sounds like an "open relationship" (in multiple ways) when the conversation turns to gay sexuality and secrecy. Lee jokes that he knows about the things Tsai does "in secret" but feels he can't tell (implying the closet), but Tsai then insists that "you can tell if you want. Of course I have my pleasures. There are times when I need to release myself. We all do. We're all human. But it's hard for us to enjoy those places" (implying gay bathhouses). Lee says, "I don't enjoy those places, actually." Later in the conversation Tsai ponders, "Why do I want to talk about this issue? I guess I won't have another opportunity. Going back to my sense of belonging. At one point in my life, the gay sauna gave me a sense of belonging. Like the father in *The River*. I went to one of them, but nothing happened. Because to be intimate with someone, there has to be a mutual attraction. But to be honest, it often turns out to be . . . You know that sometimes I'd go to some places. . . . Because there are guidebooks to such places overseas. You've been to some of those places with me." Lee then insists, "I always stood outside waiting for you to come out, or we'll agree on a place to meet. If you didn't show up I was going to call the police." Lee expresses rather maternal concern for Tsai's health in such "risky" places. Tsai then explains to him how "those places can be risky but they give me a feeling. Simply put, they give me a sense of belonging, like being home. Because I know that in that world, we're all the same. Very often, nothing would happen, but that feeling of restlessness in me would subside." We might compare this description to Samuel R. Delany's revelations about the gay bathhouse in his memoir *The Motion of Light in Water*.[66]

Transitioning to a metalevel of conversation (which occurs at several points),[67] Tsai remarks, "I feel at ease with you because I can tell you these things." He explains how "for a long time I didn't have this sense of belonging. It's the same when I get into relationships. Sometimes the other party will get jealous of you. They think that I love only you. They will feel that way. Like that guy from Italy, he was angry that I called you daily from Italy. He didn't understand. I told him I must hear your voice. I must make sure you are safe. Our relationship is weird like that." But they agree that such short phone calls are more like a mother and son (suggesting the telephone cord as umbilical cord). Yet, as Carol Mavor has argued regarding the way Barthes writes about maternal love in *A Lover's Discourse*, this maternal framing is still remarkably queer.[68]

Tsai remarks that, "You said you didn't want to play a gay man all the time. I was aware of your resistance to such role. You were under an agency and other directors wanted you. But I never stopped you."[69] Tsai asks Lee, "Has my sexual orientation ever given you trouble?" Lee responds incredulously, "Huh?" Tsai rephrases the question: "My sexual orientation, has it ever bothered you?" Lee says, "Not really," and he asks, "What has it got to do with me? Except when people are interested in me they do tend to ask a lot of questions first. But I don't think it's a big issue." Tsai asks him if his parents know about Tsai's sexual orientation, and Lee responds that he never asked his father, and he can't tell if his mother does, but "one time she was criticizing a homosexual on television and she stopped all of a sudden when she realized I was there." Tsai jokingly asks, "Why did they let their child work and live with me?"

Uncharacteristic of Tsai's other films known for an almost complete absence of spoken dialogue, *Afternoon* consists mostly of speech (although starting the conversation seems like a struggle, and there are some awkward silences).[70] Watching it unfold, the viewer wonders: is this really a dialogue, or is it instead a monologue?[71] Tsai does most of the talking, sometimes reflecting philosophically that Lee is his muse because "I feel that I can only enter my inner world through you" and "you exist because you don't seem to exist." At one point he even talks about Lee in the third person: "The one person I can't bear to let go of is Lee Kang-sheng. It's strange. I can't shift my camera away from him. . . . I don't know how he feels." This recalls the essential imbalance of Plato's *Symposium* and *Phaedrus*, texts by Maurice Blanchot like *The One Who Was Standing Apart from Me*, and especially Barthes's *A Lover's Discourse*.[72]

But beyond the European theory of Barthes's Lacanian or Winnicottian understanding of the maternal relation in love, Tsai and Lee's conversation also suggests the urgency of questions of queer kinship in the Sinophone context. Queer kinship is a central topic in Stanley Kwan's documentary *Yang ± Yin: Gender in Chinese Cinema* (1996), featuring an early interview with Tsai about his relationship with his father, and Kwan's conversation with his mother at the end of the documentary could be seen as providing a model for Tsai's "coming out" *for the record* on film in *Afternoon*.[73] Discussions of queer kinship in the Sinophone context must include not only the successful campaign for *tongxing* (same-sex) marriage in Taiwan, but also questions of cohabitation, mutual support, inheritance, and caretaking in times of illness, including the AIDS crisis, a subject addressed in Tsai's early television documentary *My New Friends* (1995) in which Tsai himself physically stands in for the two HIV-positive young gay men he interviews.[74] In a brief statement while accepting the Teddy (queer film) Award at the Berlinale for his postretirement feature film *Days* (2020), Tsai dedicated the film to "my country" Taiwan and celebrated the marriage equality decision (the translator noted that Taiwan was the "first country in Asia" to pass "gay marriage").[75] And yet, the film *Days* itself features a more liminal, queer, cross-class, inter-Asian, intergenerational, and commercial sexual relationship between Lee and a Laotian migrant in Thailand, Anong Houngheuangsy. Their massage session with a "happy ending" is filmed in a hotel room in Bangkok, followed by a shared meal in a nearby restaurant. The "bounded intimacy" of *Days* portrays queer sex work as a form of care work, since the film returns to treatments for Lee's actual neck pain first incorporated into the plot of *The River*.[76]

In his sustained attention to queer uses of space (especially rented and "abandoned" spaces), queer intimacy and queer ethics (especially of cruising and caring for strangers), and the aging body (including mourning and melancholy), Tsai's cinematic body of work—with Lee's body, as Hu notes in the epigraph—offers a deliberate disorientation of sexuality and love that holds great promise for a queer theory of love, "desire in uneasiness," and how to live together.

Expanded Cinema, Sleepovers, and Cruising the Museum

ERIK MORSE: A number of people have told me that they have fallen asleep during your films. Given the very minimalist, atmospheric style of most of your work . . . it could be that there is something quite comforting about your filmmaking style that lures viewers into a kind of hypnotic somnolence. Do you ever fall asleep while watching films?

TSAI MING-LIANG: Often! In fact, just before you called I was watching a Bollywood film but I fell asleep. I also fall asleep watching kung fu films. It's not a reflection of their quality; it's just a habit of mine. . . . I don't mind if my films make some people fall asleep but then I really don't mind criticism either; I feel that it doesn't have anything to do with me.

> —Erik Morse, "Time & Again," interview with Tsai
> Ming-liang

Given Tsai Ming-liang's well-established mode of auteurist self-curation, is he ultimately "at home" in the museum?[1] In 2014, *Stray Dogs at the Museum: Tsai Ming-liang Solo Exhibition* at the Museum of National Taipei University of Education (MoNTUE) provocatively invited audiences—recruited from the student body, but also including the elderly and families with children—to literally camp out in the museum overnight with round-the-clock screenings of Tsai's "final" commercial feature film *Stray Dogs* (2013)[2] and *Afternoon* (2015), his long, filmed career-retrospective conversation with Lee Kang-sheng (aka Hsiao [Xiao] Kang) that also explores their queer kinship. Ironically, *Afternoon* acts as itself a kind of "solo exhibition" wherein Tsai does most of the talking. The three floors of the museum were transformed into a forest or brushland filled with dried trees and leaves, pillows painted like Taiwanese cabbages (a reference to a scene in *Stray Dogs*),[3] foam mattresses, sleeping bags, and tents. The trees were downed by a tropical storm (Typhoon Matmo), found, collected, and installed in the relatively small museum—some still remain in the museum café, along with a video projection of a mattress. As we have seen, the mattress is a recurring motif in Tsai's oeuvre, suggesting erotic space and the spatial conditions of sleep and "sleepy cinema," the topics (*topoi*) addressed in this conclusion.

Sleepovers and Expanded Cinema

Tsai explains the scenario of *Stray Dogs at the Museum* in his "Notes" in the bilingual (Chinese and English) museum catalogue:

> The movie continued throughout the night. People slept if tired;
>   children went in their tents.
> Adults lay in front of the screens. The exhibition hall was full of people
>   resting and sleeping that it got tough to
> move and walk along.
> Xiao Kang's close-up kept an eye [on] their dreams
> Some people couldn't sleep, they woke up and watch[ed] my movie.[4]

We can picture the films "watching over" the watching or sleeping *spectators* or *audience* (as viewing and listening are both at work, plus an added tactile dimension) and perhaps entering their dreams. This is an idea also explored by Tsai's contemporary queer Southeast Asian interlocutor Apichatpong Weerasethakul's expanded cinema installation/sleepover *Sleepcinemahotel* (International Film Festival Rotterdam, 2018).[5] But how do such installations "expand" cinema?[6]

Tsai's poetic phrasing suggests a remarkable fusion of audiences and spaces (Figure 16): "Numerous audiences lay together in the dry forest at the museum."[7] In their exhibition catalogue essays, Chang Hsiao-hung and Sing Song-yong explore Tsai's unique combination or enfolding of the cinema and museum. Chang poses several questions: "How is it possible for the museum to plunge into 'becoming-cinema'? How is it possible for the cinema to turn into 'becoming-museum'? How does *Stray Dogs* make the museum not the museum anymore?"[8] Rather than a difference of *typology* between the cinema and museum, Chang instead proposes *topology*, the "'folding' rolling and motion of topology" or "the possibility of becoming between 'post-cinema' and 'post-museum.'"[9] Sing discusses the "museum-ification of cinema and the cinematization of the museum," noting how, as a museum-ification of cinema, "*Stray Dogs at the Museum* originated from Tsai Ming-liang's idea conceived at the start of making the film *Stray Dogs:* the museum would be the site to screen this film."[10]

Describing how *the white cube became a black box,* Sing elaborates the metamorphosis involved:

FIGURE 16. *Stray Dogs at the Museum* (Lin Chunni, 2015). Expanded cinema: multiple screens showing *Stray Dogs* (Tsai Ming-liang, 2013) in the Museum of National Taipei University of Education transformed into a forest for the continuous overnight screening with audience members in sleeping bags.

In addition to transforming the museum into movie theaters, the co-curators Tsai Ming-liang and Lin Mun-lee endeavor to integrate each location and props [trees, foam mattresses, cabbages] in the worlds of the films into the exhibition venue . . . all these are obviously for turning the museum into a context or scene for the story. The trees or the allopatric-like ruins make the visitors feel like being in the films. Entering the entrance of the second floor constructed by branches and walking over the entire space along the pathway, one sees screens surrounding the venue show several projected rushes and long takes.[11]

Rather than merely screening the final cut of the film *Stray Dogs* the way it was edited for theatrical cinematic exhibition, Sing explains how "the projected images that are absent from the film and the rushes excluded from the final cuts reappear in the exhibition venue respectively. In my view, we shall not simply understand this as undoing or deconstructing a single image but rather as the construction of form among images."[12] While in one sense this formal experiment is the becoming-movie-theater of the museum, Tsai still insists that he wants the exhibit to plant the seed in young people gathered in the museum (students and children) to also want to see his films screened in theaters.[13]

Tsai also attempts to "lower" the lofty status of the museum, turning it into something quotidian and common, as noted by Sing: "If Tsai was capable of transforming food markets and public toilets into fantastical stages for singing and dancing in *The Hole* (1998) and *The Wayward Cloud* (2005), or the National Palace Museum and the National Taiwan Museum of Fine Arts into sauna-like dark tunnels in *Erotic Space* (2007) and *Erotic Space II* (2010), his endeavor to devalue MoNTUE as a delicate art institution that symbolizes paradigm seems reasonable."[14] As discussed in my previous chapters, Tsai's approach to queer camp and the Taiwanese equivalent working-class "*song*"[15] draws out the erotic potential and "eventness"[16] of spaces including public toilets and movie theaters, but also museums (in Sing's examples), suggesting or invoking what John Paul Ricco's queer sex space theory terms "minor architecture" associated with cruising, "an architecture of promiscuous spatiality, sociality, and sexuality," or spaces for "queer erotic itinerancy."[17]

The scenario created by Tsai suggests the museum becoming park, ramble,[18] and squat (Figure 17). The installation thus poses provocative questions about Tsai and his audience's sense of home and homelessness in Taipei.[19] What different kind of jarring *mise en abyme* is created with a museum audience in sleeping bags watching a homeless family find shelter in an abandoned building? In some sense, Tsai continues to rent out spaces in which to stage a sense of disorientation or temporary loss of orientation. We can only wonder: was the museum temporarily a cruising ground as well?

Cruising the Museum

Ricco's own curatorial practice in *disappeared* (1996) explored trajectories of and through minor architectures, including Tom Burr's installation *Approximation of a Chicago Style Blue Movie House (Bijou)* featuring porn theater chairs and Derek Jarman's nonrepresentational film *Blue* (1993).[20] We can compare Burr's installation with Tsai's gallery installation pieces using movie theater seats—*It's a Dream* (2007) at the Venice Biennale and International Film Festival Rotterdam (IFFR)—

FIGURE 17. *Stray Dogs at the Museum* (Lin Chunni, 2015). Sleepover in the sylvan museum: the projection of different scenes from *Stray Dogs* (Tsai Mingliang, 2013), including the landscape mural in an abandoned building at night and the homeless family eating boxed lunches, casting a blue-green glow over audience members in sleeping bags.

and gay sauna architecture and props (mattresses and toilet paper)—
Erotic Space (2007) at the National Palace Museum and *Erotic Space II*
(2010) at the National Taiwan Museum of Fine Arts.[21] In the *Stray Dogs
at the Museum* exhibition catalogue, IFFR film curator Gertjan Zuilhof
discusses both installations in his anecdotal photo essay "Take a Seat."[22]
He explains that while the *It's a Dream* installation was originally for
Venice, for him it was also the Rotterdam installation (*Is It a Dream?*):
"After the Venice show they wanted to throw away the chairs which I
thought was a waste and so we shipped them from one harbor city to
another."[23] He includes a photograph of a woman asleep in the rows of
theater chairs, which are installed next to a wall of mirrors expanding
them into virtual space, a picture "made by the Malaysian filmmaker
Tan Chui-mui, so it is nice to know the chairs come from a Malaysian
cinema. She took the photo when we were reconstructing the installation. Since it was a dream installation, she made a double exposure
and pretended to sleep. Or maybe she really fell asleep, because this
filmmaker can sleep anywhere."[24] This helps expand our understanding of the *It's a Dream* film and installations discussed in my preface
as a microcosm of Tsai's cinema, and the notions of sleepy cinema
addressed in this conclusion.

　　Zuilhof describes *Erotic Space* in terms that fit both Sing's and Ricco's
descriptions of the minor architecture of cruising: "TML made a number of small cabins, inspired by erotic massage places that had his home
movies on monitors in them. I still think it was one of his most intense
installation works. In his room it was dark as the night (the museum
had a problem with that I recall) and the atmosphere very intimate.
Viennese choirboys on one of the videos became strangely erotic. You
could take place on a mattress in a cabin which continues the idea of
watching in comfort as a red line in this contribution."[25] Zuilhof's Dutch-
to-English phrasing wherein "you could take place on a mattress" (rather
than "take a place on") suggests how Tsai's *Erotic Space* activates the
taking-place or "eventness" of gay sauna architecture, also harking back
to his early film *The River* (1997).[26] Zuilhof's "red line" suggests both a
limit and a thread, and for me, it connotatively evokes the Dutch sex
worker organization De Rode Draad (The Red Thread), itself invoking

The Scarlet Letter,[27] pointing to the policing of sexuality including sex work, pornography, promiscuity, and gay/queer cruising in saunas and movie theaters.[28]

What is notable is that the *Erotic Space* exhibition did not feature pornography, or representations of explicit sex. But like Tsai's *No No Sleep* (2015) being mistaken for gay porn by some YouTube users,[29] Zuilhof testifies to the *sexual disorientation* the installation caused, and the way it eroticized otherwise nonpornographic footage (and the space of the gallery, through the diffuse eroticism of the darkness),[30] which is worth comparing to Burr's *Blue Movie* installation.[31]

Tsai's ongoing practice of recycling old movie theater chairs also recalls his "eco-camp" practices of recycling and conservation discussed in chapter 3.[32] Tsai explains his ethos in *Stray Dogs at the Museum*:

> Basically, my exhibition is to retrieve the real things back, a bit similar to the concept in *It's a Dream*. After filming in an old theater, I thought the theater wouldn't be around for anymore longer, and afterward those 1000 theater seats would disappear, and what will be left? Besides the film images, I thought I could salvage more from the theater, so I kept the seats. But they too would disappear someday. The film is probably the last to vanish from the world, but it will for sure be gone one day. This is how I see things in the world, and thus I prefer to make the best of everything. The application of the dried branches is similar to my searching for an abandoned building when filming *Stray Dogs*. . . . The projection screen for this exhibition is the used paper in the production of *The Monk from the Tang Dynasty*.[33]

We have also seen the queer reparative impulse of Tsai's scouting, conservation, and recycling activity in *Goodbye, Dragon Inn* (2003), filming in the Fu Ho theater before its closure, and *Visage* (2009), exploring the bowels of the museum rather than its showcase galleries.[34] Ironically, while defending his need for his entire crew to be allowed to film in the Louvre's ancient sewer, Tsai invokes a field trip: "I lost my temper over this and told the Louvre that we were filmmakers not schoolboys on a field trip to a museum."[35] Yet in *Stray Dogs at the Museum*, Tsai explains that student field trips to the Louvre are what inspired him to organize his film screening at MoNTUE for students and children.[36]

Roland Barthes's Collège de France course "The Preparation of the Novel" provided me earlier with a way of understanding the preparatory work of the film-within-the-film in Tsai's "film of commission" *Visage*.[37] In this course he also "opens a dossier"—for his students to complete—on a distinction (and slippage) between the work as *mise en abyme* and maquette (an artist's preliminary model or sketch). Like I did in the epigraph to the book you are now reading, Barthes invokes the work of Marcel Proust, but then turns to a porn theater to make his point:

> A very sophisticated case: *In Search of Lost Time:* virtually, both a work *"en abyme"* (the novel that the narrator wants to write, whose failure he's documenting (the failure of wanting-to-write)) + work-as-maquette, because the novel in question turns out to be *In Search of Lost Time* itself. As if the maquette were dissolving, fading into the background to make space for all that it draws in and attracts: a world (or a triple world: of love, of worldliness, and of art). There's an instability, an unstable slippage between the *mise-en-abyme* and the *maquette*—the issue being production (action). Example, a porn film: on the screen, a scene: the movie theater in which a porn film is being screened = *"mise-en-abyme"*; no movement other than what's happening on the screen in the film → the spectators in the movie theater in the film begin to reproduce the gestures of the scene they're watching → "maquette" (third degree, if the real spectators were to become erotic partners).[38]

Tsai's *Goodbye, Dragon Inn* and Samuel R. Delany's *Times Square Red, Times Square Blue* provide similar examples of cruising and erotic activity in the cinema, sometimes in the form of *mise en abyme* and sometimes as maquette or model.[39] Discussing a rare cameo by Tsai and queer film critic Lee You-hsin seated in the audience at the start of *Goodbye, Dragon Inn,* Song Hwee Lim notes, "Situated against the context of Tsai's film in which the labyrinthine spaces of the Fu Ho theatre are appropriated as a site for gay cruising, the queer inscriptions by

Tsai and Lee in this shot . . . insert a queer spectatorship, criticism, and auteurship right at the center of the foreground screen."[40] This has also been my own goal in foregrounding queer cruising in the cinema.

In Barthes's essay "Leaving the Movie Theater," he confesses that he likes to *leave* a movie theater, describing his bodily and affective state: "he's *sleepy*, that's what he's thinking, his body has become something *sopitive*, soft, limp and he feels a little disjointed, even . . . irresponsible."[41] In *Roland Barthes' Cinema*, Philip Watts notes the way Barthes's essay suggests "the power of the cinema resides not in its capacity to hypnotize us or render us passive, but rather in its ability to transform the sensory experience of the world around us . . . to alter the way the body and desire encounter spaces, objects, and people."[42] Inspired by Barthes's and Watts's implicit challenge to ideology criticism and "apparatus theory," my conclusion has considered the affective and bodily states of the "sleepy" audience member (during or after the screening) as well as films and expanded cinema installations that might be described as inducing or evoking "sleepy" states (which includes dreaming).

Does "slow cinema"—marked by long takes where "nothing happens"—automatically provoke sleeping in the movie theater?[43] Or, instead, do special-effects-driven action films induce sleep or "zoning out"? Might the term "sleepy" represent a productive third term to the binary division between being "awake" and being "asleep" (including the ideological implications of either vigilance or passivity)? Can the notion of "sleepy cinema" bring embodiment back to discussions of spectatorship and the cinema as an alternative public sphere or heterotopia?[44]

Soma-aesthetics or *somaesthetics* is employed by Gong Jow-jiun to understand how in *Stray Dogs at the Museum* emphasis is "redirected to visitors' bodies, as they stride from the two dimensions of projected images into the durational deferred and three-dimensional crystalline structure of Tsai's exhibition."[45] Proposing an exchanging or reshaping of somatic engagement with movie theaters and museums, Gong suggests that moving *Stray Dogs* into the museum "frees audience members' bodies and promotes the affectivization of movie going, thereby deconstructing the aesthetic regime of the movie theater," which "not only replaces gazing in a movie theater and glimpsing at video art with glancing at a film exhibition, but also urges an unrestrained flow of animacy by deploying different physical activities within the museum dispositif."[46] The word *dispositif* here perhaps brings us back to the illusionary cinematic *apparatus* of apparatus theory (which Barthes and Watts help to steer us away from). It also might return us to Michel Foucault's analysis of systems of power relations, including institutional, colonial, disciplinary, and architectural forms, along with the *deployment* of sexuality (including concepts of sexual orientation and sexual identity).[47] But Gong's tracing of unrestrained flows of animacy in *Stray Dogs at the Museum* suggests something more akin to Michel de Certeau's *antidiscipline*,[48] pointing to embodied spatial practices—in haunted, rented, and cruisy urban spaces—that are wayward, errant, itinerant, and queer.

Acknowledgments

For introducing me to Tsai Ming-liang's films, I am forever grateful to Michelle Stewart. I also want to thank several other friends and mentors from my time at the University of Minnesota: Cecilia Aldarondo, Susan Andrews, Cesare Casarino, Leo Chen, Gretchen Gasterland-Gustafsson, Thomas O. Haakenson, Kjel Johnson, Jason McGrath, John Mowitt, Tom Roach, Julietta Singh, Nathan Snaza, Graeme Stout, and the late, dearly missed Gary Thomas. Many thanks to the editors of *Jump Cut,* Julia Lesage and the late Chuck Kleinhans, for publishing (in 2008) my first piece on Tsai Ming-liang's *Goodbye, Dragon Inn,* which formed the basis for this book. *Senses of Cinema* journal also provided an important venue and resource. The Queer Diaspora conference in 2010 at National Taiwan University in Taipei also inspired this project, in particular the presentations by Fran Martin and Gayatri Gopinath, whose work has been foundational to me.

Earl Jackson's wonderful hospitality, mentorship, and introductions in Taiwan have made this book possible, along with the hospitality of Hugo Wu Ching Hsien, Tang-Mo Tan, and Corrado Neri, and initial travel funding provided by a UNF Florida Blue Ethics Center Fellowship. Earl arranged my meeting with Josephine Chuen-juei Ho and her colleagues at the Center for the Study of Sexualities at National Central University. They hosted me as a visiting scholar in 2017 with the generous support of a Ministry of Science and Technology (MOST) grant, written by Amie Parry and Fifi Naifei Ding, and a sabbatical leave from the University of North Florida. I am forever grateful to Fifi for her hospitality, mentorship, and friendship during my stay in Taiwan. I also want to express my gratitude for the warm welcome and support of my NCU English department colleagues Katherine Chou, Hans Tao-Ming Huang, Chien-Ting Lin, Wenchi Lin, Peng-yi Tai, Grace Wu, Jonathan Te-hsuan Yeh, and Peng Yi, and the assistance of Jenny Yang and Tiffany Yeh. I want to thank the graduate students in my seminar on "Gender, Sexuality, and Cinema" at NCU, and Lala Lau for her insights about Chinese queer terminology and translation. For their friendship and guidance during my stays in Taiwan, I am also grateful to Bruce Chao, Henry Chu, Brian Hioe, Teri Silvio, Tinus Stander (Bouncy Babs, with thanks to Maxime Savage for the introduction), Xander Synaptic (Spectral Codex), Nick Van Halderen (Taipei Popcorn), and Orlando Yuan-yang Wang. I am also deeply indebted to Beth Tsai for her willingness to share sources collected for her essential *Oxford Bibliography* on Tsai Ming-liang, and for her friendship and ongoing collaboration (I eagerly await the publication of her book *Taiwan New Cinema at Film Festivals*).

Thanks to Sealing Cheng in Hong Kong for helping to arrange my visit to the Chinese University of Hong Kong to give a talk to the Gender Studies seminar, which also enabled me to meet Song Hwee Lim, whose impact on my thinking about Tsai Ming-liang is profound. I am so grateful to Song Hwee Lim for connecting me with Claude Wang at Homegreen Films to arrange an interview with Tsai Ming-liang at his studio in New Taipei City, along with my NCU colleague Jonathan Te-hsuan Yeh, who also helped translate our conversation. I am immensely grateful to Tsai for generously sharing his time and his insights on space and queerness in his films. Any errors of translation or interpretation are entirely my own.

I am thankful for opportunities to present my research at several conferences, and for the resulting connections and friendships. The International Academic Forum's Asian Conference on Arts and Humanities in Japan provided an important early venue. IAFOR's *Journal of Literature & Librarianship* also published my first piece on Tsai and sexual disorientation, and I am grateful for Sim Wai Chew's input at the conference, which informed my revisions. The Asian Cinema Studies Society conferences in Macau and Singapore have been so crucial for my evolving understanding of Tsai Ming-liang and Sinophone cinemas. I am grateful for the insights and friendship of Jason Coe, Victor Fan, Elmo Gonzaga, Earl Jackson, Gina Marchetti, Corrado Neri, Zoran Lee Pecic, Phoebe Pua, Elliott Shie, Shu-mei Shih, Valerie Soe, Tan See Kam, Ying Xiao, and Jamie Zhao.

Additional conferences have enabled me to present and develop my work on Tsai and queer Sinophone cinema, including: the Practice of (in)Visibility conference at the University of Brighton, UK, where I am so grateful to have met Flair Donglai Shi; the Signifying Spaces: Theory, Method, Textual Practice conference in Lublin, Poland, where it was lovely to travel with Earl Jackson; CoGen2018: Gender and Sexuality Justice in Asia at Monash University Malaysia in Kuala Lumpur, which also made it possible for me to visit Tsai's filming locations and his hometown of Kuching in Sarawak, and meet Saw Tiong Guan to discuss his documentary on Tsai, *Past Present*.

I also appreciate the opportunity to present my work on Tsai's transnational films at conferences forced online due to the Covid-19 pandemic: the Queer Migrations: Transnational Sexualities in Theory and Practice conference, hosted by the Centre for Research in the Arts, Social Sciences, and Humanities (CRASSH) at the University of Cambridge, UK, with many thanks to convenors Geoffrey Maguire, Leila Mukhida, and Tiffany Page, keynote speaker Gayatri Gopinath, and fellow presenters Nadia Atia and J. Daniel Luther; and the East Asian Popular Culture Association conference hosted by Kyushu University, Fukuoka, Japan. I have been struck by the multiple ironies of speaking about transnational travel and diaspora during pandemic lockdown, addressing Tsai's films, which depict isolation, social alienation, and fear of disease, during a very real global pandemic that has corresponded with an appalling revival of anti-Asian rhetoric that resulted in violence toward members of the Asian diaspora in the West.

While it, too, was postponed in 2020 and moved online in 2021, the annual Society for Cinema and Media Studies conference has provided me a real sense of community (even virtually) through the Adult Film History Scholarly Interest Group and the Queer and Trans Caucus, along with crucial opportunities to present early chapter drafts. Many thanks to Peter Alilunas, Brandon Arroyo, Heather Berg, Chris Berry, Shi-Yan Chao, David Church, Lynn Comella, Antoine Damiens, Glyn Davis, Desirae Embree, Victor Fan, Scott Ferguson, Finley Freibert, Elena Gorfinkel, Lucas Hilderbrand, Adam Herron, Matt Hipps, Harry Karahalios, Patrick Keilty, Daniel Laurin, Juan Llamas, Jean Ma, Laura Helen Marks, Peter Marra, Shaka McGlotten, Nicholas Mendoza, Darshana Mini, Gary Needham, Hoang Tan Nguyen, Susanna Paasonen, Lakshmi Padmanabhan, Ryan Powell, Elizabeth Purchell, Celeste Reeb, Allison Rittmayer, Amy Rust, Casey Scott, Irhe Sohn, John Paul Stadler, Eliza Steinbock, Kyle Stevens, Billy Stevenson, Whitney Strub, Alanna Thain, Beth Tsai, Maureen Turim, Johnny Walker, Thomas Waugh, Fan Yang, and Jamie Zhao. I am also grateful to the following scholars and artists for their insights on queer sexuality, language, and cinema: Fiona Anderson, A. Anthony, Sam Ashby, Hongwei Bao, Ricardo Abreu Bracho, Rachel Sagner Buurma, Cui Zi'en, Joseph N. Goh, David Greven, David Halperin, Mie Hiramoto, Katrien Jacobs, Dredge Kang, Wenqing Kang, Travis SK Kong, Wendy Lee, Petrus Liu, Heather Love, Christopher Lupke, Nicola Mai, Greggor Mattson, Corey McEleney, Tommaso Milani, Mireille Miller-Young, Bradford Nordeen, Hiram Perez, Juliana Piccillo, John Paul Ricco, Lisa Rofel, Jordan Stein, Fred Barney Taylor, Stephen Vider, Alvin Wong, and Fan Wu.

For their camaraderie and insights into queer culture, drag, and diaspora in Taipei, Singapore, and New York City, I thank Anteus Mathieu Carter-Ransome (C'était Bontemps), Matthew de Leon (Untitled Queen), Mei-yann Hwang (Dr. Wang Newton), Joe E. Jeffreys, Alexey Kim, Jon Mangan (Magnolia La Manga), Alejandro Rodríguez (Lady Quesa'Dilla), Maxime Savage (Heliø), Lila Schallert-Wygal (Mothership), Tinus Stander (Bouncy Babs), Eugene Tan (Becca D'Bus), and Nick Van Halderen (Taipei Popcorn).

In Jacksonville, I have learned so much about queer cinema and drag culture from my close circle of friends, with many thanks to Trinity Baker, Graciela Cain (Geexella), Juliet Galleon, Christine Miller, BeBe

Palmer, Hayden Palmer, Ryan Reno, Alex Royal, and Erin Tuzuner. I am particularly grateful to Hayden Palmer for being a fabulous traveling companion and cinephile kindred spirit, and for his crucial assistance with this project. I am also grateful to Caitlín Doherty, Cassie Derickson, Nan Kavanaugh, and Matthew Patterson at the Museum of Contemporary Art Jacksonville, and Shana David-Massett and Tim Massett at Sun-Ray Cinema.

At the University of North Florida, I am fortunate to have colleagues I also consider good friends. I want to express my gratitude to my interdisciplinary faculty writing group for their crucial guidance on early drafts of these chapters: Chris Gabbard, Stephen Gosden, Laura Heffernan, Tru Leverette, Jennifer Lieberman, Betsy Nies, Sarah Provost, and Jessica Q. Stark. I would also like to thank: my English department colleagues, Keith Cartwright, Tim Donovan, Sam Kimball, Jason Mauro, Alex Menocal, Jillian Smith, and Brian Striar; my colleagues in Languages, Literatures, and Cultures, Constanza López, Clayton McCarl, Shira Schwam-Baird, and Yongan Wu; my Asia Council colleagues (in Philosophy and History), Paul Carelli, Aaron Creller, Chau Kelly, Sarah Mattice, and the late N. Harry Rothschild; and my union colleagues in the UNF chapter of the United Faculty of Florida, Carolyne Ali-Khan, Maria Atilano, James Beasley, Elizabeth R. Brown, Ash Faulkner, Gregory Gundlach, Kally Malcom-Bjorklund, and Claudia Sealey-Potts. I also want to thank the students in my East Asian Cinemas courses and my graduate seminars Gender, Sexuality, and Cinema and Drag and Camp Cinema.

At the University of Minnesota Press, I am grateful to Anne Carter, Zenyse Miller, Leah Pennywark, Jason Weidemann, former editor Richard Morrison, copyeditor Marilyn Campbell, and the anonymous manuscript readers for their helpful guidance and direction.

For their love and support, I thank my parents Jill and Peter de Villiers and my sister Charlotte Cathro. Finally, thank you Samuel Trask for traveling the world with me.

Notes

Preface

1. The version I am discussing can be found on the region-2 DVD of *Chacun son cinéma, ou, Ce petit coup au coeur quand la lumière s'éteint et que le film commence*, curated by Gilles Jacob (Paris: StudioCanal, 2007) and online at https://www.dailymotion.com/video/x2barh. On a related temporal disorientation in the work of Marcel Proust, see Roland Barthes, "*Longtemps, je me suis couché de bonne heure*," in *The Rustle of Language*, trans. Richard Howard (1986; rpt. Berkeley: University of California Press, 1989), 277–90; 283. Also see the surrealist approach to visualizing Proustian temporal and spatial disorientation in the film adaptation of *Time Regained. Marcel Proust's Time Regained (Le temps retrouvé, d'après l'oeuvre de Marcel Proust)*, DVD, directed by Raoul Ruiz (1999; Brooklyn, N.Y.: Kimstim Films, 2017).

2. I will elaborate on this label for Tsai's longtime actor and creative partner Lee Kang-sheng (aka "Hsiao [Xiao] Kang") in later chapters, but simply remark on the common yet odd modifier "male" to the idea of the artistic muse, and the complexity of their relationship and "queer" mode of kinship (Lee is younger than Tsai but here plays his father, and their relationship in interviews sometimes borders on the romantic). As Erik Bordeleau puts it, Tsai "constantly reiterates how he loves to film Xiao Kang's face and rear end, and how he will never make a film without him." Erik Bordeleau, "The Care for Opacity: On Tsai Ming-Liang's Conservative Filmic Gesture," *NECSUS*, November 22, 2012, https://necsus-ejms.org/the-care-for-opacity-on-tsai-ming-liangs-conservative-filmic-gesture/.

3. See Song Hwee Lim, *Tsai Ming-liang and a Cinema of Slowness* (Honolulu: University of Hawai'i Press, 2014), 74.

4. On Tsai's queer kinship with Lee Kang-sheng as his male muse, see chapter 5. Here I am borrowing Barthes's reading of Proust in "*Longtemps, je me suis couché de bonne heure*," 283.

5. Tsai pays homage to the *wuxia pian* or martial arts/swordsman/chivalrous combat picture in *Goodbye, Dragon Inn (Bu san)*, DVD, directed by Tsai Ming-liang (Taipei: Homegreen Films, 2003), discussed in chapter 2 of this book, and 1960s Mandarin-language musicals in *The Hole (Dong)*, DVD, directed by Tsai Ming-liang (1998; New York: Fox Lorber, 2000) and *The Wayward Cloud (Tian bian yi duo yun)*, DVD, directed by Tsai Ming-liang (2005; New York: Strand Releasing, 2008), discussed in chapter 3. The extent to which Tsai's approach to cinematic homage is "queer" is central to these chapters.

6. Quotation of the English subtitles of Tsai's film *It's a Dream*. The song is "是夢是真" (Shì mèng shì zhēn) sung by Gong Qiuxia with music and lyrics by Chen Gexin, a musical interlude from the film *Torrents* (激流) from 1943.

7. *I Don't Want to Sleep Alone (Hei yan quan)*, DVD, directed by Tsai Ming-liang (Taipei: Homegreen Films, 2006). On the queer Sinophone politics of Tsai's return home to Malaysia, see Kenneth Chan, "Queerly Connecting: The Queer Sinophone Politics of Tsai Ming-liang's *I Don't Want to Sleep Alone*," in *Queer Sinophone Cultures*, ed. Howard Chiang and Ari Larissa Heinrich (London: Routledge, 2013), 160–75; and Kai-man Chang, "Sleeping with Strangers: Queering Home and Identity in *I Don't Want to Sleep Alone*," in *Cinematic Homecomings: Exile and Return in Transnational Cinema*, ed. Rebecca Prime (New York: Bloomsbury, 2015), 250–68.

8. Michel Foucault, "Of Other Spaces," *Diacritics* 16, no. 1 (1986): 22–27.

9. Gilles Deleuze, *Cinema 2: The Time-Image*, trans. Hugh Tomlinson and Robert Galeta (Minneapolis: University of Minnesota Press, 1995), 77. Also see chapter 2 in this volume on *Goodbye, Dragon Inn* as queer metacinema.

10. *The River (He liu)*, DVD, directed by Tsai Ming-liang (1997; New York: Leisure Time Features, 2001). While cruising features prominently in *The River*, the film has been analyzed so perceptively and thoroughly already, by Fran Martin, Song Hwee Lim, Rey Chow, Kai-man Chang, Guo-Juin Hong, and Carlos Rojas, that I have chosen not to spend as much time on it in this book. See Fran Martin, *Situating Sexualities: Queer Representation in Taiwanese Fiction, Film, and Popular Culture* (Hong Kong: Hong Kong University Press, 2003), 163–84; Song Hwee Lim, *Celluloid Comrades: Representations of Male Homosexuality in Contemporary Chinese Cinemas* (Honolulu: University of Hawai'i Press, 2006), 200–241; Rey Chow, *Sentimental Fabulations: Contemporary Chinese Films* (New York: Columbia University Press, 2007), 181–95; Kai-man Chang, "Drifting Bodies and Flooded Spaces: Visualizing the Invisibility of Heteronormativity in Tsai Ming-liang's *The River*," *Post Script* 28, no. 1 (Fall 2008): 45–63; Guo-Juin Hong, "Anywhere but Here: The Postcolonial City in Tsai

Ming-Liang's Taipei Trilogy," in *Taiwan Cinema: A Contested Nation on Screen* (New York: Palgrave Macmillan, 2011), 159–81; Guo-Juin Hong, "Theatrics of Cruising: Bath Houses and Movie Houses in Tsai Ming-liang's Films," in *Queer Sinophone Cultures*, ed. Howard Chiang and Ari Larissa Heinrich (London: Routledge, 2013), 149–59; and Carlos Rojas, "Along the Riverrun: Cinematic Encounters in Tsai Ming-liang's *The River*," in *The Oxford Handbook of Chinese Cinemas*, ed. Carlos Rojas (New York: Oxford University Press, 2013), 626–46.

11. See Chang, "Drifting Bodies and Flooded Spaces."

12. Jeff Reichert and Erik Syngle, "Ghost Writer: An Interview with Tsai Ming-liang," trans. Shujen Wang, *Reverse Shot*, December 13, 2004, http://www.reverseshot.org/interviews/entry/331/tsai-ming-liang. Also see Tsai Ming-liang, "Chasing the Film Spirit," *Metrograph Edition*, March 2, 2016, http://metrograph.com/edition/article/12/chasing-the-film-spirit.

13. Gaston Bachelard, *The Poetics of Space*, trans. Maria Jolas (Boston: Beacon Press, 1969).

14. *Past Present*, film, directed by Saw Tiong Guan (2013, video courtesy of the director). Also see Allan Koay, "Tsai Ming-liang: Then and Now," *The Star*, February 9, 2014, https://www.thestar.com.my/lifestyle/entertainment/movies/news/2014/02/09/tsai-mingliang-then-and-now/.

15. See *Chacun son cinéma*, https://www.festival-cannes.com/en/films/chacun-son-cinema.

16. Nicholas de Villiers, "We Are the World Cinema: *Chacun son cinéma, ou, Ce petit coup au coeur quand la lumière s'éteint et que le film commence*," *Senses of Cinema* 45 (2007), http://sensesofcinema.com/2007/feature-articles/chacun-son-cinema/.

17. Roland Barthes, "Leaving the Movie Theater," in *The Rustle of Language*, 345–49; 346. Also see Philip Watts, *Roland Barthes' Cinema* (New York: Oxford University Press, 2016), 75.

18. Barthes, "Leaving the Movie Theater," 345.

19. See Alex Espinoza, *Cruising: An Intimate History of a Radical Pastime* (Los Angeles: Unnamed Press, 2019).

20. See Jonathan Crary, *24/7: Late Capitalism and the Ends of Sleep* (London: Verso, 2013), 126–27; and Elena Gorfinkel, "Cinema, the Soporific: Between Exhaustion and Eros," *Kracauer Lectures in Film and Media Theory*, https://www.kracauer-lectures.de/en/winter-2017-2018/elena-gorfinkel/.

21. See Beth Tsai, "The Many Faces of Tsai Ming-liang: Cinephilia, the French Connection, and Cinema in the Gallery," *International Journal of Asia Pacific Studies* 13, no. 2 (2017): 141–60. Also see: Gertjan Zuilhof, "Take a Seat: A Short Anecdotal Photo-essay on Tsai Ming-liang's Installations," in *Stray Dogs at the Museum: Tsai Ming-liang Solo Exhibition* (Taipei: Museum of National

Taipei University of Education, 2016), 219–26; 224; International Film Festival Rotterdam site for *It's a Dream*, https://iffr.com/en/2008/films/is-it-a-dream.

22. See *Stray Dogs at the Museum*, film, directed by Chunni Lin (Taipei: Museum of National Taipei University of Education [MoNTUE]/Homegreen Films, 2016), uploaded to Vimeo by the director, https://vimeo.com/166801249. The DVD is also included in the book documenting the event, *Stray Dogs at the Museum: Tsai Ming-liang Solo Exhibition*. The films screened at the museum were *Stray Dogs (Jiao you)*, DVD, directed by Tsai Ming-liang (2013; New York: Cinema Guild, 2015) and *Afternoon (Na ri xia wu)*, film, directed by Tsai Ming-liang (Taipei: Homegreen Films, 2015).

23. See Emilie Yueh-Yu Yeh and Darrel William Davis, "Camping Out with Tsai Ming-liang," in *Taiwan Film Directors: A Treasure Island* (New York: Columbia University Press, 2005), 217–48.

Introduction

1. I call it "coming out" because he discusses his sexuality explicitly in this long recorded conversation with Lee Kang-sheng on film. However, Tsai told me that he came out a long time ago when he wrote and directed the play *The Wardrobe in the Room* (1983)—in a conversation between the author, Tsai Ming-liang, and Jonathan Te-hsuan Yeh, December 8, 2017, New Taipei City. I am very grateful to Jonathan Te-hsuan Yeh for translating during our conversation. On the meanings of the wardrobe/closet and the confessional queer subtext of Tsai's play, see Lim, *Celluloid Comrades*, 134. I am inspired and indebted to Lim's concept of Tsai's filmmaking practice as a form of *écriture queer*. Cf. discussions of Tsai's career and films in relation to the closet in Hee Wai-Siam, "Coming Out in the Mirror: Rethinking Corporeality and Auteur Theory with Regard to the Films of Tsai Ming-liang," in *Transnational Chinese Cinema: Corporeality, Desire, and Ethics of Failure*, ed. Brian Bergen-Aurand, Mary Mazzilli, Hee Wai-Siam (Piscataway, NJ: Transaction Publishers, 2014), 113–36; and Shi-Yan Chao, *Queer Representations in Chinese-Language Film and the Cultural Landscape* (Amsterdam: Amsterdam University Press, 2020), 230–42. In line with my argument in *Opacity and the Closet: Queer Tactics in Foucault, Barthes, and Warhol* (Minneapolis: University of Minnesota Press, 2012), I appreciate Tsai's attribution of "the closet" to those who would closet him.

2. See Beth Tsai, *Taiwan New Cinema at Film Festivals* (Edinburgh: Edinburgh University Press, forthcoming).

3. See Tsai's list of awards at https://www.imdb.com/name/nm0158857/awards.

4. I hope to build on Kai-man Chang's argument that Tsai Ming-liang "has emerged from the second wave of Taiwan New Cinema to become the foremost advocate of homosexual themes in Taiwanese films," situating Tsai's

films within "the rise of the tongzhi movement and its subsequent mainstreaming which coincided with Tsai's filmic career" in order to understand "how Tsai's films engage in the issues of gender and sexual inequalities and why he refuses his films' being labeled as gay films" in "Drifting Bodies and Flooded Spaces," 45. Cf. Yi Wang, "Positioning Taiwanese Queer Cinema on the Global Stage," *Taiwan Insight,* March 17, 2021, https://taiwaninsight.org/2021/03/17/positioning-taiwanese-queer-cinema-on-the-global-stage/. I discuss the problem of labeling Tsai's films "gay" in chapter 1.

   5. See Hong, "Theatrics of Cruising," 150. On situated knowledge, or "what is local about the global queer," see Helen Hok-Sze Leung, "Archiving Queer Feelings in Hong Kong," *Inter-Asia Cultural Studies* 8, no. 4 (2007): 559–71; 570. Cf. Michiel Baas, "Queer Asia: Advances in a Field in Motion," *Intersections: Gender and Sexuality in Asia and the Pacific,* no. 37 (March 2015), http://intersections.anu.edu.au/issue37/baas_review_essay.pdf.

   6. See *Queer Diaspora: The 2010 International Conference on Queer Diaspora Plenary Sessions Paper Collection* (Taipei: National Taiwan University, 2010); Gayatri Gopinath, *Unruly Visions: The Aesthetic Practices of Queer Diaspora* (Durham, N.C.: Duke University Press, 2018), especially chapter 2, "Queer Disorientations, States of Suspension"; Howard Chiang and Alvin K. Wong, "Queering the Transnational Turn: Regionalism and Queer Asias," *Gender, Place & Culture: A Journal of Feminist Geography* 23, no. 11 (2016): 1643–56; Howard Chiang and Alvin K. Wong, "Asia Is Burning: Queer Asia as Critique," *Culture, Theory, and Critique* 58, no. 2 (2017): 121–26.

   7. Hong, "Theatrics of Cruising," 150.

   8. Zoran Lee Pecic, *New Queer Sinophone Cinema: Local Histories, Transnational Connections* (London: Palgrave, 2016), 18.

   9. See Brian Hu, "The Post-Retirement Films of Tsai Ming-liang," http://festival.sdaff.org/2014/still-walking-the-post-retirement-films-of-tsai-ming-liang/. Tsai's "postretirement" feature-length film *Days,* a queer diasporic meditation on sex work as care work (which I plan to address in a future publication), was released in 2020 and won the jury Teddy Award (queer film prize) at the 70th Berlinale. *Days (Rizi),* film, directed by Tsai Ming-liang (New York: Grasshopper Film, 2020). See Darren Hughes, "A State of Uncertainty: Tsai Ming-liang on *Days,*" *Cinema Scope,* no. 82 (2020), https://cinema-scope.com/cinema-scope-magazine/a-state-of-uncertainty-tsai-ming-liang-on-days/. See also the Teddy Award website for *Days:* https://www.teddyaward.tv/en/program?tag=2020-02-29&id_film=855.

   10. See Peter Wollen, "The *Auteur* Theory," in *Movies and Methods: An Anthology,* ed. Bill Nichols (Berkeley: University of California Press, 1976), 529–42. For an early treatment of Tsai as an auteur (especially his water motif) see Jean Pierre Rehm, Olivier Joyard, and Danièle Rivière, eds., *Tsaï Ming-Liang* (Paris:

Editions Dis Voir, 1999). The text features an interview with Tsai in which he states directly, "Actually, water for me is love, that's what they lack. What I'm trying to show is very symbolic, it's their need for love" (113). See also Yvette Biro, "Perhaps the Flood: The Fiery Torrent of Tsai Ming-Liang's Films," *PAJ: A Journal of Performance and Art* 26, no. 3 (2004): 78–86; Rey Chow, "Afterword: Liquidity of Being," in *The Chinese Cinema Book*, 2nd ed., ed. Song Hwee Lim and Julian Ward (London: British Film Institute, 2019), 269–76. On Tsai's use of old-fashioned Mandarin popular music, see his interview in Michael Berry, *Speaking in Images: Interviews with Contemporary Chinese Filmmakers* (New York: Columbia University Press, 2005), 386. See also Mark Betz, "The Cinema of Tsai Ming-liang: A Modernist Genealogy," in *Reading Chinese Transnationalisms: Society, Literature, Film*, ed. Philip Holden and Maria Ng (Hong Kong: Hong Kong University Press, 2006), 161–72. It is worth noting that Tsai's metacinematic, sexual and juvenile delinquency, and real estate themes already appear in his early television movie, set in the gentrifying West Gate District (Ximending) in Taipei, *All Corners of the World (Haijiao tianya)*, written and directed by Tsai Ming-liang (Taipei: Chinese Television System, 1989), available online at: https://youtu.be/CQ72D-QE0Ak. The entry for *All Corners of the World* at the International Film Festival Rotterdam refers to the area as Taipei's "red-light district," https://iffr.com/en/1994/films/all-corners -of-the-world, while Carlos Rojas discusses its significance as a youth and movie theater district for Tsai as an auteur in "'Nezha Was Here': Structures of Dis/placement in Tsai Ming-liang's *Rebels of the Neon God*," *Modern Chinese Literature and Culture* 15, no. 1 (2003): 63–89.

11. Hsiao [or Xiao] Kang is a diminutive nickname meaning "Little Kang." In an interview with Danièle Rivière, Tsai explains his relation to the actor's body: "For me it's very important to work with Lee Kang-sheng for example, because I'm very familiar with how he acts. . . . Lee Kang-sheng may have changed between two shoots, but I always find it easy to get back into working with him. For instance, over the last two years his body has changed a lot. Recently I had lunch with him and some friends and they said to him: 'You've really filled out!' I don't find it a problem working with the same actors all the time because I know that people who follow my films go to see them all. Lee Kang-sheng, who is already very close to the characters he plays, is actually two things in one, and the audience can see how the real person has changed as well." Danièle Rivière, "Scouting," trans. Andrew Rothwell, in *Tsaï Ming-liang*, ed. Rehm, Joyard, and Rivière, 79–119; 108. In an interview with Michael Berry Tsai's language is almost romantic: "At one point he [Lee] came to complain to me and said that he didn't want to do any more films with me after *The Hole*. He signed a contract with a Hong Kong agent and went off to shoot Ann Hui's film *Ordinary Heroes*. But I didn't really take his words to heart; I figured that

he would go off and do his thing, but I knew that he would be back when we had to make another film. But he was very adamant and said that he didn't want to be in my movies because I never gave him a real part that he could sink his teeth into. . . . But I knew that if he went out and worked with other directors, he'd be back." Berry, *Speaking in Images*, 381. See also Brian Hu, "The Unprofessional: An Interview with Lee Kang-sheng," *Asia Pacific Arts*, July 21, 2005, archived at https://web.archive.org/web/20080130151810/http://www.asiaarts.ucla.edu/article.asp?parentid=27006.

12. See Fran Martin, "Introduction: Tsai Ming-liang's Intimate Public Worlds," *Journal of Chinese Cinemas* 1, no. 2 (2007): 83–88; Biro, "Perhaps the Flood"; Hu, "The Unprofessional"; Chang, "Drifting Bodies and Flooded Spaces," especially his discussion of bathhouses.

13. A note on the structure of this book: While Tsai sometimes traces the evolution of relations between the same or at least similar characters across individual films, for example between the man and woman in *What Time Is It There?* (2001), *The Skywalk Is Gone* (2002), and *The Wayward Cloud* (2005), I argue that my nonchronological approach corresponds with Tsai's disorientation of time, space, and sexuality throughout his corpus—a disorientation of time, space, and character relations that he makes part of the disjunctive structure of his "final" feature film *Stray Dogs* (2013), which is actually the last film I discuss. *What Time Is It There? (Ni na bian ji dian)*, DVD, directed by Tsai Ming-liang (2001; New York: Fox Lorber, 2002); *The Skywalk Is Gone* (2002) appears as a DVD extra on *Goodbye, Dragon Inn*.

14. See Lim, "Positioning Auteur Theory in Chinese Cinema Studies," 223–45.

15. See Howard Chiang and Alvin K. Wong, "Introduction—Queer Sinophone Studies: Interdisciplinary Synergies," in *Keywords in Queer Sinophone Studies*, ed. Howard Chiang and Alvin K. Wong (London: Routledge, 2020), 1–15. They explain how "both the notions of the queer and the Sinophone resist the doxa and hegemony of binary thinking, essentialism, and disciplinarity," noting how Shu-mei Shih's foundational definition of the Sinophone "has done the work of disrupting the essentialist ontology of Chineseness or that thing called 'China' to the same degree that queer has dismantled the hegemonic identity politics of previous gay and lesbian studies. . . . The China vs. the West methodological assumption reproduces China-centrism in the way that diasporic, exilic, and Chinese settler subjects in Southeast Asia, Hong Kong, Taiwan, Latin America, and anywhere outside the People's Republic of China (PRC) are often seen as 'not Chinese enough.' . . . 'not speaking Chinese' is a historical and postmodern fact of linguistic and ethnic heterogeneity in Peranakan and other creolized Sinophone people whose very social existence displaces China-centrism. For Shih, the diaspora paradigm, in addition

to marginalizing those Sinitic-language communities and creolized people who do not speak Chinese, is also highly problematic in the way that it ties long-distanced diaspora subjects back to the mythic homeland of China, so much so that long-distanced nationalism can and often [does] reproduce zealous Chinese nationalism behind the populism of the PRC and its increasing authoritarian threat to Hong Kong, Taiwan, Vietnam, and certain parts of Africa" (3–4). See Shu-mei Shih, *Visuality and Identity: Sinophone Articulations across the Pacific* (Berkeley: University of California Press, 2007); Shu-mei Shih, "Theory, Asia, and the Sinophone," *Postcolonial Studies* 13, no. 4 (2010): 465–84. Cf. Petrus Liu, "Why Does Queer Theory Need China?" *positions* 18, no. 2 (2010): 291–320.

16. See Martin, *Situating Sexualities*, 11–13.

17. Agata A. Lisiak, "Making Sense of Absence," *City* 19, no. 6 (2015): 837–56; 839. On Taiwan's colonial history, Yoshihisa Amae notes that "some pro-independence scholars view Taiwan as having been under colonial rule for the past 400 years, various colonizers having been Dutch, Spanish, Koxinga, Qing, Japanese, and Chinese nationalists." Yoshihisa Amae, "Pro-colonial or Post-colonial? Appropriation of Japanese Colonial Heritage in Present-day Taiwan," *Journal of Current Chinese Affairs* 40, no. 1 (2011): 19–62; 52.

18. Martin, *Situating Sexualities*, 11.

19. For a crucial history of Chinese-language translations and inflections of queer theory (including gay shame, gay melancholy, and queer or *tongzhi* camp), see Chao, *Queer Representations*, 202–18. See also Martin, *Situating Sexualities*, 3–4, 26. For important critiques of "global English" as the language of theory, see Shih, "Theory, Asia, and the Sinophone," and Leung, "Archiving Queer Feelings in Hong Kong." I have benefited profoundly from the extensive annotated *Oxford Bibliography* of Chinese, English, and French publications on Tsai Ming-liang by Beth Tsai: http://www.oxfordbibliographies.com/view/document/obo-9780199791286/obo-9780199791286-0289.xml. I also want to thank Beth Tsai for her generosity as an interlocutor and fellow researcher on Tsai's films and their local and transnational reception.

20. See Nicholas de Villiers, "'Chinese Cheers': Hou Hsiao-hsien and Transnational Homage," *Senses of Cinema*, no. 58 (2011), http://www.sensesofcinema.com/2011/feature-articles/"chinese-cheers"-hou-hsiao-hsien-and-transnational-homage/.

21. Lim, *Tsai Ming-liang and a Cinema of Slowness*. In an interview with *Slant* magazine, Tsai joked that "My films have been labeled 'slow, boring, queer, colorless, anticlimactic, opaque . . .' Is it praise? Slander? What can I say? My films are my films." I hope it will be clear that both Lim and I are using these terms—especially slow, queer, and opaque—as praise, not slander. See Clayton Dillard, "Interview: Tsai Ming-liang on *Rebels of the Neon God*, Lee

Kang-sheng, & More," trans. Aliza Ma, *Slant Magazine*, April 6, 2015, https://www.slantmagazine.com/film/interview-tsai-ming-liang/.

22. See the introduction to Pecic, *New Queer Sinophone Cinema*, 1–23.

23. Jean Ma, *Melancholy Drift: Marking Time in Chinese Cinema* (Hong Kong: Hong Kong University Press, 2010).

24. Chao, *Queer Representations*, 216. See also the discussion of queer melancholy and Chinese queer diaspora in Shi-Yan Chao, "Performing Authorship in a Queer Time and Place: A Case Study of Yonfan," *Reconstruction: Studies in Contemporary Culture* 16, no. 2 (2016).

25. Ma, *Melancholy Drift*, 13.

26. Ma, *Melancholy Drift*, 10.

27. See Jonathan Flatley, *Affective Mapping: Melancholia and the Politics of Modernism* (Cambridge, Mass.: Harvard University Press, 2008); Anne Anlin Cheng, *The Melancholy of Race: Psychoanalysis, Assimilation, and Hidden Grief* (New York: Oxford University Press, 2001); Heather Love, *Feeling Backward: Loss and the Politics of Queer History* (Cambridge, Mass.: Harvard University Press, 2009); and Ann Cvetkovich, *Depression: A Public Feeling* (Durham, N.C.: Duke University Press, 2012). I am also using the term "melancholy" in a more vernacular sense than the clinical term "melancholia."

28. I am inspired by work on "minor" aesthetic categories and affects, like Sianne Ngai's work on the zany, the cute, the interesting, and noncathartic "ugly feelings," and Jonathan Flatley's work on "mood." Sianne Ngai, *Ugly Feelings* (Cambridge, Mass.: Harvard University Press, 2007) and *Our Aesthetic Categories: Zany, Cute, Interesting* (Cambridge, Mass.: Harvard University Press, 2015). Jonathan Flatley, "Reading for Mood," *Representations* 140, no. 1 (Fall 2017): 137–58.

29. Sigmund Freud, "Mourning and Melancholia," in *The Standard Edition of the Complete Psychological Works of Sigmund Freud*, ed. and trans. James Strachey (1917; rpt. London: Hogarth Press, 1958), 16:243–58; cf. Roland Barthes, *Mourning Diary*, text established and annotated by Nathalie Léger, trans. Richard Howard (New York: Farrar, Straus and Giroux, 2010).

30. See Espinoza, *Cruising*.

31. See Crary, 24/7, 126–27.

32. Fran Martin's "*Vive L'Amour*: Eloquent Emptiness" is a crucial earlier publication theorizing space in relation to queer sexuality in Tsai's films, especially in regard to heteronormative conceptions of "jia" (family home) in Chinese. See Fran Martin, "*Vive L'Amour*: Eloquent Emptiness," in *Chinese Films in Focus: 25 New Takes*, ed. Chris Berry (London: British Film Institute, 2003), 175–82. See also Martin, *Situating Sexualities*. Cf. the discussions of place and space in Rojas, "Nezha Was Here"; and Kai-man Chang, "Gender Hierarchy

and Environmental Crisis in Tsai Ming-liang's *The Hole*," *Film Criticism* 33, no. 1 (Fall 2008): 25–44.

33. On Tsai's treatment of urban space, rapid construction/demolition, and gentrification, see Lisiak, "Making Sense of Absence."

34. *Rebels of the Neon God (Qingshaonian Nezha)*, DVD, directed by Tsai Ming-liang (1992; New York: Fox Lorber, 2003); *Vive L'Amour (Ai qing wan sui)*, DVD, directed by Tsai Ming-liang (1994; New York: Strand Releasing, 1996). Hong, "Anywhere but Here," 159–81; Chang, "Gender Hierarchy."

35. See Allan Bérubé, "The History of Gay Bathhouses," in *Policing Public Sex: Queer Politics and the Future of AIDS Activism*, ed. Strange Bedfellows (Boston: South End Press, 1996), 187–220; Dianne Chisholm, *Queer Constellations: Subcultural Space in the Wake of the City* (Minneapolis: University of Minnesota Press, 2004).

36. Eve Kosofsky Sedgwick, *Touching Feeling: Affect, Pedagogy, Performativity* (Durham, N.C.: Duke University Press, 2003), 9. Cf. Esther Newton, *Mother Camp: Female Impersonators in America* (Chicago: University of Chicago Press, 1972); Judith Butler, *Gender Trouble: Feminism and the Subversion of Identity* (New York: Routledge, 1990); and Judith Butler, "Imitation and Gender Insubordination," in *Inside/Out: Lesbian Theories, Gay Theories*, ed. Diana Fuss (New York: Routledge, 1991), 13–31.

37. Sedgwick, *Touching Feeling*, 8.

38. On space/place, see Yi-Fu Tuan, *Space and Place: The Perspective of Experience* (Minneapolis: University of Minnesota Press, 1977). For an important phenomenological consideration of disorientation in terms of bodies, space, and cinema, see Vivian Sobchack, "Breadcrumbs in the Forest: Three Meditations on Being Lost in Space," in *Carnal Thoughts: Embodiment and Moving Image Culture* (Berkeley: University of California Press, 2004), 13–35. Note that while gender difference is central to Sobchack's consideration of disorientation (along with some discussion of race and class), queerness is relegated to a footnote (32n28). The same is true for Dominic Lash's *The Cinema of Disorientation: Inviting Confusions* (Edinburgh: Edinburgh University Press, 2020). The following is an attempt to redress this problem.

39. Michael Moon, *A Small Boy and Others: Imitation and Initiation in American Culture from Henry James to Andy Warhol* (Durham, N.C.: Duke University Press, 1998), 15–30.

40. Moon, *A Small Boy and Others*, 15.

41. Moon, *A Small Boy and Others*, 16–17.

42. Sara Ahmed, *Queer Phenomenology: Orientations, Objects, Others* (Durham, N.C.: Duke University Press, 2006). See also Katharina Lindner, "Questions of Embodied Difference: Film and Queer Phenomenology," *NECSUS*, Autumn 2012, https://necsus-ejms.org/questions-of-embodied-difference-film

-and-queer-phenomenology/; Murat Aydemir, "Queer Orientation with Gus Van Sant's *Elephant*," *Culture, Theory, and Critique* 57, no. 1 (2016): 32–47.

43. See Ahmed, *Queer Phenomenology*, especially chapter 3, "The Orient and Other Others." Cf. Hong, "Theatrics of Cruising," 150; Chiang and Wong, "Queering the Transnational Turn" and "Introduction—Queer Sinophone Studies"; Howard Chiang, "(De)Provincializing China: Queer Historicism and Sinophone Postcolonial Critique," in *Queer Sinophone Cultures*, ed. Howard Chiang and Ari Larissa Heinrich (London: Routledge, 2013), 38. See also the clever titles of Richard Fung's *Orientations: Lesbian and Gay Asians* (1984) and *Re:Orientations* (2016). Richard Fung artist page on *V tape*, https://www.vtape.org/artist?ai=160. Cf. *Oriented* (2015), a documentary about three gay Palestinian friends in Tel Aviv. *Oriented*, DVD, directed by Jake Witzenfeld (2015; Los Gatos, Calif.: Netflix, 2016).

44. Roland Barthes, *"Longtemps, je me suis couché de bonne heure,"* and "Preface to Renaud Camus's *Tricks*," in *The Rustle of Language*, 277–90; 291–95.

45. See Mark W. Turner, *Backward Glances: Cruising the Queer Streets of New York and London* (London: Reaktion Books, 2003); Espinoza, *Cruising*; Roland Barthes, *The Pleasure of the Text*, trans. Richard Miller (New York: Farrar, Straus and Giroux, 1975), 4; Nicholas de Villiers, "A Great 'Pedagogy' of Nuance: Roland Barthes's *The Neutral*," *Theory & Event* 8, no. 4 (2005), http://muse.jhu.edu/journals/theory_and_event/v008/8.4devilliers.html.

46. For an important caution about Eurocentric ways of reading Tsai's intertextual relations to French culture, see Fran Martin, "The European Undead: Tsai Ming-liang's Temporal Dysphoria," *Senses of Cinema*, July 2003, http://sensesofcinema.com/2003/feature-articles/tsai_european_undead/. Cf. Michelle E. Bloom, *Contemporary Sino-French Cinemas: Absent Fathers, Banned Books, and Red Balloons* (Honolulu: University of Hawai'i Press, 2017). See also Emily Barton, "Queer in Time: Tsai, Léaud, and the New Wave(s)," *Reel Honey*, March 15, 2019, http://reelhoney.com/what-time-is-it-there-queer-tsai-leaud/.

47. For Barthes's discussion of retirement and retreat, see Roland Barthes, *The Neutral: Lecture Course at the College de France (1977–1978)*, trans. Rosalind Krauss and Denis Hollier (New York: Columbia University Press, 2005).

48. John Paul Ricco, *The Logic of the Lure* (Chicago: University of Chicago Press, 2002); José Esteban Muñoz, *Cruising Utopia: The Then and There of Queer Futurity* (New York: New York University Press, 2009); Samuel R. Delany, *Times Square Red, Times Square Blue* (New York: New York University Press, 2001); and "Cruising the Seventies," https://www.crusev.ed.ac.uk. See also Fiona Anderson, *Cruising the Dead River: David Wojnarowicz and New York's Ruined Waterfront* (Chicago: University of Chicago Press, 2019); Espinoza, *Cruising*, 32.

49. In Chinese, gay cruising areas are referred to as *yuchang* or "fishing holes"—see Qing Yan, "Shanghai's Gay Bars: Here and Queer for 20 Years," *Sixth Tone*, July 17, 2017, https://www.sixthtone.com/news/1000530/shanghais-gay-bars-here-and-queer-for-20-years. See also Chang's discussion of cruising in "Drifting Bodies and Flooded Spaces." Many thanks to Lala Lau for gathering various Chinese expressions for cruising.

50. Helen Hok-Sze Leung, "Queerscapes in Contemporary Hong Kong Cinema," *positions: east asia cultures critique* 9, no. 2 (Fall 2001): 423–47.

51. See Espinoza, *Cruising*; and Delany, *Times Square Red*.

52. Marcel Proust, *Swann's Way, In Search of Lost Time*, Vol. 1, trans. C. K. Scott-Moncrieff, Terence Kilmartin, and Andreas Mayor, rev. D. J. Enright (New York: Modern Library, 1992). See also Barthes, "*Longtemps, je me suis couché de bonne heure*": "Emerging from sleep, the work *(the third form)* rests on a provocative principle: the *disorganization* of Time (of chrono-logy)" (281).

53. See Jonas Mekas, "Notes after Reseeing the Movies of Andy Warhol," in *Andy Warhol Film Factory*, ed. Michael O'Pray (London: British Film Institute, 1989), 28–41.

54. *No No Sleep*, film, directed by Tsai Ming-liang (2015), available online at http://www.editmedia.org/teaching-material/no-no-sleep-tsai-ming-liang-2015/. *Sleep*, film, directed by Andy Warhol (1963), available on YouTube: https://youtu.be/KaiEM2lUoZg. *I Don't Want to Sleep Alone* is discussed in greater detail in chapter 1.

55. Wu Cheng'en, *The Monkey King's Amazing Adventures: A Journey to the West in Search of Enlightenment*, trans. Timothy Richard (North Clarendon, Vt.: Tuttle, 2008). Tsai's "Walker" series is also known as "Slow Walk, Long March"—see Song Hwee Lim, "Walking in the City, Slowly: Spectacular Temporal Practices in Tsai Ming-liang's 'Slow Walk, Long March' series," *Screen* 58, no. 2 (2017): 180–96.

56. See Gorfinkel, "Cinema, the Soporific."

57. I have a working knowledge of Mandarin Chinese, but interviewed Tsai with the help of Jonathan Te-hsuan Yeh, my colleague during my 2017 sabbatical as a visiting scholar at National Central University in Taiwan, and a respected author and translator of queer theory in Mandarin (for a discussion of Yeh's authoritative Mandarin translation of "camp," see Chao, *Queer Representations*, 203–4; and Jonathan Te-hsuan Yeh, "Liangzhong 'Luying/yin' de Fangfa: 'Yongyuan de Yin Xueyan' yu Niezi zhong de Xingbie Yuejie Yanchu" 〈兩種「露營／淫」的方法：〈永遠的尹雪豔〉與《孽子》中的性別越界演出〉 [Go camping: Gender crossing performances in "Yung-yuan te Yin Hsueh-yen" and Nieh-tzu], 中外文學 *Chung-wai Literary Monthly* 26, no. 12 [1998]: 67–89). Jonathan and I worked together on translating and sharing my interview questions beforehand, and he reviewed my notetaking and

translation of our conversation with Tsai immediately after for accuracy (Tsai preferred the form of a long conversation to an audio-recorded interview).

58. One of many "pilgrimages" I have taken to research Tsai's filming locations and to get a sense of how he transforms them on film.

59. See "The Heart of Prajna Paramita Sutra" translation by the Chung Tai Translation Committee: http://sunnyvale.ctzen.org/wp-content/uploads/2019 /07/heart-sutra-v1.2.18-20131216.pdf. The Diamond Sutra is quoted in Tsai's film *Journey to the West* (2014) at the end: "All conditioned phenomena/Are like a dream, an illusion, a bubble, a shadow/Like dew or a flash of lightning;/ Thus we shall perceive them." [一切有為法・如夢幻泡影・如露亦如電・應 作如是觀]. See "The Diamond of Perfect Wisdom Sutra," translation by the Chung Tai Translation Committee: http://sunnyvale.ctzen.org/wp-content/up loads/2019/07/diamond-sutra-v1.9.17-201312011.pdf.

60. See Shiho Fukada, "Internet Café Refugees," *Japan's Disposable Workers,* http://disposableworkers.com/?page_id=37.

61. In chapter 5, I will suggest how a comparison could be made between Tsai's *Stray Dogs* and two films by Kore-eda Hirokazu about families in Tokyo struggling to survive abandonment and the effects of the recession: *Nobody Knows* (2004) and *Shoplifters* (2018). *Nobody Knows (Dare mo shiranai),* DVD, directed by Kore-eda Hirokazu (2004; Santa Monica, Calif.: MGM Home Entertainment, 2005); *Shoplifters (Manbiki kazoku),* film, directed by Kore-eda Hirokazu (New York: Magnolia Pictures, 2018).

62. I asked Tsai if he chose Ikebukuro West Gate area because it has an unofficial Chinatown, but he said that was not why: it was more because that area had a subway and an overpass, and a video-lit busy pedestrian crosswalk that looks like Shibuya. On the disorienting train shots, see Nadin Mai, "*No No Sleep*—Tsai Ming-liang (2015)," *The Art(s) of Slow Cinema,* May 17, 2015, https:// theartsofslowcinema.com/2015/05/17/no-no-sleep-tsai-ming-liang-2015/.

63. *Café Lumière (Kohi jiko),* DVD, directed by Hou Hsiao-hsien (Tokyo: Shochiku, 2003). The DVD includes the making-of documentary *Métro Lumière.* See de Villiers, "'Chinese Cheers.'" The Japanese *anime* feature film *Your Name* picks up some of the train and human interconnection motifs from Hou's film. *Your Name (Kimi no na wa),* DVD, directed by Shinkai Makoto (Flower Mound, Tex.: Funimation Films, 2016).

64. *Journey to the West (Xi you),* film, directed by Tsai Ming-liang (2014). The casting of Denis Lavant shadowing Lee Kang-sheng in the film creates a potential intertextual relation to Claire Denis's homoerotic *Beau Travail,* starring Lavant. *Beau Travail,* DVD, directed by Claire Denis (1999; New York: Criterion Collection, 2020).

65. For an explanation of sensory ethnography, see the Sensory Ethnography Lab website, https://sel.fas.harvard.edu.

66. See Amber Wu, "Museum Traces History of Local Hot Spring Culture," *Taiwan Today,* April 17, 2009, https://taiwantoday.tw/news.php?unit=18%2C2 3%2C45%2C18&post=24329. See also Amae, "Pro-colonial or Postcolonial?"

67. Tsai noted that this was the first time he had discussed this with anyone, but since the "Walker" series is based on the sixteenth-century Chinese story of the Tang dynasty Buddhist monk Xuanzang's legendary pilgrimage to India with an obedient white steed, he thought of Ando as the representative of the horse, and the scene in the spa is like they are making up with each other, with the monk showing gratitude to the horse, and they can finally rest. In Tsai's *Journey to the West,* the French actor Denis Lavant is like a representative of the Monkey (Sun Wukong, "Awakened to Emptiness"). But Tsai wants to leave these more mystical elements and references open to interpretation.

68. "无无眠," https://www.youtube.com/watch?v=Ts2XsoTkNg8. An earlier upload of the video was removed for violating YouTube's policy on nudity, but the YouTube user comments were oddly illuminating (previous URL: https://youtu.be/Qzbkw6Sg-Wk). Incidentally, a passerby in another "Walker" film, *Journey to the West,* speculates whether the camera crew means a "porno" film is being filmed.

69. See "Holding Blackness: Aesthetics of Suspension," *liquid blackness* 4, no. 7 (2017), especially the introduction by editor Alessandra Raengo, and Daren Fowler's "To Erotically Know: The Ethics and Pedagogy of *Moonlight,*" https://liquidblackness.com/liquid-blackness-journal-issue-7. While I do not want to abstract the specific context of the *liquid blackness* collective's discussion of the aesthetics of suspension in relation to blackness in contemporary cinema, Fowler's understanding of eroticism, which exceeds sexuality, between minority male subjects (Afro-Cuban and African American men in South Florida) can be productively compared to Lee and Ando's postcolonial relation in Tsai's film. Barry Jenkins's citation of Taiwan and Hong Kong cinema in *Moonlight* is also worth noting. See Greg Tate, "How Barry Jenkins Turned the Misery and Beauty of the Queer Black Experience into the Year's Best Movie," *Village Voice,* December 21, 2016, https://www.villagevoice.com/2016/12/21/how-barry-jenkins-turned-the-misery-and-beauty-of-the-queer-black-experience-into-the-years-best-movie/. See also "What Wong Kar-wai Taught Barry Jenkins about Longing," *Criterion* "Under the Influence," November 29, 2016, https://www.criterion.com/current/posts/4328-what-wong-kar-wai-taught-barry-jenkins-about-longing (with accompanying video https://youtu.be/LwmEWNXIsNk). *Moonlight,* DVD, directed by Barry Jenkins (2016; Santa Monica, Calif.: Lionsgate Home Entertainment, 2017).

70. See Gary Comenas, "Andy Warhol's *Sleep* (1963)," https://warholstars.org/sleep.html.

71. See https://www.filmlinc.org/nyff2018/films/your-face/. On *Your Face* and connections to Warhol, see Elena Gorfinkel, "To Extend into the Beyond: On Tsai Ming-liang's Late Digital Style," *Sight & Sound,* April 22, 2019, https://www.bfi.org.uk/news-opinion/sight-sound-magazine/features/tsai-ming-liang-late-digital-period-deserted-your-face; Beth Tsai, "Waiting for Sleep to Come: Slowness and Transportability in *Stray Dogs* and *Your Face*" (Paper presented to the *Society for Cinema and Media Studies* [online] conference, March 20, 2021).

72. On erotic temporality in Warhol's films *Sleep* and *Blow Job,* see Wayne Koestenbaum, *Andy Warhol: A Biography* (2001; rpt. New York: Open Road, 2015), 29–30; 85–87. Cf. Douglas Crimp, *Our Kind of Movie: The Films of Andy Warhol* (Cambridge, Mass.: MIT Press, 2012); and Blake Gopnik, "Andy Warhol, *Sleep* (1963)," *Brooklyn Rail,* September, 2017, https://brooklynrail.org/2017/09/criticspage/Andy-Warhol-Sleep-1963. On sleeping boys and queer romanticism, see José Esteban Muñoz, "The Sense of Watching Tony Sleep," *South Atlantic Quarterly* 106, no. 3 (2007): 543–51. Many thanks to Alanna Thain and Jean Ma for pointing me to Muñoz's essay.

73. A fruitful conversation emerged between two panels at the 2021 Society for Cinema and Media Studies conference (online) featuring Tsai and Warhol's films as shared reference points: "Night Moves: Collective Intimacies of Sleep Media," chaired by Alanna Thain, featuring Lakshmi Padmanabhan, "Sleeping Together in Postcolonial Time" and Alanna Thain, "Love, Labour, Loss: Sleep, Affect, and Radical Dispossession"; and the panel I cochaired with Beth Tsai titled "Sleepy Cinema: Affect, Audience, Embodiment," featuring my presentation, "Sleepy Cinema, Queer Phenomenology, and Tsai Ming-liang's *No No Sleep*"; Beth Tsai, "Waiting for Sleep to Come: Slowness and Transportability in *Stray Dogs* and *Your Face*"; Jean Ma, "From Cinephobia to Somnophilia: When Apparatus Theory Nods Off"; and Elena Gorfinkel, "Sleepworks: Poetics, Labor, Insomnious Times."

74. See Chang, "Sleeping with Strangers," 250–68.

75. Jasmine Ting, "Legendary Artist and Activist John Giorno Dies at 82," *Paper,* October 12, 2019, https://www.papermag.com/john-giorno-dies-82-2640946919.html.

76. See Chan, "Queerly Connecting," 160–75; and Chang, "Sleeping with Strangers."

77. See Chan, "Queerly Connecting," 168.

78. I am thus extending my approach to queer tactics in my previous books *Opacity and the Closet* and *Sexography: Sex Work in Documentary* (Minneapolis: University of Minnesota Press, 2017).

79. See Martin, *Situating Sexualities,* 26; Chao, *Queer Representations,* 202–18.

80. See Audrey Yue, "Trans-Singapore: Some Notes towards Queer Asia as Method," *Inter-Asia Cultural Studies* 18, no. 1 (2017): 10–24.

81. See Roland Barthes, *How to Live Together: Novelistic Simulations of Some Everyday Spaces*, trans. Kate Briggs (New York: Columbia University Press, 2012).

1. Spatial and Sexual Disorientation

1. Brian Hu, "Goodbye City, Goodbye Cinema: Nostalgia in Tsai Ming-liang's *The Skywalk Is Gone*," *Senses of Cinema*, no. 29 (2003), http://www.sensesofcinema.com/2003/feature-articles/skywalk_is_gone/.

2. See Nadia Atia and Jeremy Davies, "Nostalgia and the Shapes of History: Editorial," *Memory Studies* 3, no. 3 (2010): 181–86.

3. Hu, "Goodbye City." Cf. Lisiak, "Making Sense of Absence," 837–56.

4. See chapter 3 for an extended discussion of camp. Cf. Yeh and Davis, "Camping Out with Tsai Ming-liang," 217–48.

5. On Tsai's "*tongzhi* camp" approach to Grace Chang's music, see Chao, *Queer Representations*, 233–42.

6. Hu, "Goodbye City." Cf. the discussion of Tsai and Grace Chang in Pecic, *New Queer Sinophone Cinema*, 128–30.

7. See Chao, *Queer Representations*, 238.

8. Tsai Ming-liang interview in Berry, *Speaking in Images*, 386.

9. See Martin, "The European Undead." Cf. Bloom, *Contemporary Sino-French Cinemas*.

10. Tsai quoted in Berry, *Speaking in Images*, 387.

11. See Cheng, *The Melancholy of Race*; and Love, *Feeling Backward*.

12. Moon, *Small Boy*, 15–16. *Blue Velvet*, DVD, directed by David Lynch (1986; New York: Criterion Collection, 2019).

13. Moe Meyer, ed., *The Politics and Poetics of Camp* (London: Routledge, 1994), 3. Making a related distinction in her discussion of "The New Queer Chinese Cinema," Helen Hok-Sze Leung cites Tsai's *I Don't Want to Sleep Alone* as an example of queer cinema "without readily recognizable gay characters" since "what draws all these different films together under the rubric of 'queer cinema' is much more—and much more interesting—than the mere fact of gay representation." Helen Hok-Sze Leung, "Homosexuality and Queer Aesthetics," in *A Companion to Chinese Cinema*, ed. Yingjin Zhang (Oxford: Blackwell, 2012), 518–34; 518.

14. Meyer, *Politics and Poetics of Camp*, 3.

15. Berry, *Speaking in Images*, 385.

16. See Rachel Cheung, "Filmmaker Tsai Ming-liang on Sexuality and Being Touched by a Goddess," where Tsai explains, "I use homosexuality as subject matter but not for making money. Filmmaking is a creative process as well as

a way of self-expression. Very early on, a friend from Hong Kong who really liked my films suggested that I participate in the London LGBT Film Festival. I thanked him but I rejected the suggestion. At the time, society was very conservative and I did not want my film to be branded. But now I would not mind. It's a learning process, learning to accept homosexuality and myself." *Post Magazine*, October 20, 2016, https://www.scmp.com/magazines/post-maga zine/arts-music/article/2038590/filmmaker-tsai-ming-liang-sexuality-and -being.

17. Moon, *Small Boy,* 15–16.

18. Ahmed, *Queer Phenomenology,* 170–72.

19. In addition to Hu, "Goodbye City," and Martin, "European Undead," see Tsai, *Taiwan New Cinema at Film Festivals.*

20. Fredric Jameson, "Remapping Taipei," in *New Chinese Cinemas: Forms, Identities, Politics,* ed. Nick Browne, Paul Pickowicz, Vivian Sobchack, and Esther Yau (Cambridge: Cambridge University Press, 1994), 117–50.

21. Angelo Restivo, *The Cinema of Economic Miracles: Visuality and Modernization in the Italian Art Film* (Durham, N.C.: Duke University Press, 2002), 193n16.

22. Martin, "*Vive L'Amour,*" 180–81.

23. Chao explains how "Tsai found Yang's off-screen personality 'similar to a man's,' a trait that actually inspired him when he created her role in *Vive L'amour* 'much in accordance with that for a "man."' In an interview, he later laughed, 'I made her character more aggressive. This is sort of "gender inversion."' Yang's persona—at least in Tsai's cinematic world—is thus by no means circumscribed by femininity." Chao, *Queer Representations,* 235.

24. Ahmed, *Queer Phenomenology,* 170; Martin, "*Vive L'Amour,*" 180.

25. *2000, vu par (2000, Seen By)* website, https://www.hautetcourt.com/films/2000-vu-par/; https://www.hautetcourt.com/films/the-hole/.

26. It is worth noting that it is a French scientist on the radio who proposes names like "Taiwan virus," and "Taiwan flu." See Justin Chang's revisitation of the film during the Covid-19 pandemic, "Review: 'The Hole,' a 1998 Film Set during a Pandemic, Makes a Welcome Return," *Los Angeles Times,* September 13, 2020, https://www.latimes.com/entertainment-arts/movies/story/2020-09 -13/the-hole-review-tsai-ming-liang-pandemic. See also Ruairi McCann, "Tsai Ming-liang's *The Hole* Is One of the Great Films about Living in Isolation," *Little White Lies,* March 22, 2020, https://lwlies.com/articles/the-hole-tsai-ming -liang-living-in-isolation/; Indranil Bhattacharya, "Tsai Ming Liang's 1998 Film *The Hole* Is Must-Watch Viewing during the Ongoing Coronavirus Pandemic," *Firstpost,* March 13, 2020, https://www.firstpost.com/entertainment/tsai-ming -liangs-1998-film-the-hole-is-must-watch-viewing-during-the-ongoing-coro navirus-pandemic-8145831.html.

27. David Walsh, "An Interview with Tsai Ming-liang, Director of *The Hole*," *World Socialist Web Site*, October 7, 1998, https://www.wsws.org/en/articles/1998/10/tsai-007.html.

28. Walsh, "An Interview with Tsai Ming-liang."

29. Steven Shaviro, "Contagious Allegories: George Romero," in *The Cinematic Body* (Minneapolis: University of Minnesota Press, 1993), 83–105.

30. Lauren Berlant, *Cruel Optimism* (Durham, N.C.: Duke University Press, 2011).

31. *The Walking Dead*, television series (AMC 2010–2022); *Survival Family (Sabaibaru famirî)*, film, directed by Yaguchi Shinobu (2016; Tokyo: Toho Company, 2017); *Train to Busan (Busanhaeng)*, DVD, directed by Yeon Sang-ho (2016; Plano, Tex.: Well Go USA Entertainment, 2017).

32. Steven Shaviro, *The Cinematic Body* (Minneapolis: University of Minnesota Press, 1993), 88.

33. *Dancer in the Dark*, DVD, directed by Lars von Trier (2000; Los Angeles: New Line Home Video, 2001); *15: The Movie*, DVD, directed by Royston Tan (2003; London: Picture This! Entertainment, 2005); *The Act of Killing*, DVD, directed by Jonathan Oppenheimer (Copenhagen: Final Cut for Real, 2012).

34. See Chao, *Queer Representations*, 231–32.

35. See the explanation of Bertolt Brecht's "estrangement-effect" or "alienation-effect" *(Verfremdungseffekt)* and its employment by Roland Barthes in Ian Buchanan, *A Dictionary of Critical Theory* (London: Oxford University Press, 2010). On Tsai and Brecht, see "*Stray Dogs*: Thoughts by Patrick Brian Smith," November 18, 2014, https://anosamoursblog.weebly.com/blog/category/stray-dogs.

36. Chang, "Gender Hierarchy," 25–44. Cf. Tatsuya Matsumura, "Internal Borders, or De-translating the Construction of Male Homosexuality: Tsai Ming-liang's *The Hole* and the Imaging of 'Okama' in Contemporary Japan" (Paper presented at the QGrad Conference, UCLA, October 16, 2004).

37. See Rojas, "Along the Riverrun," 626–46. On the way *Skywalk* revisits but also revises a similar escalator scene in *The River*, see Song Hwee Lim, "Positioning Auteur Theory," 228.

38. Jacques Lacan, "God and the *Jouissance* of [The] Woman," in *Feminine Sexuality: Jacques Lacan and the École Freudienne*, ed. Juliet Mitchell and Jacqueline Rose, trans. Jacqueline Rose (New York: W. W. Norton, 1982), 137–48.

39. Chang, "Gender Hierarchy," 25; 37. Cf. Chang, "Drifting Bodies and Flooded Spaces," 45–63.

40. Chao, *Queer Representations*, 242.

41. See David Roth, "Todd Haynes's Masterpiece 'Safe' Is Now a Tale of Two Plagues," *New Yorker*, March 28, 2020, https://www.newyorker.com/culture/

culture-desk/todd-hayness-masterpiece-safe-is-now-a-tale-of-two-plagues. *Safe*, DVD, directed by Todd Haynes (1995; New York: Criterion Collection, 2014).

42. Eve Kosofsky Sedgwick, *Tendencies* (Durham, N.C.: Duke University Press, 1993), 8.

43. Leung, "Homosexuality and Queer Aesthetics," 518–19.

44. It is worth noting that like the European commissioning of *The Hole*, *I Don't Want to Sleep Alone* was commissioned as part of the New Crowned Hope festival initiated and funded by the city of Vienna to celebrate the 250th anniversary of Mozart's birth, alongside a film from Tsai's Southeast Asian queer cinema interlocutor, Apichatpong Weerasethakul. See Mark Cousins, "Beyond the Horizon," *Sight & Sound*, http://old.bfi.org.uk/sightandsound/feature/49386.

45. See Tash Aw, "Tsai Ming-liang's Shadow City," *Paris Review*, April 15, 2020, https://www.theparisreview.org/blog/2020/04/15/tsai-ming-liangs-shadow-city/. Resonating with Hu's discussion of urban nostalgia and transformation, Aw explains, "Favored by migrant workers and anyone in search of somewhere to eat and drink cheaply late at night, the kopitiam is a remnant of old Kuala Lumpur, a once-thriving business now barely profitable. But this one is right in the middle of town, where real estate is expensive. Soon, it will be sold, and the handsome, dilapidated space and its eclectic, democratic clientele will be forced move on, replaced by hipsters and luxe backpacker hostels. For both the people who frequent the coffee shop and those who live in the rooms above it, the building is a refuge for misfits and outsiders, those injured by the sharp edges of a rapidly modernizing society with little time for kindness. Shot fifteen years ago, the film feels at once utterly contemporary and anchored in a distant past, as if Tsai Ming-liang had anticipated the Kuala Lumpur of 2020 while celebrating the historic richness and squalor of the city's urban life."

46. Ian Johnston, "Butterfly Dream: Tsai Ming-liang's *I Don't Want to Sleep Alone*," *Bright Lights Film Journal*, no. 57 (2007), http://www.brightlightsfilm.com/57/sleep.php. For a critique of the *huaqiao* category, see Shih, "Theory, Asia, and the Sinophone," 480.

47. See Chang, "Sleeping with Strangers," 250–68. Cf. Ani Maitra, "In the Shadow of the Homoglobal: Queer Cosmopolitanism in Tsai Ming-liang's *I Don't Want to Sleep Alone*," in *New Intimacies/Old Desires: Law, Culture, and Queer Politics in Neoliberal Times*, ed. Oishik Sircar and Dipika Jain (New Delhi: Zubaan; and Chicago: Chicago University Press, 2017), 317–50.

48. Johnston, "Butterfly Dream."

49. I thank Saw Tiong Guan, director of the Tsai documentary *Past Present* (2013), for explaining this to me. See also "Tsai Ming-liang's *I Don't Want to Sleep Alone* Banned Then Unbanned," *Screen Anarchy*, March 11, 2007, https://

screenanarchy.com/2007/03/tsai-ming-liangs-i-dont-want-to-sleep-alone
-banned-then-unbanned.html; Chuck Stephens, "Review: I Don't Want to
Sleep Alone," *Film Comment*, May–June 2007, https://www.filmcomment.com/
article/i-dont-want-to-sleep-alone-review/; Chang, "Sleeping with Strangers,"
265n26.

    50. Johnston, "Butterfly Dream."

    51. See Song Hwee Lim, *Tsai Ming-liang and a Cinema of Slowness*, 98–101;
Chan, "Queerly Connecting," 165; Maitra, "Shadow of the Homoglobal," 328.
See also Michael Guillen's interview with Tsai Ming-liang about *I Don't Want
to Sleep Alone,* where Guillen notes *"I Don't Want to Sleep Alone* also reminded
me of something Milan Kundera wrote in his novel *The Unbearable Lightness
of Being,* where he said that the person you love is not the person you have sex
with; the person you love is the person you sleep with. I felt this truth in your
film." And Tsai responds, "[Making a gesture of sweeping goosebumps from
his arm.] I am very touched by your comment." Michael Guillen, "2006 TIFF—
The Evening Class Interview with Tsai Ming-Liang," *Evening Class*, September
14, 2006, https://theeveningclass.blogspot.com/2006/09/2006-tiff-evening
-class-interview-with.html.

    52. Moon, *Small Boy*, 19.

    53. Referring to the "half-finished building" used in the film, Ani Maitra
explains that "Construction at this massive site, located near the Pudu Prison
in Kuala Lumpur, was actually abandoned after the Southeast Asian financial
crisis of 1997. In Tsai's rendition of this failed project, Rawang is the only
labourer left at the site, and his only Sisyphean task seems to be pumping out
stagnant water from the base of the building. . . . Through Rawang's peculiar
relationship with the building, the failed project, and hence the 1997 crisis,
Tsai represents stagnation not in opposition to but as an effect of rapid economic progress and the over-accumulation of capital." Maitra, "Shadow of the
Homoglobal," 335–36.

    54. See Chan, "Queerly Connecting," 172.

    55. Moon, *Small Boy*, 15. Cf. René Girard, *Deceit, Desire, and the Novel: Self
and Other in Literary Structure*, trans. Yvonne Freccero (1961; rpt. Baltimore:
The Johns Hopkins University Press, 1966); and Mikkel Borch-Jacobsen, *The
Freudian Subject*, trans. Catherine Porter (Stanford, Calif.: Stanford University
Press, 1988).

    56. Moon, *Small Boy*, 16.

    57. *Vive L'Amour* and *I Don't Want to Sleep Alone* can be juxtaposed with the
love triangle in François Truffaut's *Jules and Jim*. *Jules and Jim (Jules et Jim)*,
DVD, directed by François Truffaut (1962; New York: Criterion Collection,
2005), is also worth comparing to Girard's notion of "triangular desire" published around the same time (1961). See John Oursler, "A Queer Reading of

Truffaut's Masterpiece, 'Jules and Jim,'" *PopMatters*, February 19, 2014, https://www.popmatters.com/179048-jules-and-jim-on-criterion-2495688416.html.

58. See Chang, "Sleeping with Strangers," 259–60, 265n26.

59. Moon, *Small Boy*, 16.

60. Moon, *Small Boy*, 17.

61. Johnston, "Butterfly Dream." Cf. Chang, "Sleeping with Strangers," 261; Maitra, "Shadow of the Homoglobal," 343. See also Shanon Shah, "The Malaysian Dilemma: Negotiating Sexual Diversity in a Muslim-Majority Commonwealth State," in *Human Rights, Sexual Orientation, and Gender Identity in the Commonwealth: Struggles for Decriminalization and Change*, ed. Corinne Lennox and Matthew Waites (London: University of London Press, 2013), 261–86.

62. I want to thank Sim Wai Chew for his comments pointing me in this analytic direction. See Chang, "Sleeping with Strangers," 261–63; Chan, "Queerly Connecting," 167; Maitra, "Shadow of the Homoglobal," 335–36.

63. See Chang, "Sleeping with Strangers," 250–53, 262, 264n6. See also *Queer Diaspora: The 2010 International Conference on Queer Diaspora Plenary Sessions Paper Collection* and the website for the conference, http://140.112.180.209/qd/index.php; Gopinath, *Unruly Visions*, especially chapter 2, "Queer Disorientations, States of Suspension"; Chiang and Wong, "Queering the Transnational Turn," 1643–56; and Chiang and Wong, "Asia Is Burning," 121–26. Chiang and Wong highlight "the inter-connectivity across different subregions of Asia. A key objective of our intervention is to enable specialists of East Asia, South Asia, and Southeast Asia to no longer construe the West as the only alibi for serious discussion about sexual globalisation or the ultimate neoliberal model of juxtaposition. Rather, we hope to make more transparent the modular comparability of the different regional expertise brought together here. Our project incorporates the agenda of using 'Asia as method,' as proposed by Kuan-Hsing Chen (2010) and others, by asking interlocutors in the growing field of queer Asian studies to rethink the vectors of linkage across various longstanding 'minor' regions in area studies (e.g., Korea, Thailand, Hong Kong, etc.) whose significance are made poignant via such transnational affinity, rather than always being mediated through a centre, be it China, Japan or the West" (123).

64. *Happy Together (Chun gwong cha sit)*, DVD, directed by Wong Kar-wai (1997; New York: Kino Video, 2003). Cf. Maitra, "Shadow of the Homoglobal," 342–47; Lim, *Tsai Ming-liang and a Cinema of Slowness*, 101.

65. See Chow, "Afterword," 269–76.

66. For a discussion of the music in the film, see Chang, "Sleeping with Strangers," 258, 262, 265n22. Tsai has used the theme music from Charlie Chaplin's *Limelight* (1952) again but in the form of the tune of a music box exchanged between Lee Kang-sheng and Anong Houngheuangsy in his

feature-length "postretirement" film *Days* (2020). See Lukasz Mankowski, "Interview with Tsai Ming-liang: The Longer You Take, the Time Comes Out," *Asian Movie Pulse*, March 20, 2020, https://asianmoviepulse.com/2020/03/interview-with-tsai-ming-liang-the-longer-you-take-the-time-comes-out/.

67. See Chang, "Sleeping with Strangers," 266n30. Chang explains, "Tsai's original idea for the last scene was to show the three of them having sex. However, he decided at the last minute to have them simply sleep together on the old mattress."

68. Barthes, "Leaving the Movie Theater," 346.

69. See Elena Gorfinkel, "Weariness, Waiting: Endurance and Art Cinema's Tired Bodies," *Discourse* 34, nos. 2–3 (Spring–Fall 2012): 311–47. Cf. Maitra, "Shadow of the Homoglobal," 335–36.

70. Roland Barthes, *Roland Barthes by Roland Barthes*, trans. Richard Howard (New York: Farrar, Straus and Giroux, 1977), 142.

2. Leaving the Cinema

1. Barthes, "Leaving the Movie Theater," 348. See also Watts, *Roland Barthes' Cinema*, 75.

2. Barthes, "Leaving the Movie Theater," 346.

3. Barthes, "Leaving the Movie Theater," 346.

4. It will be clear later why I have insisted on both "gay" and "queer" as adjectives here. But let me say at the outset that for me these terms are not collapsible (despite recent usage) yet are also not simply to be opposed in terms of generation, but rather in terms of a conceptual or ontological distinction. I take my cue from Moe Meyer, who argues that unlike the identities labeled "gay and lesbian," "Queer sexualities become, then, a series of improvised performances whose threat lies in the denial of any social identity derived from participation in those performances. As a refusal of sexually defined identity, this must also include a denial of the difference upon which such identities have been founded. And it is precisely in the space of this refusal, in the deconstruction of the homo/hetero binary, that the threat and challenge to bourgeois ideology is queerly executed." Meyer, ed., *Politics and Poetics of Camp*, 3. A more practical reason for the distinction is that not all men who participate in cruising and same-sex activities would identify as "gay men" (nor might they identify as "queer" but here I use the term as a concept, not an identity label).

5. *Midnight Cowboy*, DVD, directed by John Schlesinger (1969; New York: Criterion Collection, 2018); *Far from Heaven*, DVD, directed by Todd Haynes (2002; New York: Kino Lorber, 2019); Delany, *Times Square Red*. On cruising in *Far from Heaven*, see Nicholas de Villiers, "Glancing, Cruising, Staring: Queer Ways of Looking," *Bright Lights Film Journal*, no. 57 (2007), https://bright

lightsfilm.com/glancing-cruising-staring-queer-ways-looking/#.XPVZCy2Z
POQ.

6. Barthes, *Pleasure of the Text*, 4–6, 27.

7. I first published the essay expanded for this chapter as "Leaving the
Cinema: Metacinematic Cruising in Tsai Ming-liang's *Goodbye, Dragon Inn*,"
Jump Cut, no. 50 (Spring 2008), https://www.ejumpcut.org/archive/jc50.2008/
DragonInn/. Three brilliant essays have since been published that make important overlapping points and incorporate similar references to Barthes and
cruising: Jean Ma, "The Haunted Movie Theater," in *Melancholy Drift*, 95–122;
Hong, "Theatrics of Cruising," 149–59; and Fan Wu, "Cruising's Spectral Intimacies (Four Scenes)," *Mice Magazine*, no. 3 (Fall 2017), http://micemagazine
.ca/issue-three/cruising's-spectral-intimacies-four-scenes. See also Nick Pinkerton, *Goodbye, Dragon Inn* (Berlin/Melbourne: Fireflies Press, 2021); and the
online excerpt, "Cruising at the Cinema": https://mubi.com/notebook/posts/
cruising-at-the-cinema-an-excerpt-from-goodbye-dragon-inn.

8. Barthes, "Leaving the Movie Theater," 349. Cf. Chris Wood, "Realism,
Intertextuality, and Humour in Tsai Ming-liang's *Goodbye, Dragon Inn*," *Journal of Chinese Cinemas* 1, no. 2 (2007): 105–16.

9. Barthes, "Leaving the Movie Theater," 346.

10. *Sunset Boulevard*, DVD, directed by Billy Wilder (1950; Los Angeles: Para-
mount Home Video, 2002); *Scream*, DVD, directed by Wes Craven (1996;
New York: Dimension Home Video, 1998); *An Amorous History of the Silver
Screen (Yinmu yanshi)*, film, directed by Cheng Bugao (Shanghai: Mingxing
Film Company, 1931); *Electric Shadows (Meng ying tong nian)*, film, directed by
Xiao Jiang (2004; New York: Asia Society, 2005). On *Scream* as metacinema,
see Nicholas de Villiers, "Metahorror: Sequels, 'The Rules,' and the Metareferen-
tial Turn in Contemporary Horror Cinema," in *The Metareferential Turn: Forms,
Functions, Attempts at Explanation*, ed. Werner Wolf (Amsterdam: Rodopi, 2011),
357–77. See also G. Andrew Stuckey, *Metacinema in Contemporary Chinese Film*
(Hong Kong: Hong Kong University Press, 2018).

11. *Dragon Inn (Long men kezhan)*, DVD, directed by King Hu (1967; New
York: Janus Films, 2016). See Hu, "Goodbye City"; cf. Rojas, "'Nezha Was
Here,'" 63–89.

12. Delany, *Times Square Red*, xviii. See also Nicholas de Villiers, "Documentary and the Anamnesis of Queer Space: *The Polymath, or, The Life and Opinions
of Samuel R. Delany, Gentleman*," *Jump Cut: A Review of Contemporary Media*,
no. 51, http://www.ejumpcut.org/archive/jc51.2009/Polymath/index.html.

13. See Miriam Hansen's discussion of how "the cinema as a heterotopia
converges with the concept of an alternative public sphere" in early cinema's
specific *social* context of theatrical reception prior to the disciplining of spectatorship in accordance with middle-class taste. Miriam Hansen, "Chameleon

and Catalyst: The Cinema as an Alternative Public Sphere," in *The Film Cultures Reader*, ed. Graeme Turner (New York: Routledge, 2002), 390–419; 402. I would like to thank John Mowitt for suggesting this connection.

14. José Esteban Muñoz, "Ghosts of Public Sex: Utopian Longings, Queer Memories," in *Policing Public Sex: Queer Politics and the Future of AIDS Activism*, ed. Strange Bedfellows (Boston: South End Press, 1996), 355–72. Cf. Muñoz, *Cruising Utopia*.

15. Walsh, "An Interview with Tsai Ming-liang."

16. On Tsai's intratextuality and intertextuality, see Song Hwee Lim, "Positioning Auteur Theory," 223–45.

17. See Hong, "Theatrics of Cruising."

18. See chapter 1.

19. See Lim, *Celluloid Comrades*, 137–39; Rojas, "Nezha Was Here."

20. See Hu, "The Unprofessional."

21. *All Corners of the World (Haijiao tianya)*, written and directed by Tsai Ming-liang (1989), available online at: https://youtu.be/CQ72D-QE0Ak. See Rojas, "Nezha Was Here," 68–69. *A City of Sadness (Beiqing chengshi)*, film, directed by Hou Hsiao-hsien (New York: Sony Pictures Classics, 1989).

22. Brian Hu suggests that "it is as Tsai's muse that Lee Kang-sheng will forever be known. Like Mifune to Kurosawa, Ullman to Bergman, Karina to Godard, Léaud to Truffaut, Gong Li to Zhang Yimou, and Chow Yun-fat to John Woo, Lee is more than Tsai's preferred actor, but the face of his films and the cinematic embodiment of the director's worldview. Tsai's body of work is in fact Lee's body." Hu, "The Unprofessional."

23. Nick Browne, "Introduction," in *New Chinese Cinemas: Forms, Identities, Politics*, ed. Nick Browne, Paul Pickowicz, Vivian Sobchack, and Esther Yau (Cambridge: Cambridge University Press, 1994), 1–11; 6.

24. Browne, "Introduction," 7.

25. *The Terrorizers (Kong bu fen zi)*, film, directed by Edward Yang (Taipei: Inbaubel, 1986).

26. Browne, "Introduction," 7. Jameson, "Remapping Taipei," 114–57.

27. See Hong, "Anywhere but Here," 159–81.

28. Jameson, "Remapping Taipei," 119.

29. Rey Chow, *Primitive Passions: Visuality, Sexuality, Ethnography, and Contemporary Chinese Cinema* (New York: Columbia University Press, 1995), 155–56.

30. *The 400 Blows (Les quatre cent coups)*, DVD, directed by François Truffaut (1959; New York: Criterion Collection, 2004). Arguably, Tsai's *All Corners of the World* is an early attempt to make a Taipei-based *400 Blows* since it focuses on a delinquent schoolboy playing hooky. For more on Tsai's connections to Truffaut, see chapter 4.

31. Martin, "European Undead." Cf. Bloom, *Contemporary Sino-French Cinemas.*

32. Martin, "European Undead." I return to this problem in chapter 4.

33. Hu, "Goodbye City."

34. Jameson, "Remapping Taipei," 132.

35. Jameson, "Remapping Taipei," 132.

36. Michel de Certeau, *The Practice of Everyday Life*, trans. Steven Rendall (Berkeley: University of California Press, 1984).

37. De Certeau, *Practice of Everyday Life*, 103.

38. See Harold Garfinkel, *Studies in Ethnomethodology* (Englewood Cliffs, N.J.: Prentice-Hall, 1967) and *Ethnomethodology's Program: Working Out Durkheim's Aphorism*, ed. Ann Warfield Rawls (Lanham, Md.: Rowman and Littlefield, 2002).

39. Jameson, "Remapping Taipei," 132.

40. Jameson, "Remapping Taipei," 132.

41. Kenneth Chan, "*Goodbye, Dragon Inn*: Tsai Ming-liang's Political Aesthetics of Nostalgia, Place, and Lingering," *Journal of Chinese Cinemas* 1, no. 2 (2007): 89–103; 100n9.

42. Lee Edelman, "Tearooms and Sympathy; or, The Epistemology of the Water Closet," in *The Lesbian and Gay Studies Reader*, ed. Henry Abelove, Michèle Aina Barale, and David M. Halperin (New York: Routledge, 1993), 553–74.

43. See Hong, "Theatrics of Cruising," 151; Ma, *Melancholy Drift*, 119–21. I too find Tsai's films "queer" rather than "gay" because his vision of cruising goes beyond being "about" gay men or about "coming out." Certainly Tsai has experience making films about gay people, as evidenced by his AIDS documentary *My New Friends* (1995), which he describes in an interview with Danièle Rivière: "My producer at the time advised me not to look for a homosexual HIV sufferer. 'Why not?' I asked her. 'It would be stupid for people to link AIDS with homosexuality.' I went home to think about it, and came back to tell her that I would still prefer to use a homosexual. Personally I think that in Taiwan, as in many other countries in the world, there are many people with a stereotypical and rather negative view of AIDS because they think of it as a disease of homosexuals. So I thought that if they knew so little about the disease, they probably knew nothing about the life of a homosexual either." Rivière, "Scouting," 92. Cf. Rojas, "Nezha Was Here." Tsai's logic here is quite refreshing, actually, but beyond this documentary I would question whether Tsai's other films are "about" homosexuals (to use his term) in Taiwanese society. Tsai has declared, "I'm sick of people labeling my films as 'gay films' or 'dysfunctional family films.'" Berry, *Speaking in Images*, 385. I believe that sexuality is "queered" in films like *The River, The Hole, Vive L'Amour*, and *I Don't*

Want to Sleep Alone, as I argued in chapter 1 regarding "sexual disorientation." Like Delany's personal-sociological reflections on cruising in his account of Times Square porn theaters, I do not presume that all the men doing the cruising in Tsai's film are "gay men" per se. In this, I differ slightly from Kenneth Chan's reading ("*Goodbye, Dragon Inn*," 99; 99n8).

44. See Andrew Grossman, *Queer Asian Cinema: Shadows in the Shade* (Binghamton, NY: Harrington Park Press, 2000).

45. The film *Fireworks* (1947) is part of *Kenneth Anger: The Complete Magick Lantern Cycle,* DVD, directed by Kenneth Anger (San Francisco: Fantoma, 2010). See Christopher Meir, "Fireworks," *Senses of Cinema* (July 2003), http://sensesofcinema.com/2003/cteq/fireworks/.

46. It is worth noting that "sayonara" (literally "if it be thus") as an expression for "goodbye" or "farewell" implies that you will never see the person again, and thus has fallen out of use in Japan. Scott Wilson, "Say Sayonara to 'Sayonara'–70% of Japanese Don't Use This Word for Goodbye Anymore," *Japan Today,* May 22, 2016, https://japantoday.com/category/features/life style/say-sayonara-to-sayonara-70-of-japanese-dont-use-this-word-for-good bye-anymore. See also Johnny Waldman, "Sayonara: One of the Most Japanese Words in the Dictionary," https://www.spoon-tamago.com/2019/03/21/sayo nara-japanese-word-meaning/.

47. See Leo T. S. Ching, *Anti-Japan: The Politics of Sentiment in Postcolonial East Asia* (Durham, N.C.: Duke University Press, 2019).

48. John Whittier Treat, *Great Mirrors Shattered: Homosexuality, Orientalism, and Japan* (New York: Oxford University Press, 1999), 151. Cf. Tan Hoang Nguyen, *A View from the Bottom: Asian American Masculinity and Sexual Representation* (Durham, N.C.: Duke University Press, 2014).

49. Yang's character is identified in the credits as "Peanut Eating Woman" (on imdb.com), but as eating watermelon seeds by Chan, "*Goodbye, Dragon Inn,*" 92; and Ma, *Melancholy Drift,* 110.

50. All of the quotes that follow in this paragraph are from Chen Shiang-chyi's interview in the documentary.

51. Deleuze, *Cinema 2,* 271.

52. Deleuze, *Cinema 2,* 272.

53. Deleuze, *Cinema 2,* 273.

54. The three-year-old boy and grandfatherly Miao Tien are in fact a "ghostly" intertextual reference to Lee Kang-sheng's directorial debut film *The Missing* (*Bu jian*), produced around the same time as a companion to Tsai's *Goodbye, Dragon Inn* (*Bu san*). The two appear as "ghosts" or, in a more lighthearted joke, as gone "missing" in the theater in Tsai's film. (I thank Chuck Kleinhans for clarifying this for me.) Tsai provides the backstory in his interview with

Michael Berry, starting with the theater about to be torn down: "I ran into the owner again, and he told me they were preparing to tear all the seats out and rent the space. As soon as he told me that, I could feel myself starting to get anxious. I immediately called my producer and told him to rent it so we could make a short film there. . . . It was just around that time that Hsiao Kang [Lee Kang-sheng] was also planning to make his directorial debut with a short that eventually became a feature and was renamed *The Missing (Bujian)*. I liked Hsiao Kang's script so I decided to work with him on it. It was at that moment that I thought, *Why don't we each make a short in the theater?* One is called *Bujian* [lit. "don't meet"], the other is called *Busan* [lit. "don't leave"], the Chinese titles of which together form the popular idiom *bu jian bu san*, which means 'don't leave until we meet.'" Berry, *Speaking in Images*, 388.

55. John A. Lent, *The Asian Film Industry* (London: Christopher Helm, 1990), 64–65.

56. Darren Hughes, "Tsai Ming-liang," *Senses of Cinema* director profile, http://www.sensesofcinema.com/contents/directors/03/tsai.html; Stephen Teo, "King Hu," *Senses of Cinema* director profile, http://www.sensesofcinema.com/contents/directors/02/hu.html.

57. *Dragon Inn (Sun lung moon hak chan,* aka *New Dragon Gate Inn)*, DVD, directed by Raymond Lee (1992; San Francisco: Tai Seng Video Marketing, 2001).

58. Lent, *The Asian Film Industry*, 87. Cf. Rojas, "Nezha Was Here."

59. David Bordwell, *Planet Hong Kong* (Cambridge, Mass.: Harvard University Press, 2000).

60. See Lutz Koepnick, *The Long Take: Art Cinema and the Wondrous* (Minneapolis: University of Minnesota Press, 2017).

61. *Man with a Movie Camera (Chelovek s kino-apparatom)*, DVD, directed by Dziga Vertov (1929; New York: Kino Video, 2003).

62. Chan, *"Goodbye, Dragon Inn,"* 91.

63. See the preface. See also de Villiers, "We Are the World Cinema." See also the editorial by Rolando Caputo and Scott Murray in the same issue: http://www.sensesofcinema.com/2007/editorial/45index/.

64. See the remarkable documentation of old and derelict movie theaters in Taiwan on the blog *Spectral Codex:* https://spectralcodex.com/collections/taiwan-theaters/.

65. Barthes, "Leaving the Movie Theater," 348.

66. Barthes, *Pleasure of the Text*, 14.

67. A strong case could be made that the gender neutral or nonbinary pronoun "they/their" would be more effective here to describe this subject.

68. Barthes, *Pleasure of the Text*, 14.

69. Barthes, *Pleasure of the Text*, 26.

70. Quotation of the English subtitles to *Goodbye, Dragon Inn*. The song is "Liu Lian" by Yao Lee, with lyrics by Chen Dieyi. Along with Gong Qiuxia, whose song was discussed in the preface, Yao Lee was one of the "Seven Great Singing Stars" who dominated Chinese pop music in the 1940s. See Pinkerton, *Goodbye, Dragon Inn*, 137.

71. Walsh, "Interview with Tsai Ming-liang."

72. However, critics often try to show how Tsai's particular use of nostalgia avoids potentially reactionary uses: specifically, Chan reads the nostalgia in *Goodbye, Dragon Inn* in a way that "disrupts its conservative possibilities," arguing that "this nostalgia, in employing place-based politics, allows *Goodbye, Dragon Inn* to question the cultural commodification of Chinese culture in the recent Hollywood interest in the *wu xia pian*" ("*Goodbye, Dragon Inn*," 92). Likewise, Hu's "Goodbye City" draws out the ambiguity and ambivalence of nostalgia as it is deployed in Tsai's *The Skywalk Is Gone* and *Goodbye, Dragon Inn*.

73. Fredric Jameson, "Postmodernism and Consumer Society," in *Movies and Mass Culture*, ed. John Belton (New Brunswick, N.J.: Rutgers University Press, 1996), 194. See also Fredric Jameson, *Postmodernism, or, The Cultural Logic of Late Capitalism* (Durham, N.C.: Duke University Press, 1991).

74. Deleuze, *Cinema 2*, 76–77. For an example of Wim Wenders's "melancholic Hegelian reflections," see *Tokyo-Ga*, film, directed by Wim Wenders (New York: Gray City, 1985).

75. Deleuze, *Cinema 2*, 82.

76. *The Eye (Gin gwai)*, DVD, directed by the Pang Brothers (2002; Santa Monica, Calif.: Lionsgate Home Entertainment, 2003).

77. Jacques Derrida, *Specters of Marx: The State of the Debt, the Work of Mourning, and the New International*, trans. Peggy Kamuf (New York: Routledge, 1994). Cf. Colin Davis, "Hauntology, Spectres, and Phantoms," *French Studies* 59, no. 3 (2005): 373–79.

78. Several of the characters also appear quite pale and are lit with a slightly greenish light reflecting from the screen, thereby conforming to the conventions for representing "ghosts" in Chinese cinema, especially of the King Hu era. Thus, they seem more like ghosts by association with cinematic presentations of ghosts. I thank Chuck Kleinhans for pointing this out to me. Cf. G. Andrew Stuckey, "Ghosts in the Theatre: Generic Play and Temporality in Tsai Ming-liang's *Goodbye, Dragon Inn*," *Asian Cinema* 25, no. 1 (2014): 33–48.

79. Muñoz, "Ghosts of Public Sex"; Delany, *Times Square Red*.

80. Delany, *Times Square Red*, 145.

81. Delany, *Times Square Red*, 147.

82. Delany, *Times Square Red*, xviii. Cf. Muñoz, *Cruising Utopia*.

83. See the photos of the "ruins" of the Fu Ho aka Fuhe Grand Theatre (福和大戲院) in Yonghe (and discussion of *Goodbye, Dragon Inn*) at: https:// lenpep.wordpress.com/2018/02/01/fuhe-grand-theatre-福和大戲院/.

84. Paul Burston, "Confessions of a Gay Film Critic, or How I Stopped Worrying and Learned to Love *Cruising*," in *Anti-Gay*, ed. Mark Simpson (London: Freedom Press, 1997), 84–97.

85. Victor Burgin, "Barthes's Discretion," in *Writing the Image after Roland Barthes*, ed. Jean-Michel Rabaté (Philadelphia: University of Pennsylvania Press, 1997), 19–29; 29.

86. Barthes, "Leaving the Movie Theater," 349.

87. Roland Barthes, "Soirées de Paris," in *Incidents*, ed. François Wahl, trans. Richard Howard (Berkeley: University of California Press, 1992), 51–73.

3. Queer Camp and Porn Musicals

1. Ironically, "white coat" or "white coater" is a common nickname for sexploitation films that use the alibi of medical experts to differentiate themselves from pornography. See the Something Weird Video documentary *That's Sexploitation!*, DVD, directed by Frank Henenlotter (2013; Los Angeles: Severin Films, 2016).

2. David Halperin, *How to Be Gay* (Cambridge, Mass.: Harvard University Press, 2012). For a remarkable pre-Stonewall combination of camp and sex, see Robert Scully, *A Scarlet Pansy*, ed. Robert J. Corber (New York: Fordham University Press, 2016).

3. David Church, *Disposable Passions: Vintage Pornography and the Material Legacies of Adult Cinema* (New York: Bloomsbury, 2016); *Sluts and Goddesses Video Workshop*, video, directed by Annie Sprinkle and Maria Beatty, available on demand at https://www.pinklabel.tv/on-demand/film/sluts-and-goddesses/; Carol Leigh's feminist camp videos can be found at https://vimeo.com/carolleigh. On feminist camp, see Pamela Robertson Wojcik's *Guilty Pleasures: Feminist Camp from Mae West to Madonna* (Durham, N.C.: Duke University Press, 1996).

4. Vivian Lee, "Pornography, Musical, Drag, and the Art Film: Performing 'Queer' in Tsai Ming-liang's *The Wayward Cloud*," *Journal of Chinese Cinemas* 1, no. 2 (2007), 117–37; Lim, *Tsai Ming-liang and a Cinema of Slowness*, 136–48; Chao, *Queer Representations*, 199–244. Cf. Weihong Bao, "Biomechanics of Love: Reinventing the Avant-garde in Tsai Ming-liang's Wayward 'Pornographic Musical,'" *Journal of Chinese Cinemas* 1, no. 2 (2007): 139–60.

5. On queer and camp translations and the aesthetic of "*tongzhi* camp," see Chao, *Queer Representations*, 201–18.

6. On the reception of Japanese porn actress vocalization in East Asia (including Taiwan and Korea), see Aljoša Pužar, "Soundtracks of Human Mimetic

Sexual Play: The Case of East Asian Regional Sexual Vernacular," *Sexualities* (July 2020), https://doi.org/10.1177/1363460720936474.

7. When I told Tsai this story, he explained that he heard of a Taiwanese professor who showed the film for students, and one student complained to the administration, and they made the teacher apologize to the student. I told him: this sounds like the United States.

8. See Andrei Plakhov, "'The Wayward Cloud': Histoire d'Eau," *55th Berlinale* report at FIPRESCI (the international federation of film critics), https://fipresci.org/report/the-wayward-cloud-histoire-deau-by-andrei-plakhov/. *The Umbrellas of Cherbourg (Les parapluies de Cherbourg)*, DVD, directed by Jacques Demy (1964; New York: Criterion Collection, 2014).

9. Tsai explains his Kafkaesque scenario (which also evokes AIDS and SARS) in an interview with David Walsh, "An Interview with Tsai Ming-liang." *The Hole* was commissioned as part of a series for French television: *2000, vu par (2000, Seen By)*. It is worth noting that it is a French scientist on the radio who proposes names like "Taiwan virus," and "Taiwan flu." See Justin Chang's revisitation of the film during the Covid-19 coronavirus pandemic, "Review: 'The Hole.'" See also Ruairi McCann, "Tsai Ming-liang's *The Hole*"; Bhattacharya, "Tsai Ming Liang's 1998 Film *The Hole*." The uncanny relevance of *The Hole* is also worth comparing to Todd Haynes's AIDS allegory (and critique of heteronormativity) in *Safe* (1995), as analyzed by Roth, "Todd Haynes's Masterpiece." I borrow the concept of contagious allegory from Shaviro's discussion of George Romero's zombie films, to which Tsai's disaster film is worth comparing. "Contagious Allegories," 83–105.

10. Chang, "Gender Hierarchy," 28.

11. Chang, "Gender Hierarchy," 33–34. Cf. the discussion of Tsai and Grace Chang in Pecic, *New Queer Sinophone Cinema*, 128–30.

12. Chang, "Gender Hierarchy," 36.

13. Chang, "Gender Hierarchy," 37.

14. Chang, "Gender Hierarchy," 41.

15. Chang, "Gender Hierarchy," 42n8.

16. Put variously by Lacan in "God and the *Jouissance* of [The] Woman": "there is no sexual relation" (143), "the absence of sexual relation" (141), and "in the case of the speaking being the relation between the sexes does not take place" (138). See also Kirsten Hyldgaard, "Sex as Fantasy and Sex as Symptom," *Umbra: A Journal of the Unconscious*, http://www.gsa.buffalo.edu/lacan/sexasfantasy.html. Cf. Elizabeth Grosz, *Jacques Lacan: A Feminist Introduction* (New York: Routledge, 1990), 137. Lacan might also be helpful for reading an enigmatic erotic scene in *The Hole* in which the woman in the downstairs apartment participates in phone sex (that Chang suggests is both real and virtual [Chang, "Gender Hierarchy," 37]). Grosz explains: "Lacan counterposes

a resistant and residual *jouissance* of the woman, an ecstasy that man has (mis)taken for divinity. Woman experiences a *jouissance beyond the phallus*. But if this enigmatic *jouissance* is attributed to woman as her mark of resistance to the Other, at the same time, this *jouissance* is, by that fact, strictly outside of articulation and is thus *unknowable*" (139). This is clearly what makes feminists ambivalent about Lacan, and while I have tried to indicate how Lacan might help us read *The Hole*, I don't think that Tsai's work is therefore Lacanian. Tsai certainly focuses on *jouissance*, but in the end I have found Barthes's use of this same vocabulary more appropriate. I am also mindful of the danger of too heavily "applying" French theory to Tsai's work. See Wood, "Realism, Intertextuality, and Humour in Tsai Ming-liang's *Goodbye, Dragon Inn*," 105–16. Despite having used André Bazin and Julia Kristeva to speculate about *Goodbye, Dragon Inn*, Wood concludes: "Although it is often tempting to compose grand stories in which Tsai fulfills the fantasies of European critical theory, ultimately what makes Tsai's cinema so compelling is its light-hearted playfulness" (113). Though Lacan is quite aware of the "comedy" of romance, a Lacanian reading may not help us pick up on the comic, camp effects in Tsai's *The Hole*, either.

17. Grosz, *Jacques Lacan*, 137.

18. Matthew Flisfeder and Clint Burnham, "Love and Sex in the Age of Capitalist Realism: On Spike Jonze's *Her*," *Cinema Journal* 57, no. 1 (Fall 2017): 39. *Her*, DVD, directed by Spike Jonze (2013; Burbank, Calif.: Warner Home Video, 2014).

19. Flisfeder and Burnham, "Love and Sex," 39.

20. "A hole is a hole is a hole," *Urban Dictionary*, https://www.urbandictio nary.com/define.php?term=A%20hole%20is%20a%20hole%20is%20a%20 hole.

21. See Martin, "European Undead: Tsai Ming-liang's Temporal Dysphoria." Cf. Bloom, *Contemporary Sino-French Cinemas*. I borrow the term and concept of "trajectories of identification" in the postcolonial context from Allan Cameron's "Trajectories of Identification: Travel and Global Culture in the Films of Wong Kar-wai," *Jump Cut*, no. 49 (2007), http://www.ejumpcut.org/archive/ jc49.2007/wongKarWai/index.html.

22. See Hu, "Goodbye City."

23. See Rojas, "Along the Riverrun," 626–46; and Rojas, "'Nezha Was Here,'" 63–89. On the regulation and importation of porn in Taiwan, see Pinkerton, *Goodbye, Dragon Inn*, and the online excerpt, "Cruising at the Cinema."

24. Similarities between pornography and musical genres could be compared with analogies between pornography and ethnography. See de Villiers, *Sexography*, 2.

25. Judith Butler, *Excitable Speech: A Politics of the Performative* (New York: Routledge, 1997), 68.

26. Linda Williams, *Hard Core: Power, Pleasure, and the "Frenzy of the Visible"* (Berkeley: University of California Press, 1989), 124.

27. Williams, *Hard Core*, 149.

28. Lim, *Tsai Ming-liang and a Cinema of Slowness*, 142.

29. Sigmund Freud, "Three Essays on the Theory of Sexuality," in *The Freud Reader*, ed. Peter Gay (New York: W. W. Norton, 1989), 239–93.

30. D. A. Miller, *Place for Us: Essay on the Broadway Musical* (Cambridge, Mass.: Harvard University Press, 2000), promotional blurb.

31. Susan Sontag, *Against Interpretation and Other Essays* (New York: Octagon, 1982), 280. For queer critiques of Sontag's definition of camp, see: Meyer, ed., *Politics and Poetics of Camp*; D. A. Miller, "Sontag's Urbanity," in *The Lesbian and Gay Studies Reader*, ed. Henry Abelove, Michèle Aina Barale, and David M. Halperin (New York: Routledge, 1993), 212–20; and Nicholas de Villiers, "'The Vanguard—and the Most Articulate Audience': Queer Camp, Jack Smith, and John Waters," *Forum*, no. 4 (2007), http://www.forumjournal.org/article/view/577.

32. Lee, "Pornography," 133.

33. Lee, "Pornography," 131. See also Martin, "*Vive L'Amour*," 227. Qiu Miaojin, *Notes of a Crocodile*, trans. Bonnie Huie (1994; rpt. New York: NYRB Classics, 2017).

34. Lee, "Pornography," 132; Halperin, *How to Be Gay*, 159, 211; Manuel Puig, *Kiss of the Spider Woman* (1978; rpt. New York: Vintage, 1991); *Kiss of the Spider Woman*, DVD, directed by Hector Babenco (1985; New York: Strand Releasing, 2008).

35. Lee, "Pornography," 135–36; Lim, *Tsai Ming-liang and a Cinema of Slowness*, 146–48.

36. A woman in Charlie Chaplin drag can also be seen in the metacinematic camp classic *Sunset Boulevard*, DVD, directed by Billy Wilder (Los Angeles: Paramount Home Entertainment, 2008) and in François Truffaut's *Jules and Jim*. See Oursler, "Queer Reading."

37. For a reading of Madonna's performances and costumes as drag, see Ann Cvetkovich, "The Powers of Seeing and Being Seen: *Truth or Dare* and *Paris Is Burning*," in *Film Theory Goes to the Movies*, ed. Jim Collins, Hilary Radner, and Eva Preacher Collins (New York: Routledge, 1993), 155–69.

38. Halperin, *How to Be Gay*, 159; 211.

39. José Esteban Muñoz, *Disidentifications: Queers of Color and the Performance of Politics* (Minneapolis: University of Minnesota Press, 1999); cf. Nicholas de Villiers, "Drag," in *Gender: Laughter*, ed. Bettina Papenburg (New York: Macmillan Reference USA, 2017), 263–78. World of Wonder provides many

examples of drag queens' complex disidentification with/as sex workers: "Drag Queens React to Straight Porn: Alyssa Edwards, Alaska, Raven, Raja, Delta Work, Pandora & More!" https://youtu.be/YSxWXj2xcuE; "UNHhhh Ep 49: 'PornOh Honey' w Trixie Mattel & Katya Zamolodchikova," https://youtu .be/4SOT1FgYgKs; "UNHhhh Ep 92: 'Crime Part 2' with Trixie Mattel and Katya Zamolodchikova," https://youtu.be/m1xxNlY6TuU.

40. Newton, *Mother Camp*; *The Boys in the Band*, DVD, directed by William Friedkin (1970; New York: Kino Lorber, 2015).

41. Halperin, *How to Be Gay*, 209–10.

42. Halperin, *How to Be Gay*, 191–93; 208.

43. *Vapors*, film, directed by Andy Milligan (1965): https://youtu.be/6DrCy jzwoWw. The bathhouse encounter in Tsai's *The River* is strikingly wordless by comparison. For an important discussion of the dynamic of racial difference/sameness (in relation to colonial histories) in cruising and bathhouses see Wu, "Cruising's Spectral Intimacies."

44. Bérubé, "History of Gay Bathhouses," 202. *The Women*, DVD, directed by George Cukor (1939; Burbank, Calif.: Warner Home Video, 2002).

45. See the documentaries *Wigstock: The Movie*, DVD, directed by Barry Shils (1995; Beverly Hills, Calif.: MGM Home Entertainment, 2003) and *Wig*, video, directed by Chris Moukarbel (Santa Monica, Calif.: HBO Films, 2019).

46. Halperin, *How to Be Gay*, 210. A remarkable contemporary example of combining sex and camp (via porn history) can be seen in Elizabeth Purchell's video mashup of post-Stonewall urban gay adult video *Ask Any Buddy* (2020): https://www.ask-any-buddy.com/.

47. Newton, *Mother Camp*, 109.

48. Halperin, *How to Be Gay*, 147.

49. Jack Babuscio, "Camp and the Gay Sensibility," in *Camp Grounds: Style and Homosexuality*, ed. David Bergman (Amherst: University of Massachusetts Press, 1993), 27.

50. Adam Balz, "*The Wayward Cloud*," *Not Coming to a Theater Near You*, April 22, 2009, http://www.notcoming.com/reviews/waywardcloud.

51. Babuscio, "Camp and the Gay Sensibility," 28–29.

52. Linda Williams, "Film Bodies: Gender, Genre, and Excess," *Film Quarterly* 44, no. 4 (Summer 1991): 2–13.

53. Williams, "Film Bodies," 11.

54. Chao, *Queer Representations*, 237.

55. Or between Tsai's cinema and horror movies: see Stuckey, "Ghosts in the Theatre," 33–48.

56. On Tsai and Brecht, see "*Stray Dogs*: Thoughts by Patrick Brian Smith."

57. *Annie Hall*, DVD, directed by Woody Allen (1977; Santa Monica, Calif.: MGM Home Entertainment, 2002).

58. A similar scene of "shadow puppet" eating can be seen in Zhang Yimou's metacinematic short film entry to the Cannes compilation *Chacun son cinéma* (2007) titled *En regardant le film*/看電影: https://www.dailymotion.com/video/x2bb3a.

59. Tsai Ming-liang interviewed by La Frances Hui, Asia Society, available on YouTube: "Filmmaker Tsai Ming-Liang on Human Relationships, Sexual Desire," https://youtu.be/oas4h6Vu3Wg.

60. See "Sumomo," *Behind the Name*, https://www.behindthename.com/name/sumomo/submitted.

61. See Pužar, "Soundtracks of Human Mimetic Sexual Play," for a nuanced discussion of sexual "faking": "The mimetic process here is suspended in what can be seen as a liminal space between full and ecstatic immersion into 'playing a role' on the one hand, and laborious utilitarian 'faking' on the other (a form of demanding emotional labor, usually gender-bound). Such a process, furthermore, always relies on acknowledging some elusive pre-standing 'reality' of pleasure, that is, it builds upon collective belief in some imaginary primordial sound of pleasure that, at some point in history, presented a biological-ethological blueprint for pornographic sonic scripts. . . . 'willing suspension of disbelief' still underpins spectators' (or auditors') fantasy of the natural or organic voice of pleasure, and their buying into the 'truth' of sexual vocalizations and other sounds. In order to exemplify the sonic nexus of porn and non-porn and to elaborate on the emergence of mimetic sonic play from within this nexus, I will present a specific type of East Asian sexual vocalization (initially Japanese, and largely copulatory) and will try to read it as an important part of (prevalently female) mimetic sexual play."

62. Lee, "Pornography," 125–26.

63. See Helen Bandis, Adrian Martin, and Grant McDonald, "The 400 Blow Jobs," *Rouge* (2005), http://www.rouge.com.au/rougerouge/wayward.html. They argue: "It is not enough to say that the scene is dark and shocking, and that the film is thus an accusation of pornography, an exposé of sexual alienation and commodification (Shiang-chyi transformed into a compliant porn body-double). Nor is it accurate to charge Tsai with misogyny, or a wholesale contempt for human sexuality. For, on one level, Tsai's cinema has always been, in a crucial sense, matter-of-factly pornographic, showing (in a less heightened register) many of the same actions we see here: masturbation (often extravagantly inventive), quickie sex with prostitutes in cars, anonymous gay bathhouse encounters (all the way to the father–son clinch in *The River* [1997]). . . . One must grasp and experience the ambiguous 'fusion' of Shiang-chyi and Hsiao-kang in *The Wayward Cloud* in the context of the entire film, the entire series formed by this film, *What Time Is It There?* and the short *The Skywalk Is Gone* (2003), and even within the entire œuvre of Tsai." Cf. Lee,

"Pornography," 127. See also Balz, *"The Wayward Cloud"*: "During the film's screening at the Berlin Film Festival, many patrons left the theatre during the final scene, I assume in disgust. There's an undeniable perversity to the last ten minutes, something so nonchalantly deliberate and direct you yourself may want to find a dark, calm corner."

64. See Andrea Dworkin and Catharine MacKinnon, *Pornography and Civil Rights: A New Day for Women's Equality* (Minneapolis: Organizing against Pornography, 1988). *Videodrome*, DVD, directed by David Cronenberg (1983; New York: Criterion Collection, 2004).

65. Lee, "Pornography," 121.

66. Song Hwee Lim, "Manufacturing Orgasm: Visuality, Aurality, and Female Sexual Pleasure in Tsai Ming-liang's *The Wayward Cloud*," author's postprint on *Open Research Exeter*, 15, https://ore.exeter.ac.uk/repository/bitstream/handle/10871/11747/Song%20Lim%20JCC%202011.pdf. [Cf. Song Hwee Lim, "Manufacturing Orgasm: Visuality, Aurality, and Female Sexual Pleasure in Tsai Ming-liang's *The Wayward Cloud*," *Journal of Chinese Cinemas* 5, no. 2 (2011): 141–55.]

67. Lim, "Manufacturing Orgasm," 18–19.

68. In "Manufacturing Orgasm," Lim includes a note that "It is debatable whether Tsai can be accused of misogyny since his representation of the comatose body is not (female) gender specific. In his next film, *Heiyanquan/I Don't Want to Sleep Alone* (2006), Tsai introduces a male comatose body (played by Lee Kang-sheng) sexually abused by his mother forcing the hand of the household maid (played by Chen Shiang-chyi) into the disposable incontinent pants worn by the comatose body and masturbating him" (27n8).

69. *Boogie Nights*, DVD, directed by Paul Thomas Anderson (1997; Los Angeles: New Line Home Video, 1998).

70. See Lauren Rosewarne, "Radical Feminists' Objections to Sex Work Is Profoundly Un-feminist," *The Conversation*, August 8, 2017, https://theconversation.com/radical-feminists-objection-to-sex-work-is-profoundly-un-feminist-81333. For a comparison of the exploited work of porn actors and migrant laborers in Tsai's films, see See Chang, "Sleeping with Strangers," 256–57. See also Andrew Huang, "Interview with Tsai Ming-liang," *Taiwan News*, February 18, 2005, reprinted at http://interviewreprint.blogspot.com.

71. See Elena Gorfinkel, "Weariness, Waiting," 311–47. See also the Wild Bunch press kit for *The Wayward Cloud* available from: https://www.wildbunch.biz/movie/the-wayward-cloud/.

72. See Rehm, Joyard, and Rivière, eds., *Tsaï Ming-Liang*, which features an interview with Tsai in which he states directly, "Actually, water for me is love, that's what they lack. What I'm trying to show is very symbolic, it's their need for love" (113).

73. I am grateful to Fifi Neifei Ding for pointing this out to me. See Cao Xueqin, *The Dream of the Red Chamber*, trans. Henry Bencraft Joly (North Clarendon, Vt.: Tuttle/Periplus Editions, 2010).

74. Chang, "Gender Hierarchy," 38. See also the illuminating five-part series of articles on the semiotics of *The Wayward Cloud* by Harry Tuttle, *Screenville*, https://screenville.blogspot.com/2005/12/wayward-cloud-14.html.

75. Stephens, "Review: *I Don't Want to Sleep Alone*."

76. Johnston, "Butterfly Dream."

77. Conversation between the author, Tsai Ming-liang, and Jonathan (Te-Hsuan) Yeh, December 8, 2017, New Taipei City. See also Linda Jaivin interview with Tsai Ming-liang at the "Taiwan, the View from the South" conference at Australian National University (ANU), published to YouTube as "In Conversation with Director Tsai Ming-Lang: *Stray Dogs*," January 19, 2015, https://youtu.be/IlSrm5zJ2Ag.

78. Lee, "Pornography," 118. Cf. Corrado Neri, "Tsai Ming-liang and the Lost Emotions of the Flesh," *positions: east asia cultures critique* 16, no. 2 (Fall 2008): 389–407.

79. Halperin, *How to Be Gay*, 175–76. Compare Vivian Lee's description of the final porn-shoot scene in *The Wayward Cloud* as "almost comical" in its absurdity. Lee, "Pornography," 126.

80. On Tsai's mixture of high/low genres, see Lee, "Pornography"; and Bao, "Biomechanics."

81. Yeh and Davis, "Camping Out with Tsai Ming-liang," 235.

82. Yeh and Davis, "Camping Out with Tsai Ming-liang."

83. My thanks to Jonathan Te-hsuan Yeh for discussing this with me. The circulation of this translation can be seen here: 酷兒 & 敢曝 Queer & Camp": http://edumovie.culture.tw/activities_info.php?id=467 and in the theme of the 2017 Taiwan International Queer Film Festival, "酷兒 & 敢曝 Queer & Camp": https://en.tiqff.com/films/2017. See Chao, *Queer Representations*, 203–4; and Yeh, "Liangzhong 'Luying/yin' de Fangfa," 67–89.

84. Sedgwick, *Touching Feeling*, 149.

85. Sedgwick, *Touching Feeling*, 150.

86. In *Past Present* (2013).

87. Muñoz, *Disidentifications*, x.

88. See J. Hoberman, *On Jack Smith's Flaming Creatures* (New York: Granary Books, 2001). Cf. de Villiers, "Queer Camp, Jack Smith, and John Waters."

89. Steve Gallagher, "You Don't Know Jack," *Filmmaker*, Spring 2007, https://filmmakermagazine.com/archives/issues/spring2007/features/jack_smith.php. See also *Jack Smith and the Destruction of Atlantis*, DVD, directed by Mary Jordan (2006; London: Arts Alliance, 2008).

90. Chao, *Queer Representations*, 232, 241–42.

91. Richard Dyer, "It's Being So Camp as Keeps Us Going," in *Only Entertainment* (London: Routledge, 1992), 135–47; Chao, *Queer Representations*, 227, 238–41.

92. Sedgwick, *Tendencies*, 222. The Wild Bunch press kit for *The Wayward Cloud* includes the note: "There's always an ordinary-looking door—a secret door that you'd push open whenever no one's looking. You've never met anyone else inside, so you think you're the only person in the world who watches pornography."

93. See Pužar, "Soundtracks of Human Mimetic Sexual Play."

94. Cf. Chao, *Queer Representations*, 236.

95. Tim Robey, "Sex with Watermelons: Porn Meets Slow Cinema in *The Wayward Cloud*," *The Telegraph*, June 12, 2015, https://www.telegraph.co.uk/film/mubi/the_wayward_cloud/.

96. Helen Hester, *Beyond Explicit: Pornography and the Displacement of Sex* (Albany: State University of New York Press, 2014).

97. Linda Williams, "Pornography, Porno, Porn: Thoughts on a Weedy Field," *Porn Studies* 1, nos. 1–2 (2014): 36.

98. Moon, *Small Boy*, 15–16; Gayle Rubin, "Thinking Sex: Notes for a Radical Theory of the Politics of Sexuality" (1984), in *The Lesbian and Gay Studies Reader*, ed. Henry Abelove, Michèle Aina Barale, and David M. Halperin (New York: Routledge, 1993), 3–44.

99. I will return to Tsai's method of recycling in the conclusion to this book discussing the installation of *Stray Dogs at the Museum*. *Stray Dogs at the Museum: Tsai Ming-liang Solo Exhibition* (Taipei: Museum of National Taipei University of Education, 2016).

100. Guy Schaffer, "Queering Waste through Camp," *Discard Studies*, February 27, 2015, https://discardstudies.com/2015/02/27/queering-waste-through-camp/.

101. Schaffer, "Queering Waste through Camp."

102. Schaffer, "Queering Waste through Camp."

103. Lauran Whitworth, "*Goodbye Gauley Mountain*, Hello Eco-camp: Queer Environmentalism in the Anthropocene," *Feminist Theory* 20, no. 1 (2019): 73–92; quotation from abstract. See also Annie Sprinkle and Beth Stephens with Jennie Klein, *Assuming the Ecosexual Position: The Earth as Lover* (Minneapolis: University of Minnesota Press, 2021).

104. Whitworth, "*Goodbye Gauley Mountain*, Hello Eco-camp."

4. Different Time Zones

1. *The Tenant (Le locataire)*, DVD, directed by Roman Polanski (1976; Los Angeles: Paramount Home Video, 2003); *Three Colors Trilogy (Blue, White, Red) (Trois couleurs [Bleu, Blanc, Rouge])*, DVD, directed by Krzysztof Kieślowski

(1993–94; Los Angeles: Miramax, 2003); *Caché*, DVD, directed by Michael Haneke (2005; Culver City, Calif.: Sony Pictures Home Entertainment, 2006); *Amour*, DVD, directed by Michael Haneke (2012; Culver City, Calif.: Sony Pictures Home Entertainment, 2013).

2. Cameron, "Trajectories of Identification." Cf. Martin, "European Undead."

3. *Face (Visage)*, DVD, directed by Tsai Ming-liang (Paris: Rézo Films, 2009).

4. On French auteur theory and Tsai's approach to intertextuality and intratextuality (including his French reception), see Lim, "Positioning Auteur Theory," 223–45. See also Tsai, "Many Faces of Tsai Ming-liang," 141–60. On Tsai's success in France, see Chang, "Sleeping with Strangers," 263n4. Chang explains, "Since his fourth feature *The Hole*, commissioned by French TV station La Sept Arte in 1998, Tsai has been remarkably successful in obtaining both Taiwanese government's subsidy and foreign financial assistance. It is safe to say that Tsai's films have attracted more French than Taiwanese audiences. The first book on his oeuvre was actually written in French, published by Dis Voir in 1999. The book was later translated into Mandarin Chinese and English in 2001. What is more, Tsai received a distinguished medal of the Knight of Order of Arts and Letters from the French government in 2002" (263n4). In an interview with *Slant* magazine, Tsai discusses what European financing (especially Arte in France) has enabled in terms of his creative control over production and distribution: "From *The Hole* onward, my films have been French co-productions, which gave me the chance to start my own production company. From *What Time Is It There* onward, I began to control every aspect of my work, from production to distribution. This has given me utmost freedom." Dillard, "Interview."

5. *Le Voyage du Ballon Rouge*, DVD, directed by Hou Hsiao-hsien (2007); *Le Ballon Rouge*, DVD, directed by Albert Lamorisse (1956); *There Is Only One Sun*, video, directed by Wong Kar-wai (2007), available online: https://vimeo.com/28933554; *I Travelled 9000 Km to Give It to You* is included in *Chacun son cinéma, ou, Ce petit coup au coeur quand la lumière s'éteint et que le film commence*, DVD, curated by Gilles Jacob (Paris: StudioCanal, 2007); *In the Mood for Love (Faa yeung nin wa)*, DVD, directed by Wong Kar-wai (2000; New York: Criterion Collection, 2004) and *2046*, DVD, directed by Wong Kar-wai (2004; Culver City, Calif.: Sony Pictures Home Entertainment, 2005).

6. Bloom, *Contemporary Sino-French Cinemas*.

7. See Rachel Sagner Buurma and Laura Heffernan, "Notation after the 'Reality Effect': Remaking Reference with Roland Barthes and Sheila Heti," *Representations* 125, no. 1 (Winter 2014): 80–102. They coin the term "novels

of commission," which I adapt here for "films of commission." On Tsai's "homework" and scouting for *Visage*, see "Filmmaker Tsai Ming-liang on *Face* (2009)," *Asia Society*, April 5, 2010, https://youtu.be/8mxZTyCluUs.

8. John Urry, *The Tourist Gaze*, 2nd ed. (London: SAGE Publications, 2002). Urry explains, "When tourists see two people kissing in Paris what they capture in the gaze is 'timeless romantic Paris'" (3).

9. Andrew Sun, "Would You Drink Hot Water on a Scorching Summer's Day? Many Hongkongers Do," *South China Morning Post*, October 31, 2018, https://www.scmp.com/lifestyle/food-drink/article/2170974/would-you -drink-hot-water-scorching-summers-day-many.

10. See Barton, "Queer in Time."

11. Barton, "Queer in Time."

12. Cf. Martin, "*Vive L'Amour*: Eloquent Emptiness," 175–82, where she has more to say about space and queerness; *Queer Diaspora*; Gopinath, *Unruly Visions*; J. Jack Halberstam, *In a Queer Time and Place: Transgender Bodies, Subcultural Lives* (New York: New York University Press, 2005); and Shi-Yan Chao, "Performing Authorship."

13. See Martin, "European Undead," note 24.

14. Robin Wood argues that in *Rebels of the Neon God* (1992), "Lee's character might be seen as crypto-gay," and then "Lee's characters are explicitly gay (if perhaps hesitant)" in *Vive L'Amour* (1994) and *The River* (1997), but starting with *The Hole* (1998), "the Lee character becomes abruptly heterosexual" and in "Lee's subsequent roles he is consistently heterosexual—even, in *What Time Is It There?* (2001), mildly homophobic." Robin Wood, "Sleep Therapy," *Artforum* (May 2007): 70. I am skeptical whether crypto- versus explicitly gay is necessarily the best explanation for these earlier films, as previous chapters have suggested, but Wood is making this argument in order to point to the end of *I Don't Want to Sleep Alone* (2006) as suggesting "a 'free' sexuality, based purely on attraction and affection, hence not at all on traditional notions of gender, family, monogamy, and sexual difference—a film for our future, if we have one" (70). I agree, but I find this potential in the earlier films as well. Moreover, I am more closely aligned with Jean Ma's insistence that "The deceptive stability of the inside/outside binary of sexual identity offers little for the utopic imaginings of *Goodbye, Dragon Inn*, a film that moves far beyond the purview of what Song Hwee Lim terms an 'Anglo-American centric, identity-politics-based framework' that privileges the coming-out narrative as the *urform* of gay filmmaking," and I agree with her critique of "the tendency to impose an epistemology of the closet rooted in the West as the single standard against which gay liberationist enterprises in other parts of the world are to be measured as inevitably *retardataire* and inadequate

to the present." Ma, *Melancholy Drift*, 119. Lim, "Positioning Auteur Theory," 223–24, 240.

15. Martin, "European Undead."

16. Martin, "European Undead." Also see Mark Betz, "The Cinema of Tsai Ming-liang: A Modernist Genealogy," in *Reading Chinese Transnationalisms: Society, Literature, Film*, ed. Philip Holden and Maria Ng (Hong Kong: Hong Kong University Press, 2006), 161–72.

17. Martin, "European Undead."

18. See the description of the conference "Queer Migrations: Transnational Sexualities in Theory and Practice," convened by Geoffrey Maguire, Leila Mukhida, and Tiffany Page, November 23–27, 2020: http://www.crassh.cam .ac.uk/events/28576.

19. "Filmmaker Tsai Ming-liang on *Face* (2009)."

20. See Bloom, *Contemporary Sino-French Cinemas*, 93.

21. Lee Kang-sheng has directed *The Missing (Bu jian)* (2003), which was paired with Tsai's *Goodbye, Dragon Inn*, as well as the film *Help Me, Eros* (2007). *Help Me, Eros (Bang bang wo ai shen)*, film, directed by Lee Kang-sheng (2007; New York: Strand Releasing, 2008).

22. *Day for Night (La nuit américaine)*, directed by François Truffaut (1973; New York: Criterion Collection, 2015).

23. See Martin, "European Undead"; Ma, *Melancholy Drift*, 93. The credits of *What Time Is It There?* feature the dedication "To my father, and Lee Kang-Sheng's father."

24. See Freud, "Mourning and Melancholia," 16:243–58; cf. Flatley, *Affective Mapping*; and Barthes, *Mourning Diary*.

25. My translation. See Culture 8, "*Le Voyage du Ballon Rouge*," interview with Simon Iteanu, Juliette Binoche, and Vincent Julé (2008), https://youtu .be/7X9mIwY4SJU.

26. See de Villiers, "'Chinese Cheers.'" *Café Lumière (Kohi jiko)*, DVD, directed by Hou Hsiao-hsien (2003; New York: Fox Lorber, 2005).

27. Leo Goldsmith, "World Tourist," *Reverse Shot*, no. 26, http://www .reverseshot.com/article/8_flight_red_balloon.

28. Culture 8, "*Le Voyage du Ballon Rouge*."

29. See Martin, "European Undead." Cf. Buurma and Heffernan's invocation of Pierre Bourdieu's *Distinction: A Social Critique of the Judgment of Taste* (New York: Routledge, 1984), while also suggesting a different approach to "how meaning and value accrue around artworks and models of personhood through the ways people take note of and pay attention to them." Buurma and Heffernan, "Notation after the 'Reality Effect,'" 96.

30. On his approach to the Louvre, see Tsai Ming-liang, "On the Uses and Misuses of Cinema," with an introduction by Erik Bordeleau, trans. Beth Tsai,

Senses of Cinema, no. 58 (March 2011), http://sensesofcinema.com/2011/feature
-articles/on-the-uses-and-misuses-of-cinema/.

31. *Absolutely Fabulous* S4:E3 "Paris," television program, directed by Bob
Spiers, written by Jennifer Saunders, aired September 14, 2001 (BBC).

32. See Erik Morse's interview with Tsai about *Visage* where Tsai explains,
"Personally, I am more interested in the architectural elements of the Louvre;
film is also an architectural concept. I spent almost three years scouting the
various hidden locations; at first, the gallery didn't understand why I needed
access to ventilation pipes, sewer systems, or ancient wells no longer in use.
Luckily, I met a fireman who assisted me in exploring the various hidden
spaces. One of these discoveries was an abandoned sewer channel beneath the
plaza of the rear palace. It's a perfect size; although manmade, its stone surface possesses a kind of beauty that can only come with age. . . . For the scene
in the sewer, I was told that only seven people at a time were allowed in the
water, which made the shoot impossible. I lost my temper over this and told
the Louvre that we were filmmakers not schoolboys on a field trip to a museum.
After this, the museum became a bit more accommodating." Erik Morse, "Time
& Again," trans. Vincent Cheng, *Frieze*, no. 137 (March 2011), https://frieze
.com/article/time-again.

33. Highlighting miscommunication, Bloom notes that Lee Kang-sheng
doesn't recognize the name Mizoguchi when Léaud says it because he knows
the different, Mandarin version of the Chinese characters (kanji) as "Goukou."
Bloom, *Contemporary Sino-French Cinemas*, 96.

34. On Salomé and Orientalism, see Bram Dijkstra, *Idols of Perversity: Fantasies of Feminine Evil in Fin-de-Siècle Culture* (New York: Oxford University
Press, 1988).

35. Lim, *Tsai Ming-liang and a Cinema of Slowness*, 65; cf. Bloom, *Contemporary Sino-French Cinemas*, 93.

36. *All the Boys Are Called Patrick (Charlotte et Véronique, ou, Tous les garçons
s'appellent Patrick)*, film, directed by Jean-Luc Godard (1957; New York: Criterion Collection, 2004). We could also connect these scenes to a multilingual
pickup scene in Wong Kar-wai's *Chungking Express. Chungking Express (Chung
Hing sam lam)*, DVD, directed by Wong Kar-wai (1994; New York: Criterion
Collection, 2008).

37. The framing in the bushes echoes the framing in a scene from *Day for
Night* where a member of the crew tells the director (played by Truffaut) that
he must leave the set because his mother has died.

38. "Filmmaker Tsai Ming-liang on *Face* (2009)."

39. See Volker Hummel, "*The Missing*: An Interview with Lee Kang-sheng,"
Senses of Cinema, no. 32 (July 2004), http://sensesofcinema.com/2004/53rd
-melbourne-international-film-festival/lee_kang_sheng/.

40. See the review of *Visage* titled "Ming-liang Tsai's self-portrait" on imdb .com by someone who attended a retrospective of Tsai's films and heard Tsai introduce the film: https://www.imdb.com/title/tt1262420/; reviewer profile "j-m-d-b": https://www.imdb.com/user/ur4334960/?ref_=tt_urv.

41. Buurma and Heffernan, "Notation after the 'Reality Effect,'" 88.

42. Buurma and Heffernan, "Notation after the 'Reality Effect,'" 87. Roland Barthes, *The Preparation of the Novel, Lectures, Courses, and Seminars at the Collège de France (1978–1979 and 1979–1980),* trans. Kate Briggs (New York: Columbia University Press, 2010), 20.

43. Buurma and Heffernan, "Notation after the 'Reality Effect,'" 88.

44. Buurma and Heffernan, "Notation after the 'Reality Effect,'" 89; 88; 97.

45. Cf. the scathing criticism of the Louvre's commission of Tsai's *Visage* by Harry Tuttle (nom de plume of Benoit Rouilly), "Backstabbing French Commission," *Screenville,* November 25, 2009, http://screenville.blogspot.com/20 09/11/backstabbing-french-commission.html.

46. Buurma and Heffernan, "Notation after the 'Reality Effect,'" 89.

47. See Lim, *Tsai Ming-liang and a Cinema of Slowness,* 111–12. Lim connects this scene with Lee, Tsai, and the stags to a Buddhist idea of life as fleeting or drifting in Tsai's work.

48. See Bloom's *Contemporary Sino-French Cinemas* for a thorough accounting of the intertextual connotations each of the actresses bring with them to Tsai's film.

49. Lim, "Positioning Auteur Theory."

50. We could also connect the flooded apartment in *Rebels of the Neon God* to the flooded apartment in Wong Kar-wai's *Chungking Express* (1994), featuring a kind of "pathetic fallacy" comparable to Tsai's treatment of water in several of his films: a wet hand towel is described as crying and "still an emotionally charged towel." This can in turn be linked to the description of a derelict house "crying" in Tsai's final feature film *Stray Dogs.*

51. For an analysis of this haunting ending, see Ma, *Melancholy Drift,* 93.

52. Noting "the stereotypes of Taiwanese film most familiar to Western audiences in film festivals and art houses," Brian Hu discusses how "*The Skywalk Is Gone* employs many of the long takes characteristic of the Taiwan New Cinema movement. The extreme long takes evoke Hou's films, and the fragmentation of urban space into squares of windows and buildings is reminiscent of Yang's *Taipei Story* (1985) and *Yi Yi* (2000). However, as mentioned earlier, the takes are exaggeratedly long (a staple of Tsai's cinema) and the fragmentations are ridiculous to the point that they become optical illusions that fool the viewer. This playful, self-mocking attitude towards the traditions of Taiwanese art film shows that the movement as we know it is dead." Hu, "Goodbye City."

53. This quote is the epigraph to Martin's "European Undead," taken from Tsai Ming-liang's "Director's Notes" on the *What Time Is It There?* DVD.

54. Bloom, *Contemporary Sino-French Cinemas,* 105.

55. See Cameron, "Trajectories of Identification."

56. Bloom, *Contemporary Sino-French Cinemas,* 103.

57. Ahmed, *Queer Phenomenology,* 170.

58. "Filmmaker Tsai Ming-liang on *Face* (2009)."

59. See the remarkable "A Note on 'Salomé'" by Robert Ross, where he explains that Oscar Wilde's "'SALOMÉ' has made the author's name a household word wherever the English language is not spoken. Few English plays have such a peculiar history. Written in French in 1892 it was in full rehearsal by Madame Bernhardt at the Palace Theatre when it was prohibited by the Censor. Oscar Wilde immediately announced his intention of changing his nationality, a characteristic jest, which was only taken seriously, oddly enough, in Ireland. The interference of the Censor has seldom been more popular or more heartily endorsed by English critics. . . . When 'Salomé' was translated into English by Lord Alfred Douglas, the illustrator, Aubrey Beardsley, shared some of the obloquy heaped on Wilde. . . . It has been remarked that Wilde confuses Herod the Great (Mat. xi. 1), Herod Antipas (Mat. xiv. 3), and Herod Agrippa (Acts xiii), but the confusion is intentional, as in mediæval mystery plays Herod is taken for a type, not an historical character, and the criticism is about as valuable as that of people who laboriously point out the anachronisms in Beardsley's designs." Project Gutenberg ebook of *Salomé,* by Oscar Wilde, https://www.gutenberg.org/files/42704/42704-h/42704-h.htm.

60. Sedgwick, *Touching Feeling,* 150.

61. Sobchack, "Breadcrumbs in the Forest," 26.

62. Gender difference is central to Sobchack's consideration of disorientation (along with some discussion of race and class) but queerness is relegated to a footnote. Sobchack, "Breadcrumbs in the Forest," 32n28.

63. Cf. Barthes, *Pleasure of the Text,* 14.

64. Sedgwick, *Tendencies,* 20.

65. Bloom, *Contemporary Sino-French Cinemas,* 104.

66. Barton's reading of the cemetery scene in *What Time* also stresses queer intimacy and queer temporality: "Standing in the cemetery where Truffaut lies, Tsai creates a concrete connection between the Paris-obsessed Hsiao-kang and Shiang-chyi. . . . The film posits a juxtaposition between film-historic time, through Léaud and Truffaut's presence, and a kind of queer time, through Léaud's presence in Tsai's film. As Truffaut cared for Léaud during his young adult life—paying for his apartment and lifestyle and giving him work on film sets—the two men are thought by some to have shared a homoerotic relationship, or at least a homoromantic one. Léaud's presence in *What*

Time Is It There? therefore signals a kind of longing for a queer film history. By including him, Tsai creates a genealogy between the French New Wave and the Second Taiwanese New Wave that is queer in its inflections." Barton, "Queer in Time."

67. Bloom, *Contemporary Sino-French Cinemas*, 102–4. On the film *Salomé* and its queer cast reputation, see Jennifer Horne, "Alla Nazimova," in *Women Film Pioneers Project*, ed. Jane Gaines, Radha Vatsal, and Monica Dall'Asta (New York: Columbia University Libraries, 2013), Center for Digital Research and Scholarship, https://wfpp.cdrs.columbia.edu/pioneer/ccp-alla-nazimova/; Kenneth Anger, *Hollywood Babylon* (San Francisco: Straight Arrow Books, 1975), 113; and "*Salomé* (1923 film)," https://en.wikipedia.org/wiki/Salomé_(1923_film). *Salomé*, DVD, directed by Charles Bryant and Alla Nazimova (1923; Los Angeles: Image Entertainment, 2003). On the fate of Oscar Wilde's grave, see Dalya Alberge, "Oscar Wilde's Lipstick-Covered Paris Tomb to Be Protected," *The Guardian*, November 26, 2011, https://www.theguardian.com/culture/2011/nov/27/oscar-wilde-grave-paris-cemetery.

68. See "Gay Cruising Areas in Paris," https://www.queereurope.com/cruising-map-paris/. On the long history of cruising in the Jardin des Tuileries, see Espinoza, *Cruising*, 52–53.

69. "Filmmaker Tsai Ming-liang on *Face* (2009)." Cf. Erik Bordeleau, "Lee Kang-sheng et Tsai Ming-liang: Une relation idiorythmique?" *Hors Champ*, September 7, 2011. Cf. Bordeleau, "Care for Opacity."

70. *Alphaville (Alphaville, une étrange aventure de Lemmy Caution)*, DVD, directed by Jean-Luc Godard (1965; New York: Criterion Collection, 1998).

71. See the New York Film Festival page for *Your Face*: https://www.filmlinc.org/nyff2018/films/your-face/.

72. Bloom, *Contemporary Sino-French Cinemas*, 93; cf. "Laetitia Casta," *Wikipedia*, https://en.wikipedia.org/wiki/Laetitia_Casta.

73. Gilles Deleuze, *Cinema 1: The Movement Image*, trans. Hugh Tomlinson and Barbara Habberjam (Minneapolis: University of Minnesota Press, 1986), 103.

74. Deleuze, *Cinema 1*, 99.

75. Deleuze, *Cinema 1*, 99.

76. *Persona*, DVD, directed by Ingmar Bergman (1966; New York: Criterion Collection, 2014).

77. Deleuze, *Cinema 1*, 99.

78. Deleuze, *Cinema 1*, 100.

79. Ahmed, *Queer Phenomenology*, 171.

80. See the entry "Face (sociological concept)," *Psychology Wiki*, https://psychology.wikia.org/wiki/Face_(sociological_concept).

81. See "Vogue (Madonna song)," *Wikipedia,* https://en.wikipedia.org/wiki/Vogue_(Madonna_song).

82. "Gaining and Losing Face in China," *China Culture Corner,* October 10, 2013, http://chinaculturecorner.com/2013/10/10/face-in-chinese-business/. Thanks to Yongan Wu for sharing this information.

83. "Face (sociological concept)."

84. Chao, *Queer Representations,* 212. See also Martin, *Situating Sexualities,* 196–205.

85. Sedgwick, *Touching Feeling,* 149. Cf. Sontag, *Against Interpretation,* 280; 290–91.

86. Roland Barthes, *Empire of Signs,* trans. Richard Howard (New York: Farrar, Straus and Giroux, 1982), 102. For a brilliant reading of Barthes and queerness/Orientalism in *Empire of Signs,* see Benjamin Hiramatsu Ireland, "Memoirs of a Gaysha: Roland Barthes's Queer Japan," *Barthes Studies,* no. 4 (2018), http://sites.cardiff.ac.uk/barthes/files/2018/11/HIRAMATSU-IRELAND-Memoirs-of-a-Gaysha.pdf.

87. *Irma Vep,* DVD, directed by Olivier Assayas (1996; New York: Kino Lorber, 2017).

88. "Filmmaker Tsai Ming-liang on *Face* (2009)." Cf. Tuttle, "Backstabbing French Commission."

89. Buurma and Heffernan, "Notation after the 'Reality Effect,'" 89.

90. Bloom, *Contemporary Sino-French Cinemas,* 92.

91. Ahmed, *Queer Phenomenology,* chapter 3 (109–56).

5. Haunted, Rented, Queer Spaces

1. De Certeau, *Practice of Everyday Life,* 103.

2. Here I have included some of the locations of Tsai's late "Walker" series, including *No No Sleep* (2015) set in Tokyo, *Journey to the West* (2014) set in Marseille, and *The Walker* (2012) set in Hong Kong. See David Eng, "Slowness as an Act of Rebellion: On Tsai Ming-liang's *Walker,*" *Entropy,* May 22, 2014, https://entropymag.org/slowness-as-an-act-of-rebellion-on-tsai-ming-liangs-walker/. While most of Tsai's films in Taiwan are set in Taipei/New Taipei City (focusing on the areas of Ximending and Yonghe), he has also set films in two other major cities, Kaohsiung and Taichung.

3. I say *allegedly* final because Tsai has gone on to make a feature-length film *Days (Rizi)* (2020). Instead, Tsai has retired from "commercial" feature filmmaking. See Hu, "Post-Retirement Films of Tsai Ming-liang." See also Neil Young, "Of Cabbages and Kings: Tsai Ming-liang's 'Stray Dogs,'" *Neil Young's Film Lounge,* https://www.jigsawlounge.co.uk/film/reviews/straydogs/.

4. De Certeau, *Practice of Everyday Life,* xix.

5. Lisiak, "Making Sense of Absence," 849.

6. Carrefour is a French multinational corporation known for "hypermar-ket" chains. It has a major presence in Taiwan, which could be connected to the themes of globalization in Tsai's films discussed in chapter 4.

7. Tony Rayns, "Review: *Stray Dogs*," *Film Comment*, May–June 2014, https://www.filmcomment.com/article/review-stray-dogs-tsai-ming-liang/.

8. I am indebted to Sara Ahmed's connection of Michael Moon's concept of sexual disorientation to questions of space and queer phenomenology. Ahmed, *Queer Phenomenology*; cf. Moon, *Small Boy*, 15–16.

9. On Tsai and Lee's relationship as *idiorrhythmic*, see Bordeleau, "Une rela-tion idiorythmique?"

10. The DVD is also included in the book documenting the event, *Stray Dogs at the Museum*.

11. Muñoz, *Cruising Utopia*, 40.

12. Muñoz, *Cruising Utopia*, 43. Derrida, *Specters of Marx*. Cf. Davis, "Haunt-ology, Spectres, and Phantoms," 373–79.

13. *The Polymath, or, The Life and Opinions of Samuel R. Delany, Gentleman*, DVD, directed by Fred Barney Taylor (New York: Maestro Media, 2007). See de Villiers, "Documentary and the Anamnesis of Queer Space." See also Eliz-abeth Purchell's brilliant gay adult video collage *Ask Any Buddy* (2020). As the website explains, "The piece uses fragments from 126 theatrical feature films spanning the years 1968–86 to create a kaleidoscopic day in the life snapshot of urban gay culture in the era—or at least how it looked in the movies. From casual tearoom cruising to actual police raids, *Ask Any Buddy* uses rare foot-age shot at dozens of real bathhouses, bars, movie theaters, pride parades and legendary hotspots like New York's West Side Piers to explore both the sex film genre's unique blend of fantasy and reality and its role in documenting a subculture that was just starting to come into visibility in the years immedi-ately following the Stonewall Riots." Purchell's "remix" approach to this visual archive has remarkably disorienting and reorienting effects on queer time and space/place, in some ways complementary to my discussions of Tsai's films' queer "reparative reading."

14. De Certeau, *Practice of Everyday Life*, 96.

15. In an interview, Tsai explained: "when I was scouting locations for *What Time Is It There?* I discovered the theater in a small town outside of Taipei. I got to know the owner and shot the segment there. A few months later I ran into the owner again and he told me that he was going to have to close the theater. Audiences were small and it was now mainly a cruising place for gay men. It was just an impulse—I leased the theater for six months. I had no idea what I was going to do and thought I'd just make a short film, but I wanted to try to capture something of it on film. I feel like it was the theater that was calling me to make the film." Reichert and Syngle, "Ghost Writer:

An Interview with Tsai Ming-liang." For pictures of the "ruins" of the old movie theater, see: https://lenpep.wordpress.com/2018/02/01/fuhe-grand-the atre-福和大戲院/.

16. See Chan, "*Goodbye, Dragon Inn,*" 89–103.

17. Reichert and Syngle, "Ghost Writer."

18. Delany, *Times Square Red.*

19. Hu, "Goodbye City."

20. See Jennifer Pan, "Tsai Ming-Liang's *Wayward* Boundaries," *Asian American Writers' Workshop: The Margins,* July 18, 2012, https://aaww.org/tsai-ming-liangs-wayward-boundaries/.

21. Rayns, "Review: *Stray Dogs.*"

22. Rayns, "Review: *Stray Dogs.*"

23. Rayns, "Review: *Stray Dogs.*"

24. Sigmund Freud, "The Uncanny," in *The Standard Edition of the Complete Psychological Works of Sigmund Freud,* ed. and trans. James Strachey (1919; rpt. London: Hogarth Press, 1955), 17:219–53.

25. Addressing questions of hypocrisy, cultural capital, and ethics, Chen Tai-song explains, "there are some people who have been accusing of Tsai Ming-liang for his film *Stray Dogs* and his collaboration with Farglory Construction Group; they think it collapses the legitimacy of Tsai's using this film to depict the underprivileged. . . . The date was February 28. Farglory Capital Apartments hosted a talk, 'Expounding on *Stray Dogs,*' at the site of its Xinzhuang residential development, to celebrate the Golden Horse award won by *Stray Dogs,* in which the production of which the Farglory Group had supplied location permission and advertisement placards for filming. . . . Beyond the walking advertisement of having Lee's character hold up continuously their advertising placard in the movie, at the minimum this would generate a cultured image of supporting the arts that would suffice to package the construction product, along with an added aura of celebrity status generated by Tsai. . . . Even if the film contains critiques on urban alienations, on the construction companies' price-war effects on housing, and on the endless demands of land capital that have constituted the marginalization of the disadvantaged minority, the tone of this film have [sic] remained overall subtle and reserved." Chen Tai-song, "Emotive Images and Its Reproduction in *Stray Dogs,*" in *Stray Dogs at the Museum: Tsai Ming-liang Solo Exhibition* (Taipei: Museum of National Taipei University of Education, 2016), 173.

26. See Erik Bordeleau, "Soulful Sedentarity: Tsai Ming-Liang at Home at the Museum," *Studies in European Cinema* 10, nos. 2–3 (2013): 179–94. On Tsai's running theme of "homelessness at home," see Hong, "Anywhere but Here," 159–81.

27. Rayns, "Review: *Stray Dogs.*"

28. Rayns, "Review: *Stray Dogs*."

29. "Excursion" or "a day out" is also a common composition writing assignment, as we see the children working on late in the film. For a more thorough intertextual reading of the Chinese, English, and French titles of the film, see Louis Lo, "Enduring the Long Take: Tsai Ming-liang's *Stray Dogs* and the Dialectical Image," *CLCWeb: Comparative Literature and Culture* 21, no. 5 (2019), https://docs.lib.purdue.edu/cgi/viewcontent.cgi?article=3264&context=clcweb.

30. Rayns, "Review: *Stray Dogs*."

31. *Face (Visage)*, DVD, directed by Tsai Ming-liang (Paris: Rézo Films, 2009).

32. Muñoz, *Cruising Utopia*, 43.

33. *Tokyo Godfathers*, DVD, directed by Kon Satoshi (2003; New York: Sony Pictures Entertainment, 2004).

34. Walsh, "Interview with Tsai." Cf. Chen, "Emotive Images," 173.

35. See Louis Lo's critique of the idea that Tsai is aiming for audience "empathy" with the suffering of the homeless figure in "Enduring the Long Take."

36. J. Hoberman, "'Disorder' and 'Stray Dogs' Capture the Look of Cities Falling Apart," *New York Times*, April 9, 2015, https://www.nytimes.com/2015/04/12/movies/homevideo/disorder-and-stray-dogs-capture-the-look-of-cities-falling-apart.html.

37. See, for example, *The Walking Dead*, television series (AMC 2010–2022); *Survival Family (Sabaibaru famirî)*, film, directed by Yaguchi Shinobu (2016; Tokyo: Toho Company, 2017); *Train to Busan (Busanhaeng)*, DVD, directed by Yeon Sang-ho (2016; Plano, Tex.: Well Go USA Entertainment, 2017). Tsai's approach to disaster/dystopia/survival genres is closer to Lauren Berlant's discussion of "living on" in *Cruel Optimism*.

38. Delany, *Times Square Red*, 90.

39. Jaivin, "In Conversation with Director Tsai."

40. Cf. Biro, "Perhaps the Flood," 83.

41. *Stray Dogs* press kit (2013) qtd. in Lisiak, "Making Sense of Absence." On the economic context of the unfinished construction site in *I Don't Want to Sleep Alone*, see Maitra, "In the Shadow of the Homoglobal," 335–36.

42. See the discussion of Detroit "ruin porn" in David Church, "Queer Ethics, Urban Spaces, and the Horrors of Monogamy in *It Follows*," *Cinema Journal* 57, no. 3 (Spring 2018): 3–28. For an "urban exploration" project documenting derelict movie theaters in Taiwan that I believe rises above "ruin porn," see the blog *Spectral Codex*, https://spectralcodex.com/collections/taiwan-theaters/.

43. On the suffix "porn," see Hester, *Beyond Explicit*.

44. Cf. Lisiak's claim that "Tsai depicts, but does not romanticize subversive urban behaviours. Neither does he fetishize urban ruins. The lives of his

protagonists who try to get by with their lives in dilapidated buildings are hardly enviable. Tsai shies away from poverty porn and aestheticization of urban blight." Lisiak, "Making Sense of Absence," 849.

45. Walsh, "Interview with Tsai."

46. In "Enduring the Long Take," Lo explains how the mural was made by "Taiwanese artist Kao Jun-Honn in a separate project *Taiwan Motor Transport/Return* (臺汽/回到), and was discovered accidentally by Tsai. Kao's work is part of 'The Ruin Image Crystal Project' (廢墟影 像晶體計畫) in 2013. . . . He enlarged a historical photograph titled *Lalung, Formosa*, taken by a Scottish journalist, John Thomson, who visited Taiwan in 1871. . . . Kao's act of reproducing a pre-colonial, orientalized image of the 'beautiful island' via the eye of a western photographer on the wall of the Material House of Taiwan Motor Transport Co. Ltd. in present-day Taiwan is charged with criticism. Both the gaze of the colonizers (though Scotland did not colonize Taiwan) and the neoliberal economy of present-day Taiwan are problematized. The mural is reproduced in charcoal, with the two aboriginal children omitted. As a Taiwanese subject, Kao's act of reclaiming a lost history by reproducing and appropriating a politically-charged colonial image is confronted with the ephemeral nature of the ruined site where the mural is drawn. Different layers of temporality are juxtaposed." See also Young, "Of Cabbages and Kings."

47. Lo explains, "The dilapidated building was abandoned in 1995; the state-own[ed] company privatized in 2001 and dissolved after ten years. Both Kao and Tsai took advantage of its ruined state before the commencement of demolition and construction. While Kao's deliberate attempt to repossess Taiwan's past highlights its failed present, Tsai inserts himself into the historical discourse by incorporating the mural into his film. Not surprisingly, the building was demolished in 2017, leaving the film the only memorial of the mural. The film serves as an archive of the disappeared mural which itself records layers of alternative histories, reminding the audience that understanding has to be informed by a sense of historical co-existence which allows different historical narratives in dialogue with each other." Lo, "Enduring the Long Take."

48. See Lisiak, "Making Sense of Absence"; Tuan, *Space and Place*; Ackbar Abbas, *Hong Kong: Culture and the Politics of Disappearance* (Minneapolis: University of Minnesota Press, 1997); Ma, *Melancholy Drift*.

49. *The Polymath*; *Still Life (San xia hao ren)*, DVD, directed by Jia Zhangke (2006; New York: New Yorker Films, 2008); *Disorder (xianshi shi guoqu de weilei)*, DVD, directed by Huang Weikei (2009; dGenerate Films Collection/Icarus Films, 2012). J. Hoberman links Tsai's *Stray Dogs* with Huang's *Disorder* in his review, "'Disorder' and 'Stray Dogs' Capture the Look of Cities Falling Apart."

50. De Villiers, "Documentary and the Anamneses of Queer Space." Cf. Church, "Queer Ethics," 24–26. Church notes the irony that "The connotations of ruin porn in *It Follows*'s Detroit setting become more notable (and even literalized) . . . as it was precisely the ruination of old urban centers that opened their economically impoverished spaces to reclamation by queer patrons forming covert communities organized around public sex" (24). This suggests "both a ruin-porn aesthetic and the potential for such postindustrial spaces to be used for the very sorts of open, polyvalent sex practices that would help diffuse the monster's threat" within the plot of *It Follows* (25). *It Follows*, film, directed by David Robert Mitchell (2014; New York: RADiUS-TWC, 2015). We could link Church's reading of *It Follows* in terms of queer ethics back to Tsai's similarly gothic but also radically queer treatment of the ethics of cruising in *Goodbye, Dragon Inn*.

51. Jaivin, "In Conversation with Director Tsai."

52. Johnston, "Butterfly Dream." For a critique of the *huaqiao* category, see Shih, "Theory, Asia, and the Sinophone," 480.

53. See Gorfinkel, "To Extend into the Beyond."

54. "Living Where No One Lives," poem included in the brochure for the Venice Biennale 2017 installation of *The Deserted*, VR film, directed by Tsai Ming-liang (New Taipei City: Homegreen Films, 2017). Quotation used with permission from Homegreen Films.

55. Barthes, *How to Live Together*; Roland Barthes, *A Lover's Discourse: Fragments*, trans. Richard Howard (New York: Farrar, Straus and Giroux, 1978).

56. David Greven, "Unlovely Spectacle: D. A. Miller on *Call Me by Your Name*," *Film Int.*, March 13, 2018, http://filmint.nu/?p=23937; D. A. Miller, "Elio's Education," *Los Angeles Review of Books*, February 19, 2018, https://lareviewofbooks.org/article/elios-education/. David Halperin praises Paul Morrison for "exhorting us not to allow sex to degenerate into love" in his endorsement for Morrison's *The Explanation for Everything: Essays on Sexual Subjectivity* (New York: New York University Press, 2002); Jane Ward's "Against Gay Love: This One Goes Out to the Queers," is the final chapter of her book *Not Gay: Sex between Straight White Men* (New York: New York University Press, 2015).

57. See de Villiers, *Opacity and the Closet*.

58. See Nicholas de Villiers, "The Amicable Return of Roland Barthes," *University of Minnesota Press Blog*, July 18, 2012, https://uminnpressblog.com/2012/07/18/the-amicable-return-of-roland-barthes/.

59. See Jonathan Romney, "Film of the Week: *Afternoon*," *Film Comment*, April 1, 2016, https://www.filmcomment.com/blog/film-week-afternoon-tsai-ming-liang/. See also Nadin Mai, "*Afternoon*—Tsai Ming-liang (2016)," *Art(s) of Slow Cinema*, August 6, 2019, https://theartsofslowcinema.com/2019/08/06/afternoon-tsai-ming-liang-2016/.

60. Cf. Hee Wai-Siam, "Coming Out in the Mirror: Rethinking Corporeality and Auteur Theory with Regard to the Films of Tsai Ming-liang," in *Transnational Chinese Cinema: Corporeality, Desire, and Ethics of Failure,* ed. Brian Bergen-Aurand, Mary Mazzilli, Hee Wai-Siam (Piscataway, NJ: Transaction Publishers, 2014), 113–36. While I find Hee's essay compelling in terms of how he reads Lee as Tsai's mirror reflection in his films, I diverge here from his reading of Tsai and Lee's identities and relationship in relation to "the closet."

61. See Hughes, "A State of Uncertainty."

62. Cf. Chen Tai-song, "A Shaping Image: Perspective on *Stray Dogs at the Museum—Tsai Ming-liang Solo Exhibition*," in *Stray Dogs at the Museum,* 176–79; 178.

63. See Barthes, *How to Live Together;* and Bordeleau, "Une relation idiorythmique?"

64. Lim, *Tsai Ming-liang and a Cinema of Slowness.* See also the Fandor video *Tsai Ming-liang and Lee Kang-sheng Are a Perfect Partnership,* https://www.youtube.com/watch?v=zmhkXl8ObXM.

65. Michel Foucault, "Friendship as a Way of Life," in *Ethics: Subjectivity, and Truth (Essential Works of Foucault, 1954–1984),* ed. Paul Rabinow, 3 vols. (New York: New Press, 1998), 1:136. See also Tom Roach, *Friendship as a Way of Life: Foucault, AIDS, and the Politics of Shared Estrangement* (Albany: State University of New York Press, 2012).

66. Samuel R. Delany, *The Motion of Light in Water: Sex and Science Fiction Writing in the East Village* (Minneapolis: University of Minnesota Press, 2004).

67. Nadin Mai highlights two other metalevel comments: "Does this conversation have to be so miserable?" and "I just feel like expressing my gratitude toward you." Mai, *"Afternoon."*

68. Carol Mavor, *Reading Boyishly: Roland Barthes, J. M. Barrie, Jacques Henri Lartigue, Marcel Proust, and D. W. Winnicott* (Durham, N.C.: Duke University Press, 2008), 155. See also Diana Knight, *Barthes and Utopia: Space, Travel, Writing* (Oxford: Oxford University Press, 1997).

69. Cf. Yip Wai Yee, "After Suffering a Stroke, Taiwanese Actor Lee Kang-sheng Is Grateful for Any Role," *Straits Times,* October 12, 2016, https://www.straitstimes.com/lifestyle/entertainment/after-suffering-a-stroke-taiwanese-actor-lee-kang-sheng-is-grateful-for-any. Yip explains, "This is not the first gay character he [Lee] has portrayed, having also played gay men in films such as *Rebels of the Neon God* (1992) and *The River* (1997). 'I used to mind it when directors kept giving me only gay roles because I was afraid of being typecast. But now, I don't complain. As long as the script is good, that's good enough for me,' says the actor who has never revealed his sexual orientation." We could, of course, complicate the assignment of these characters as "gay," in line with

the discussion of this issue in chapter 1 (the opacity of the actor's orientation is also worth noting).

70. See Lisiak, "Making Sense of Absence": "In *Goodbye, Dragon Inn,* shot entirely in a Taipei movie theatre, the first sentence is uttered 45 minutes into the film and even then it is rather vague. . . . The absence of speech in Tsai's films is often tightly related to the protagonist's status as an outsider. Tsai's protagonists are underdogs in one way or another, be it because they are new in town *(What Time, I Don't Want To),* suffering from a mysterious disease *(River),* homeless *(Vive l'Amour, Stray Dogs)* or working semi-legal jobs *(The Wayward Cloud, Vive l'Amour).* In *What Time,* Shiang-chyi (Chen Shiang-chyi) is new in Paris. She understands neither the language nor the local rules of conduct in urban space" (843–44).

71. See Romney, "Film of the Week: *Afternoon.*" Mai also notes how "*Afternoon* is almost one-sided. The way we know Lee from Tsai's films is very much the way he is in real life. He is quiet, withdrawn, shows little desire. Over the course of the film, we learn that his film personnages are his true self (minus the sexual orientation). Watching him as a conversation partner is fascinating, although he isn't doing or saying much. It's more about his body language and the few sentences he does say ('You should leave the house more often.')." Mai, "*Afternoon.*"

72. Plato, *The Collected Dialogues of Plato, Including the Letters,* ed. Edith Hamilton and Huntington Cairns (Princeton, NJ: Princeton University Press, 2005). Maurice Blanchot, *The One Who Was Standing Apart from Me,* trans. Lydia Davis (Barrytown, N.Y.: Station Hill Press, 1989).

73. See Chao, *Queer Representations,* 210–13; *Yang ± Yin: Gender in Chinese Cinema* (1996), film, directed by Stanley Kwan, available at: https://archive .org/details/kwan-final. See also Chia-Chi Wu, "Queering Chinese-Language Cinemas: Stanley Kwan's *Yang+ Yin: Gender in Chinese Cinema,*" *Screen* 51, no. 1 (Spring 2010): 38–53. See also Martin, *Situating Sexualities.* For important recent discussion of kinship and the limitations of the out/closeted dichotomy in the context of Taiwan, see Amy Brainer, "New Identities or New Intimacies? Rethinking 'Coming Out' in Taiwan through Cross-Generational Ethnography," *Sexualities* 21, nos. 5–6 (2018): 914–31.

74. *My New Friends (Wo xin renshi de pengyou),* television program, directed by Tsai Ming-liang (1995). See Lim, *Celluloid Comrades,* 135–36; Rojas, "'Nezha Was Here,'" 63–89.

75. See "TEDDY AWARD Ceremony 2020": https://www.youtube.com/ watch?v=W_Wi0Od7a3o&t=2420s; see also the Teddy Award website for *Days:* https://www.teddyaward.tv/en/program?tag=2020-02-29&id_film=855.

76. See *Tsai Ming-liang and Lee Kang-sheng Are a Perfect Partnership.* On bounded intimacy, see Elizabeth Bernstein, *Temporarily Yours: Intimacy,*

Authenticity, and the Commerce of Sex (Chicago: University of Chicago Press, 2007).

Conclusion

1. See Bordeleau, "Soulful Sedentarity," 179–94. Cf. Tsai, "Many Faces of Tsai Ming-liang," 141–60.

2. In 2020, Tsai did in fact release another feature-length film, *Days.* See Hughes, "A State of Uncertainty."

3. Lee Kang-sheng's character smothers then destroys and eats a Taiwanese cabbage his daughter had "personified" with a face drawn on with lipstick. For a reading of the affective intensity of this enigmatic scene, see Lo, "Enduring the Long Take." Cf. Young, "Of Cabbages and Kings."

4. Tsai Ming-liang, "Tsai Ming-liang's Notes," in *Stray Dogs at the Museum: Tsai Ming-liang Solo Exhibition,* 105.

5. *SLEEPCINEMAHOTEL,* International Film Festival Rotterdam, https://iffr.com/en/2018/films/sleepcinemahotel. See also Giovanni Marchini Camia, "Ghosts in the Machine: A Night at the 'Hotel' Where Films Become Dreams," *The Guardian,* February 2, 2018; Beth Tsai has explored the link between Tsai and Apichatpong Weerasethakul's "sleep-in cinema" installations in "Transnational Spectator, Transmedia Exhibition: Introducing Sleep-in Cinema Where Films Become Dreams" (Paper presented to the Society for Cinema and Media Studies conference, Seattle, March 13, 2019). A fruitful conversation with shared references to Tsai and Apichatpong also emerged between two panels at the 2021 Society for Cinema and Media Studies conference (online): "Night Moves: Collective Intimacies of Sleep Media," chaired by Alanna Thain, with a presentation on Tsai by Lakshmi Padmanabhan, and the panel I cochaired with Beth Tsai titled "Sleepy Cinema: Affect, Audience, Embodiment," also featuring presentations by Jean Ma and Elena Gorfinkel. On Apichatpong's admiration for Tsai, see the documentary *Past Present,* directed by Saw Tiong Guan (2013, video courtesy of the director). Apichatpong W. also praised Tsai's *Goodbye, Dragon Inn* as "THE best film of the last 125 years" on Twitter, a statement that has been used in publicity for the film: https://twitter.com/kickthe machine/status/1324578915252228097?lang=en.

6. On the history of "expanded cinema," see Valie Export, "Expanded Cinema as Expanded Reality," *Senses of Cinema,* no. 28 (October 2003), http://sensesofcinema.com/2003/peter-tscherkassky-the-austrian-avant-garde/ex panded_cinema/.

7. Tsai Ming-liang, poetic notation, in *Stray Dogs at the Museum: Tsai Ming-liang Solo Exhibition,* 105.

8. Chang Hsiao-hung, "Slow Walk in Museum," in *Stray Dogs at the Museum: Tsai Ming-liang Solo Exhibition,* 164–65; 165.

9. Chang Hsiao-hung, "Museum Is Cinema," in *Stray Dogs at the Museum: Tsai Ming-liang Solo Exhibition*, 166–69; 168.

10. Sing Song-yong, "The Continuous Crisscrossing Shimmer: On *Stray Dogs at the Museum: Tsai Ming-liang Solo Exhibition*" (ed. David Barton), in *Stray Dogs at the Museum: Tsai Ming-liang Solo Exhibition*, 181–89; 185.

11. Sing, "Continuous Crisscrossing Shimmer," 187.

12. Sing, "Continuous Crisscrossing Shimmer," 187.

13. Tsai Ming-liang, prefatory notes, in *Stray Dogs at the Museum: Tsai Ming-liang Solo Exhibition* (no page numbering).

14. Sing, "Continuous Crisscrossing Shimmer," 189.

15. Yeh and Darrel Davis, "Camping Out with Tsai Ming-liang," 235.

16. Muñoz, *Cruising Utopia*, 43.

17. Ricco, *Logic of the Lure*, 142–48; 6–7; 20.

18. See the discussion of the Ramble in Matt Baume, "Under the Cover of Night: 10 of America's Most Famous Gay Cruising Spots, Past and Present," *Hornet*, December 13, 2019, https://hornet.com/stories/gay-cruising-spots -america/.

19. Cf. Hong, "Anywhere but Here," 159–81.

20. Ricco, *Logic of the Lure*, 51–55. *Blue*, DVD, directed by Derek Jarman (1993; London: Curzon Artificial Eye, 2014).

21. Sing, "Continuous Crisscrossing Shimmer," 189. Also see the description of *Erotic Space* at http://www.curtas.pt/solar/index.php?menu=280&sub menu=285&lang=en.

22. Zuilhof, "Take a Seat," 219–26.

23. Zuilhof, "Take a Seat," 224. See *Is It a Dream?* installation (IFFR 2008 Exploding Cinema: New Dragon Inns): https://iffr.com/en/2008/films/is-it-a -dream.

24. Zuilhof, "Take a Seat," 224. Fellow Malaysian filmmaker Tan Chui-mui also produced an omnibus film on Chinese diaspora for which Tsai brought his "Walker" series to the apartment building in which he grew up as a child: *Letters from the South* (2013), https://iffr.com/en/2014/films/letters-from-the -south.

25. Zuilhof, "Take a Seat," 225.

26. See the discussions of cruising and saunas/bathhouses in Chang, "Drifting Bodies and Flooded Spaces," 45–63; Hong, "Theatrics of Cruising," 149–59; and Wu, "Cruising's Spectral Intimacies."

27. "The Red Thread (De Rode Draad)," *Wikipedia*, https://en.wikipedia .org/wiki/The_Red_Thread_(De_Rode_Draad).

28. See Strange Bedfellows, ed., *Policing Public Sex: Queer Politics and the Future of AIDS Activism* (Boston: South End Press, 1996).

29. See my discussion of *No No Sleep* in the introduction to this book.

30. See Barthes, "Leaving the Movie Theater," 346.

31. On sexual disorientation, see Moon, *Small Boy*, 15–17.

32. See Tsai's discussion of recycling in his talk at National Central University (in an auditorium containing some of the cinema chairs salvaged from the Fu Ho theater), published as Tsai, "On the Uses and Misuses of Cinema." On "eco-camp," see Whitworth, "Hello Eco-camp," 73–92; Schaffer, "Queering Waste through Camp."

33. Sing Song-yong, Tsai Ming-liang, and Lin Mun-lee (cocurators), "Projecting Tsai Ming-liang, towards Trans-art Cinema: Film Exhibition Forum, *Stray Dogs at the Museum*," in *Stray Dogs at the Museum: Tsai Ming-liang Solo Exhibition*, 227–36; 235.

34. On the reparative impulse, see Sedgwick, *Touching Feeling*, 149. See also Tsai, "On the Uses and Misuses of Cinema."

35. Morse, "Time & Again."

36. Tsai explains, "When preparing for the filming of *Visage*, I often visited the Louvre where I always saw groups of children and some even from kindergartens. . . . All of a sudden I seemed to realize something. I became very eager to show the kids my films at art museums, especially to those children in the place where I live. One day after these children grow up and when there are enough audiences, I will have my films screened in theaters, waiting them to cue up to buy the tickets." *Stray Dogs at the Museum: Tsai Ming-liang Solo Exhibition*, prefatory notes (no page numbering).

37. Barthes, *Preparation of the Novel*. See also Buurma and Heffernan, "Notation after the 'Reality Effect,'" 80–102. They coin the term "novels of commission," which I have adapted as "films of commission." On Tsai's "homework" and scouting for *Visage*, see "Filmmaker Tsai Ming-liang on *Face* (2009)."

38. Barthes, *Preparation of the Novel*, 170.

39. Delany, *Times Square Red*. See also Purchell's brilliant gay adult video collage *Ask Any Buddy* (2020).

40. Lim, "Positioning Auteur Theory," 240.

41. Barthes, "Leaving the Movie Theater," 345.

42. Watts, *Roland Barthes' Cinema*, 75.

43. See Lim, *Tsai Ming-liang and a Cinema of Slowness*, 16–17.

44. Hansen, "Chameleon and Catalyst," 390–419; Foucault, "Of Other Spaces," 22–27. Part of this paragraph reworks the proposal for the SCMS panel I cochaired with Beth Tsai, "Sleepy Cinema: Affect, Audience, Embodiment" (presented March 20, 2021).

45. Gong Jow-jiun, "Strolling and Chatting in the Cinema, Sitting and Watching in the Museum: *Stray Dogs* and the Contemporaneity of a Film Exhibition," *Stray Dogs at the Museum: Tsai Ming-liang Solo Exhibition*, 191–201; 196.

46. Gong, "Strolling and Chatting," 200.

47. Jeremy W. Crampton, "What Is the *Dispositif?*" *Foucault Blog,* https://
foucaultblog.wordpress.com/2007/04/01/what-is-the-dispositif/. Cf. Jeremy W.
Crampton and Stuart Elden, *Space, Knowledge, and Power: Foucault and Geography* (New York: Routledge, 2007). The deployment of sexuality is discussed in
Michel Foucault, *The History of Sexuality,* vol. 1, *An Introduction,* trans. Robert
Hurley (New York: Vintage, 1990). On Foucault and China or in Sinophone
contexts, see Liu, "Why Does Queer Theory Need China?" 291–320; and Chiang, "(De)Provincializing China," 28.

48. De Certeau, *Practice of Everyday Life,* 96.

Index

abjection, 62, 97

Absolutely Fabulous, 83, 90

action films, 45, 48, 105, 125

action-image, 50

Act of Killing, The (2012, dir. Joshua Oppenheimer), 26

actor(s): Ando Masanobu as, 10; animal, 86; Fanny Ardant as, 87, 80; Norman bin Atun as, xi, 3, 88; Nathalie Baye as, 87; body of the, 77, 133n2, 138n11, 156n22; Robert Bresson on, 90; Laetitia Casta as, 83, 87, 90–92; Chen Chao-jung as, 3; Chen Shiang-chyi as, 3, 44, 66, 99; Chinese, 94; Pearly Chua as, x; Gilles Deleuze on, 91–93; director and, 91–92, 112, 133n2, 156n22; discovery of, 37; from *Dragon Inn,* 41, 45, 48; fetish, 80; French, 83–84, 87, 94, 145n64, 146n67, 174n48; Japanese, 10, 40–41, 54, 71; Hong Kong, 12, 23, 77, 94; Denis Lavant as, 146n67; Jean-Pierre Léaud, 77–79, 83, 156n22, 175n66; Lee

Kang-sheng as, ix, 3, 37, 68, 77, 80, 83, 91, 106, 111–12, 133n2, 138n11, 156n22, 183n69; Lu Yi-ching as, 3, 62, 99; Malaysian, x–xi, 88; Miao Tien as, 3, 45; Jeanne Moreau as, 87; porn, 38, 54, 62, 66, 161n6, 167n70; Shih Chun as, 41, 45, 48; Song Fang as, 82; François Truffaut and, 79–80, 83, 86–87, 156n22, 175n66; Tsai Ming-liang and, ix–x, 2–3, 37, 40–41, 44, 54, 62, 66, 72, 77, 80, 83–84, 86–88, 90–94, 99, 102, 106, 111–12, 133n2, 138n11, 145n64, 146n67, 149n23, 156n22, 167n70, 175n66, 183n69; typecasting of, 183n69; Yang Keui-mei as, 3, 99, 149n23; Sumomo Yozakura as, 54, 72. *See also* male muse

advertising, 33, 58, 60, 102, 179n25

aesthetics, 10, 17, 26–27, 37, 49, 63, 69–71, 93, 97, 107, 125–26, 141n28, 146n69, 148n13, 161n5, 181n44, 182n50

NICHOLAS DE VILLIERS is professor of English and film at the University of North Florida. He is author of *Opacity and the Closet: Queer Tactics in Foucault, Barthes, and Warhol* (Minnesota, 2012) and *Sexography: Sex Work in Documentary* (Minnesota, 2017).